THE CHANGING POLITICAL ECONOMIES
OF SMALL WEST EUROPEAN COUNTRIES

CHANGING WELFARE STATES

Advanced welfare states seem remarkably stable at first glance. Although most member states of the European Union (EU) have undertaken comprehensive welfare reform, especially since the 1990s, much comparative welfare state analysis portrays a 'frozen welfare landscape'. Social spending is stable. However, if we interpret the welfare state as more than aggregate social spending and look at long-term trends, we can see profound transformations across several policy areas, ranging from labour market policy and regulation, industrial relations, social protection, social services like child care and education, pensions, and long-term care. This series is about trajectories of change. Have there been path-breaking welfare innovations or simply attempts at political reconsolidation? What new policies have been added, and with what consequences for competitiveness, employment, income equality and poverty, gender relations, human capital formation, and fiscal sustainability? What is the role of the EU in shaping national welfare state reform? Are advanced welfare states moving in a similar or even convergent direction, or are they embarking on ever more divergent trajectories of change? These issues raise fundamental questions about the politics of reform. If policymakers *do* engage in major reforms (despite the numerous institutional, political and policy obstacles), what factors enable them to do so? While the overriding objective of the series is to trace trajectories of contemporary welfare state reform, the editors also invite the submission of manuscripts which focus on theorising institutional change in the social policy arena.

The Changing Political Economies of Small West European Countries

Uwe Becker (ed.)

AMSTERDAM UNIVERSITY PRESS

Cover illustration: Paul Cézanne, *The Card Players* (Les joueurs de cartes), 1890-1892, oil on canvas

Cover design: Crasborn Grafisch Ontwerpers BNO, Valkenburg a/d Geul
Lay-out: V3-Services, Baarn

ISBN   978 90 8964 331 5
e-ISBN   978 90 4851 454 0
NUR   740

Table of Contents

Preface and Acknowledgements

The intention of this volume is to contribute to the discussion on changing capitalist political economies and to enhance the empirical knowledge of institutional continuity and change in the small, highly corporatist political economies in the Alps, the Benelux countries and Scandinavia. Almost all of these political economies have often been in the spotlight. Many observers consider them as alternative models for socio-economic development since they combine competitiveness and a highly developed welfare system. Remarkably, these small political economies are largely absent from the literature on capitalist varieties that empirically still focuses on the US, Britain, France, Germany and Japan. This is an empirical omission, but also a missed chance for a critical review of the theory of varieties of capitalism. The character and development of the small countries' political economies qualifies very well for this matter.

The volume's origins can be traced back to the editor's involvement in an international 5th Framework research project on *The Consensual Political Cultures of the Small West European States* (2003-2006), his co-editorship (with Herman Schwartz) of the book on *Employment "Miracles"* in a few small European countries (Amsterdam University Press 2005) and his recent participation in the discussion on capitalist varieties as exemplified in his book on *Open Varieties of Capitalism* (Palgrave-Macmillan 2009). The starting shot for the volume was the organization of a workshop in Amsterdam in June 2008 and subsequently of a panel at the SASE conference in San Jose, Costa Rica on "Institutional change and continuity in the small countries' political economies". The locations of these meetings once more illustrated what a privilege it is to have a job in academia. Discussants and complimentary paper presenters in Amsterdam were Jean Claude Barbier, Frans Becker, Brian Burgoon, Jeannette Mak, Daniel Mügge, Arne Niemann, Otto Penz, Els Sol, Jeroen Towen, Barbara Vis, Jaap Woldendorp and Adrian Zimmermann. Gregory Jackson chaired the SASE-panel in San Jose. The authors of the volume are indebted to all of them for their suggestions and criticisms. They have also to thank the two reviewers and the editorial staff of the Amsterdam University Press as well as Evelien van der Molen and Lea Klarenbeek for their assistance in the preparation of the bibliography and the index as well as in proofreading.

Uwe Becker
Amsterdam, May 2011

1   Introduction

Uwe Becker

Changing capitalism is a topic that has been discussed, with increasing intensity, in the context of the debate following the publication of Peter Hall's and David Soskice's *Varieties of Capitalism* (2001). Empirically, this discussion and related comparative research have concentrated on the bigger political economies of the United States, Japan and Germany, with some attention for Britain, France and Italy. Smaller countries have largely been ignored. This volume would like to shed some light on a group of smaller European countries, all of which reveal a high degree (Belgium, Denmark, Finland, Switzerland) or even a very high degree (Austria, the Netherlands, Norway and Sweden) of corporatism, as is shown in Table 1.1. From here on, I will call them the sample countries.

Table 1.1   Siaroff's corporatism index (based on the different indices of 13 other authors)

Average Corporatism Score (scale 1 to 5; mid-1990s)			
Australia	1,688	Japan	2,912
Austria	5,000	Netherlands	4,000
Belgium	2,840	New Zealand	1,955
Canada	1,150	Norway	4,864
Denmark	3,545	Spain	1,250
Finland	3,295	Sweden	4,674
France	1,674	Switzerland	3,375
Germany	3,543	UK	1,652
Ireland	2,000	US	1,150
Italy	1,477		

Source: Siaroff 1999: 185

These countries are of special interest because most of them have been praised as models in recent years – as an alternative to the strongly liberal route as exemplified by the US. It is intriguing, therefore, to learn what politico-economic change has meant to these countries. Have they moved in the liberal direction and if so, to what extent? Or have divergent developments occurred? What happened with their welfare systems, corporate governance, labour market legislation and industrial relations in the one and a half decades preceding the sharp downturn of the world economy in 2008? Subsequent chapters will investigate these questions and also pay separate attention to how they have reacted to the process of Europeanisation. The concluding chapter delves into the question whether corporatist capitalism is a viable candidate for a European socio-economic model, with the sample countries (or at least some of them) as examples.

This introductory chapter provides an overview of the institutional changes that have taken place since the early 1990s. It puts the sample countries into broader comparative perspective (with attention for the bigger EU countries, the Anglo-Saxon world outside Europe, and Japan) and identifies a number of forces that triggered the recent changes. It is also, however, a contribution to the discussion on the appropriate mapping of capitalist varieties. This is important because we need a kind of typology that is suitable for the analysis of institutional change and for specifying the identification of the direction of change. From where to where do empirical varieties move? I will propose a typology of five types (liberal, corporatist, statist, meso-communitarian and patrimonial), of which three are relevant in this volume, and throughout the text I will strictly distinguish ideal types and empirical cases.[1] Ideal types are idealised and simplified – but not fictitious – constructions of reality. Ideal types are no ideal performers, and they are not ideal in a normative sense. Complex, historically grown cases such as political economies or democracies never represent ideal types; they approximate them.[2] Ideal types are fixed constructions, while cases are historical entities and change their location on the axes and in the space between the types. In short: ideal types are fixed, empirical cases are moving.

The Varieties of Capitalism (VoC) perspective analytically tries to capture the ways to economic performance. It conceives 'liberal' and 'coordinated' routes to international competitiveness. We will have to discuss whether this dichotomy is much too simplifying. At the outset I would like to say that, when using a dichotomy, I prefer to talk of liberal versus embedded liberal capitalism because at the ideal-typical level, (complete) coordination and market are diametrically opposed and exclude each other. The concept of embedded liberalism/capitalism, coined by Polanyi (1957), was much in use in the 1990s (see e.g. Crouch & Streeck 1997).

Empirically diverse capitalism and ideal-typical coordinates

From where to where do capitalism varieties change? Do they only move from embedded to liberal capitalism and vice versa? For much of this volume, this simple dichotomous distinction is largely sufficient because corporatism (regularly combined with a considerable level of statism) is a form of embeddedness, and the recent institutional change of the highly corporatist political economies was mainly in a liberal direction. The country chapters focus on this development. Distinguishing ideal types and cases, Figure 1.1 illustrates the movement of two highly embedded (corporatist) cases in a liberal direction, where the change that Y undergoes is more marked than that of X.

Figure 1.1   Illustration of the change of two imaginary capitalisms (X and Y) from T_1 to T_2 on the axis between the ideal types of embedded and liberal capitalism

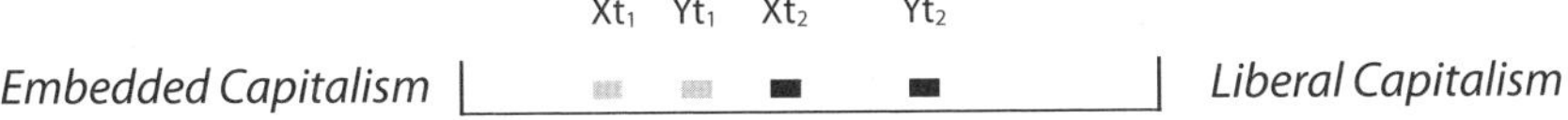

The dichotomous distinction is largely but not completely sufficient! For this reason, attention will be given to the question what a more differentiated typology should look like. There are considerable regional and national differences in capitalism with sometimes a strong role of the state, sometimes corporatist cooperation or clientelist infiltration and sometimes fragmentation of the economy into large business groups. Sometimes capitalism combines with a social-democratic environment, sometimes with a conservative one and sometimes with authoritarian regimes. Understandably, many critics have argued that the category of coordinated/embedded capitalism is too broad and that it has to be subdivided. This criticism is justified. Typologies have to simplify empirical reality, but they also have to reflect fundamental differences.

What are the criteria on which a typology of capitalist varieties should be based? Not much has been written about this, but they have to be chosen pragmatically because objective meta criteria for selecting the most appropriate criteria do not exist. Those of Hall and Soskice (2001: 6) appear to be identical with the seven institutional components they identify in capitalism: industrial relations, corporate governance, inter-firm relations, employer-employee relations within firms, training and education systems, the level of social protection, and product market regulation. Amable's list (2003: 173ff; more limited) as well as those of Boyer and Hollingsworth (1997: 2; broader, also includes 'conceptions of fairness and justice') and Schmidt (2002: 107f) are similar, with the latter offering three simple yet comprehensive criteria: 1) the structure of business relations, 2) the relations between government, firms and labour, and 3) the relations between capital and labour.

Since a typology must simplify diversity, the number of criteria should be limited. Resembling Schmidt's criteria, I propose to choose a few core criteria that point to *fundamental and overarching features* of capitalism and distinguish it from other politico-economic formations like feudalism or state socialism. Such criteria are:

I   *The relationship between capital and labour.* This involves the relationship between unions and employers as well as that between management and employees. Corporate governance is related to it, and it is connected to the firm-investor and stakeholder-shareholder relations.

II *The relation between politics and economy.* This includes the welfare system dimension, employment protection, product-market regulation, privatisation/nationalisation of companies and business sectors, the partial regulation of wages and profits, supply and demand and, related to these aspects, the scope and character of economic policy.

In case they add substantial features to capital-labour and state-market relations, culture and ideology (such as conceptions of fairness and justice) should be given the status of a separate, *third criterion*. Sometimes they do, sometimes they do not.[3] For this reason, and because the maxim of simplicity could become threatened by adding this criterion, we should only use it for constructing idea-typical sub-varieties of capitalism and circumscribe it as *the normative orientation of a political economy* that is about 'core' norms – what is considered 'normal' in a political economy – and basic ideological principles.

A number of proposals for non-dichotomous typologies have been made (for a more extensive discussion of what follows, see Becker 2009: chapter 3). In a context of analysing change, these typologies only make sense when:

- they at least implicitly reflect criteria like those just mentioned;
- they are not static by definition, which is the case in geographically termed typologies (could a Nordic[4] political economy move in a Mediterranean direction?);
- no mixed types are constructed – reality is mixed (and changing) types are not;
- cases are distinguished from ideal types, where the former only approximate the latter. Classifications, where cases belong to types, sometimes conceal considerable differences between cases – for example, between the 'liberal' US and Canada – and do not leave space for change other than the radical jump from one type to another.

Typologies worth considering are those of Robert Boyer (2004: 13f) and Vivien Schmidt (2002a: 107ff). Boyer draws distinctions between four varieties: market-based, social democratic, statist and meso-corporatist, the latter referring to the cooperation between labour and capital within (large) companies as well as between companies in different branches as it exists in East Asian countries. Boyer does not distinguish ideal types and cases, however. Vivien Schmidt does. Writing in terms of countries coming 'close' and 'closest' to the ideal types, with no one country 'entirely fitting', she is the only prominent author presenting a non-dichotomous, ideal type-based typology. Her typology of *European* varieties of capitalism consists of the types of market capitalism, state capitalism and managed capitalism.

What, then, are the ideal types we should work with? We do not need to reinvent the wheel in this field and can take types already circulating in the discussion. Although Boyer works with classifications instead of ideal type-based typologies, I will adopt from him and Schmidt three types of embedded capitalism: statist, social democratic/managed and meso-corporatist, which I would like to rename statist, corporatist and – to avoid having the concept of corporatism twice in a row – meso-communitarian capitalism. The picture of the typology and of national political economies most approximating the ideal types is this:

1 *The liberal type.* Here, the market governs every aspect of the economy, and politics unrestrictedly facilitates private property and the market – apart from regulations regarding issues like health and human safety. Besides this facilitation and the provision of residual social security and a legal and infrastructural framework, state interventionism is very limited and capital-labour relations are largely individualised and adversarial. Unions and employers' associations

are weak, and labour as well as companies highly commodified. Shareholders and private owners are the only stakeholders. Political economies most approximating this ideal type, though in different degrees, are those of the Anglo-Saxon countries, but all other capitalist countries also feature strong liberal traits. Otherwise they would not be capitalist.

2   *The statist type.* Here, the market is restricted by political regulation that attempts to determine the overall direction of the economy. Alongside private owners, the state acts as a prominent stakeholder that is assumed to know best the common interest. Statism does not directly determine the level of the welfare system and the character of the capital-labour relationship, but a hierarchical organisation of companies with limited worker rights fits this type best. Social democratic statism is not impossible, however. France has traditionally been the empirical political economy most approximating this ideal type, although statist features have also been strong in other European and East Asian countries. They are also clearly present in the countries studied in this volume (least so in Switzerland), and at a basic level, even the most liberal political economies are statist.

3   *The corporatist type.* This type first of all defines the institutionalised cooperation between capital and labour. Apart from wage bargaining, it consists of negotiations among the relevant peak organisations on long-term socio-economic targets in terms of the common interest. Corporatist regulation partially corrects market regulation. Topics such as social security and income inequality are also on the agenda, particularly in tripartite corporatism, where the state takes part directly in the negotiations. The commitment of the main socio-economic players to pragmatism, consensualism and the common interest, however contested the latter may be, is an underlying aspect of corporatism. Labour and politics are stakeholders in this system, and the former also has a voice within companies. The political economies most approximating this type are those analysed in this volume and Germany.

4   *The meso-communitarian type.* This type can be distinguished by the organisation of networks of firms as communities. Managers and workers are expected to act cooperatively on behalf of the community. The networks also act as a welfare agency. Next to basic tasks, politics is limited to enhancing the firms' global competitiveness. This type is most approximated in Japan (Anchordoguy 2005) and other Asian countries. In this volume, it is less important.

5   *The patrimonial type.* Also less relevant here, this type is characterised by an important role for political leadership based on patron-client relationships between the state and the economy. It involves a specific interaction pattern between political centre, local politicians and the top business firms. It exhibits favouritism in the distribution of privileges. It is strongly present in non-Western economies.

Figure 1.2 shows this five-dimensional typology. It illustrates a strongly corporatist case in the space between the ideal types. The figure also reflects the fact that all forms of capitalism are liberal and that corporatism, because of its macro-economic orientation, only exists together with statism.

Figure 1.2 **Illustration of the five-dimensional typology of capitalist varieties featuring an imaginary, strongly corporatist case in the field between the ideal types**

(the two types less relevant for this volume have dashed lines)

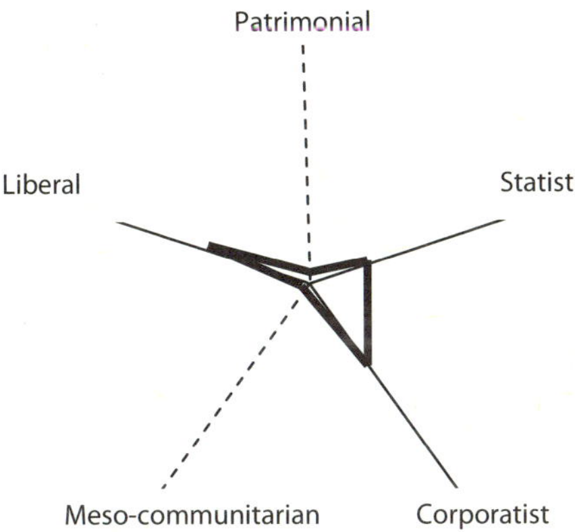

Since meso-communitarianism and patrimonialism are almost neglectable in the contemporary West European context, the types relevant in this volume are only those of liberalism, statism and corporatism. Of these, the latter two, on the basis of the third, normative criterion just mentioned, could be divided into *social democratic* ('equality of conditions', 'co-determination' at the company level) and *conservative* (concern of 'the strong' for the 'weak'; social harmony as a core value) sub-varieties.[5]

Recent contextual changes: globalisation, Europeanisation and individualisation

Before analysing institutional changes, we must first describe the environmental shifts triggering them. Institutional changes are adaptations to contextual changes. The main contextual changes in recent decades have been globalisation – particularly the intensification of global competition – the process of Europeanisation in the case of Europe, social-structural change, the related emergence of new interest constellations and relatively autonomous ideological processes. The latter notably points to neo-liberalism which in the late 1970s started to become the dominant strand in economic thinking and which received a push during the Thatcher and Reagan years. Since the 1990s, it has been repeated time and again that globalisation forces advanced economies to liberalise their markets and reduce social expenditures. Did globalisation really exert this pressure?

Globalisation is not a new phenomenon. In terms of trade relative to GDP, it was already strong in the heyday of colonialism in the early 20th century. During World War I and in the 1920s it receded, and in the years of the Great Depression, fascism and World War II, it weakened to a very low level. Thereafter, it was not until the breakdown of the Bretton Woods system in the early 1970s that globalisation received some attention again. It took until the 1990s for global trade to surpass its pre-World War I level. Since then, with the breakdown of Soviet socialism, the removal of international trade barriers and – very important for international transactions at financial markets – the introduction of the Internet, globalisation has accelerated and has become a major topic in politico-economic discussions. A new feature of this recent period of globalisation is the emergence of new competitors from outside the Western world. China and India are the most recent prominent examples.

The ongoing discussion on globalisation and its consequences is intense, but a number of widely known features seem to be undeniable and can be summarised in note form:
- Since the emergence of high-volume, low-wage production of manufactured goods in subsequent regions of Asia and, since 1990, Eastern Europe, this type of production has gradually moved offshore to these regions. It concerns labour-intensive industries characterised by batch production at individual workstations, like garment assembly, shoes, toys, luggage and cheap household goods. Some capital-intensive but medium-skill industries like ship-building and consumer

electronics also largely disappeared from the advanced economies. As a result, in almost every OECD economy, the number of manufacturing jobs has fallen considerably.

– Most recently, ICT equipment is increasingly being produced and developed in Asia, which is no longer only a competitor in low-wage sectors. Taiwan, for example, has become 'a major world technology power' (Berger 2005: 19), China is moving up the value chain and India has become an important player in business services (Havik & McMorrow 2006: 10, 17).

– The intensification of trade and the relocation of production has also brought about a changed international division of labour which in part is characterised by the compartmentalisation or modularisation of production processes – manufacturing has become 'a commodity' (Berger 2005: 83).

– One aspect that was made brutally clear to all since 2008 is that globalisation is particularly embodied in the exponential growth in international financial markets, which have increased in magnitude, speed and volatility at the same time that the ability of national governments to control their effects is decreasing (Schmidt 2002: 17).

– One implication of the surge in international financial markets and more generally the extension of the global division of labour is the increased mobility of capital (even if there are path dependencies such as sunk costs and the reliance on clusters that limit mobility). Related, though disputed, is capital's increased power vis-à-vis labour and the state.

– The current period of globalisation is ushering in not only new competitors and a new international division of labour but also new customers. For example, the more competitive that countries such as China become, the more purchasing power they gain and the more they can buy goods and services that are still produced in the most advanced economies. As a whole, this is a growth-enhancing configuration (cf. Obstfeld & Taylor 2004).

– Moreover, falling prices for imported manufactured goods has increased disposable incomes in the advanced economies and left space for an increasing shift in demand towards services and better quality manufactures.

Intensified global competition exerts pressure on countries to improve their competitiveness and in that sense leads also to pressure for politico-economic change. It does not dictate the direction of change, however. Moreover, empirical cases unequivocally demonstrating the superiority of strongly liberal political economies do not exist. The US and Britain have had strong GDP growth in the decade up to 2007/08, but this is also true for the smaller European economies analysed in this volume – with the exception of the most liberal of them: Switzerland. These countries have much less inequality and poverty than Anglo-Saxon countries, and they care more for the environment. Both well performing and less well performing economies exist in either more liberal or more corporatist forms, and the same is true for political economies approximating statist or meso-communitarian types. The causal nexus between institutional structure and economic performance seems to be weaker than is often supposed.

A sort of special European supplement to globalisation is the process of Europeanisation which has taken shape since the late 1980s and early 1990s. This process can be defined as the convergence of member states of the European Union in specific areas, induced by European treaties, legislation or policies (Falkner & Leiber 2004: 3; cf. Schmidt 2006). Relevant changes in the context of national capitalisms brought about by Europeanisation have been:

- The *Single European Act* of 1986 where a single European market was envisaged, and the *Maastricht Treaty* on the *Economic and Monetary Union* (EMU; 1992) which laid down plans for the economic and monetary integration that was realised in subsequent years.
- The establishment of the European Central Bank (ECB; 1997) and of the Euro (2002) – at least for the members of 'Euroland' (some EU member states – e.g. Denmark, Sweden and the UK – have yet to join the EMU).
- The criteria for membership in the EMU – the so-called 'Maastricht criteria' – which states that a member's budget deficit could not exceed 3% of GDP, that total public debt must be lower than 60% of GDP and that national inflation rates should not be more than 1.5 percentage points above the average of the three lowest national inflation rates in the EU.
- The establishment of the Directorate General for Competition, or DG 4. The common market is in essence a liberal endeavour aimed at breaking down national economic borders, but with the activities of DG 4, it becomes so in a pronounced way. This DG must eliminate unfair competition and mergers (including cases against companies such as Microsoft which lead to fines of hundreds of millions of Euros for the violation of certain rules) and also enforce the ban on direct forms of state subsidies to business.

– The jurisdiction of the European Court of Justice prohibiting any form of economic protection that violates the principle of equality, which for example is the case in constructions that protect private companies against hostile takeovers (cf. Höpner & Schäfer 2007: 18ff; Zumbansen & Saam 2007). Volkswagen is such a case.

It is particularly via the activities of the EU Commission's competition department that the EU reflects the dominance of neo-liberalism. EMU-Europeanisation, therefore, has 'ensured that globalisation has been more pronounced in Europe than elsewhere', and because of its restrictive stance and the related move away from Keynesianism towards monetarism, it has led to convergence in the monetary policy arena (Schmidt 2002a: 4, 14).

Two years after the Maastricht Treaty was signed, the OECD published its *Jobs Study* (1994) in which the entire neo-liberal policy creed of the time was summarised. More than the Maastricht Treaty, it reflected the wisdom that had become increasingly influential in the course of the preceding decade and at the same time strengthened this wisdom – not least by a section on 'Implementing the Jobs Study' that was included for a number of years in the OECD's *Country Surveys*. The nine recommendations made in the *Jobs Study* (1994: 2; 47-54) are:

1   Set macroeconomic policy such that it will encourage non-inflationary growth. Redirect public spending away from subsidies and make fiscal consolidation a main objective for the medium term.
2   Enhance the creation and diffusion of technological know-how by improving frameworks for its development. Intensify R&D.
3   Increase flexibility of working time (both short-term and lifetime) voluntarily sought by workers and employers.
4   Nurture an entrepreneurial climate by eliminating impediments to, and restrictions on, the creation and expansion of enterprises. Lower start-up costs and eliminate any unwarranted regulatory impediments.
5   Make wage and labour costs more flexible by removing restrictions that prevent wages from reflecting local conditions and individual skill levels. Keep minimum wages low, reduce non-wage labour costs and direct taxes.
6   Reform employment security provisions that inhibit the expansion of employment in the private sector. Loosen employment protection and permit fixed-term contracts.
7   Strengthen the emphasis on active labour market policies and reinforce their effectiveness.

8   Improve labour force skills and competences through wide-ranging changes in education and training systems.

9   Reform unemployment and related benefit systems. Restrict unemployment insurance benefit entitlements in countries where they are especially long, reduce after-tax replacement ratios where these are high, and tighten soft eligibility criteria.

A tenth recommendation, implicit in the argument of the *Jobs Study*, was sometimes added:

10   Enhance product market competition so as to reduce monopolistic tendencies and weaken insider-outsider mechanisms while also contributing to a more innovative economy.

Recommendations 3-6 and 9 are at the core of the liberal creed, but the other ones also sound familiar. After the initial publication of the *Jobs Study*, these recommendations have endlessly been repeated by politicians, economists and journalists, particularly after the Anglo-Saxon economies had entered a period of apparently unfettered prosperity in the second half of the 1990s, quickly recovering from the burst of the tech bubble in 2000/2001. Didn't this prove that liberalisation as recommended by the OECD was the best response to the new Asian and East European competitors?

Less discussed than globalisation, Europeanisation and the dominance of neo-liberal ideas is the contextual change that took place in the social structure. It can be summarised under the heading of individualisation. It could be fertile ground for the normatively individualist aspects of neo-liberalism that stress personal initiative and responsibility and – related to this – welfare cuts. Social-structural individualisation, which must be distinguished from this normative and ideological individualisation, involves the loosening of group and class ties and a process whereby individuals increasingly have to rely on themselves. Indicators are:

–   Demographic ageing (due to a low fertility rate; Ireland and the US are exceptions);
–   The decline in the number of marriages per 1,000 inhabitants (by about 30% on average in the Western world between 1970 and the early 2000s);
–   The divorce rate which has more than doubled in most countries in the same period;
–   The average household size which shrank by more than 10% towards levels of two persons per household in Scandinavia and Germany,

somewhat higher levels in the Anglo-Saxon countries, and still relatively high, though sharply declining, levels in countries such as Ireland and Italy (CoE 2003; Eurostat 2004);

— The increase in the number of tertiary education attendants – in the brief period between 1991 and 2002, the average increase was about 30%, reflecting economic requirements but also the growing impact of an individualistic meritocracy (OECD 2004a).

— Another yardstick of individualisation is the decline in union density (see Table 1.2). In many countries, trade unions lost one third to one half of their members between 1970 and 2003. Exceptions to this trend are only Canada and Italy as well as the countries featuring the 'Ghent system'. In the latter (in Belgium and Scandinavia), membership rose because unemployment benefits are administered by trade unions. To be eligible for these benefits, one has to belong to a trade union.

Table 1.2   Union density rates (% of the labour force), 1970-2003

	1970	*1990*	*2000*	*2003*
Australia	50	41	-	35
Austria	63	47	37	35
Belgium	41	54	56	55
Canada	32	33	28	28
Denmark	60	75	74	70
Finland	51	72	76	74
France	22	10	10	8
Germany	32	31	25	23
Ireland	53	51	38	35
Italy	37	39	35	34
Japan	35	25	-	20
Netherlands	37	25	23	22
New Zealand	55	51	-	22
Norway	57	59	-	53
Spain	-	13	-	16
Sweden	68	80	79	-
Switzerland	29	24	18	18
UK	45	39	31	29
US	27	15	13	12

Sources: OECD 2004b: 145; Blanchflower 2007: 3

Did social-structural individualisation lead to decreasing solidarity, enhanced normative individualisation, and thereby to diminished support for the welfare state? Principally, the first form of individualisation and solidarity need not oppose each other; the weakening of the traditional ties of families, neighbourhoods and of early voluntary working-class insurance arrangements had been at the basis of modern, state-organised solidarity, even if this is a rather anonymous solidarity. It does not, however, tell us anything about the support of different layers of society for welfare arrangements in the context of changing circumstances. A relevant question therefore is whether people currently find individual responsibility more important than they did at lower levels of social-structural individualisation. Do they (still) support welfare state solidarity? Tables 1.3 and 1.4 provide tentative answers to these questions, but the information that comparative research provides is sparse and one has to keep in mind the considerable contextual differences between the countries surveyed. In a crisis year, attitudes will be different from those uttered in times of economic growth, and specific national contexts also influence the answers given in surveys.

Table 1.3 **Support for welfare state intervention, 1996-2006**
(% that answered "definitely")

Should it be the government's responsibility to provide:	*A job for everyone who wants it*		*Health care for the sick*		*A decent living standard for the unemployed*		*To reduce income differences*	
	1996	2006	1996	2006	1996	2006	1996	2006
West Germany	28	30	51	51	17	15	25	26
East Germany	57	46	66	62	38	26	48	50
Sweden	35	29	71	63	39	27	43	37
US	14	16	39	56	13	16	17	29

Source: Svallfors 2007: 22

Table 1.3 contains answers given in the years 1996 and 2006 – both years of economic upswing. The overall trend points slightly towards more individualistic attitudes. In 2009, the answers would possibly have been less individualistic than in 2006. Remarkable in the table is the generally low level of support for a decent living standard for the unemployed; that in the US, support for state intervention has increased somewhat,[6] albeit from a comparatively low level; and that attitudes in West Germany (where

80% of Germans live) with respect to the questions posed approximate the US level and are considerably more individualistic than those in East Germany and Sweden.[7] Eurobarometer surveys in 1976, 1989, 1993 and 2001 on the causes of poverty point in the same direction. The number of people indicating that poverty is caused by laziness decreased sharply between 1976 and 1993 in all countries, but increased again after 1993 (Eurobarometer 2002: 19).

The data in Table 1.4 send a different message. This table consists of a larger sample of countries and presents data on questions similar to those asked in the survey that Table 1.3 is based upon. The attitudes in 2000 are not more individualistic than those in 1990 – rather, the trend is reversed. Perhaps this is so because of the very years the surveys were conducted. 1990 was the last year before the recession (in Scandinavia: severe crisis) of the early 1990s, while 2000 was the year of the bursting tech bubble. Table 1.4 is important as a contrast to Table 1.3 because the comparison of the data shows the dependency of attitudes on context and also that the differences between countries can be different in different surveys. The differences between Sweden and Germany are relatively small in Table 1.3, and in 1990 Americans ranked the possibility for unemployed people to refuse a job offer higher than most European countries surveyed.

Table 1.4   **Valuation of competition and individual responsibility (10-point scale*)**

	Competition is good. It stimulates people to work hard and develop new ideas		People who are unemployed should take any job available or lose their unemployment benefits	
	1990	2000	1990	2000
France	4,03	4,73	4,40	4,53
Britain	3,81	4,01	5,33	4,92
Germany	3,25	3,80	4,42	4,09
Austria	...	3,19	...	3,87
Italy	4,11	4,16	3,63	3,41
Netherlands	4,28	4,68	4,89	5,23
Belgium	4,03	4,80	4,63	4,89
Denmark	3,93	4,02	4,57	4,87
Sweden	3,22	3,46	3,86	3,95
Finland	...	4,28	...	5,07
Ireland	3,70	3,81	5,28	5,60
US	3,17	...	4,61	...

*1 = competition is good; unemployed people have to take any job; 10 = competition is harmful; unemployed people may refuse a job offer.
Sources: EVS 1990 and EVS 2000, own calculations

It seems that there is no clear trend in the support of welfare state interventionism, implying that social-structural individualism (or 'atomisation') does not have structurally strengthened individualist attitudes. At least, this is what one can say on the basis of the limited evidence. Broadening this by looking at election results over the past twenty years would show that voters have shifted to the right of centre and that social democratic parties have also made a move away from the left (Swank 2006: 848). Perhaps this indicates a slightly increased normative individualism.

Some overall political-economic changes: mid-1990s to mid-2000s

When the environment of national political economies changes, it might create space for change within these political economies, and their institutional structure will come under pressure to (be) adapt(ed) in one or the other way. This is true, for example, for the structure of education and vocational training systems and the level of welfare benefits. Pressure to change does not necessarily bring about real change, and if it takes place then its direction is not strictly determined by the changing context – at least in most cases. When EU regulation requires member states to take specific steps, we have a case of stricter determination; for the rest, however, the course of adjustment largely depends on the relevant actors' interpretation of the situation, their knowledge, which is shaped by learning but also by fads and (perhaps) opportunism, and the power relations among them. In the past quarter century, this mix brought about a move towards neo-liberalism. In individual countries, this development might have been less pronounced, but the general trend is beyond doubt. Ideal-typical varieties of capitalism do not change (they are analytical constructions), but empirical political economies did.

What have been the main changes? It is difficult comparatively and exactly to identify the major and less major changes, but rising income inequality and poverty rates have been recurring themes of political debate in most Western countries, including the strongly corporatist ones. Probably related to decreasing union density and the somewhat changed social attitudes, income inequality (as measured by the Gini coefficient) has increased, though from a low level, in all of our sample countries except in Belgium and the Netherlands (see Table 7.3 in the final chapter), and in most other Western countries this is also the case. Remarkably, it has declined somewhat in the highly liberal political economies of Australia, Britain and Ireland. In the case of poverty (50% or less of the median income), the picture is similar, with declining rates only in Belgium and Norway (slightly in both cases) among the sample countries, and elsewhere in Britain, France and Italy.

Another major change related to Europeanisation and globalisation has been the loosened regulation of trade and product markets. This loosening, above all in non-manufacturing sectors, took place mostly in the period from the late 1980s to the mid-1990s (Simmons et al. 2006: 783, 786; Siegel 2007: Table 2). Significant changes have also occurred in the fields of privatisation and company finance (hedge funds and private equity) as well as in the power relationship between capital and labour as expressed by the wage share. Privatisation, as measured by the revenues it generated, has been another process that was boosted in the 1990s (Simmons et al. 2006: 786), but it is difficult to find out how much of it was motivated by competitiveness considerations and ideological factors and how much by budgetary reasons. In the first case, the conviction that the market works better would have been central; in the latter, financial need would have been the main motivation, as has particularly been the case for (candidate) member states of the EMU.

In the case of hedge funds and private equity, the situation is similar. Until 2008, the assets they managed had grown explosively. In that year, hedge funds' total managed assets were 25 times the volume they managed in 1988 (see Figure 1.3). For private equity funds the situation is not much different, although their spectacular increase only occurred in the years after 2002 (cf. ITUC 2007: 13). National data for a large number of countries are not available, however.[8] By inference, the same is true for the value of these assets in relation to the total of assets. The latter information would tell us

Figure 1.3   Hedge funds, development of assets managed, 1988-2008 in billion $

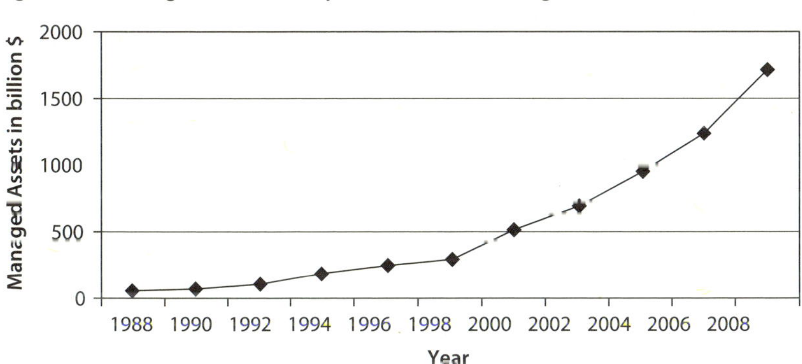

Source: Van Hedge Fund Advisor International

about the direct impact of these funds on national economies. In any case, we can say that these funds have grown significantly and that the larger the relative amount of assets they managed, the more substantial the influence or even control of these financial companies with a decidedly short-term orientation. And the stronger this short-term orientation is, the more liberal markets are.

Furthermore, both these fund types, but particularly hedge funds, embody the increasing commoditisation of productive property and employment by buying and selling companies, or parts of them, in the manner consumers buy clothes. They are also exponents of the debt bubble that has ballooned since the mid-1990s and that started to burst in 2008. As unregulated limited partnerships of financially strong individuals and institutions (pension funds, no longer outstanding examples of a long-term orientation,[9] are prominently represented), their operations heavily rely on borrowed money – which until the current financial crisis (2008-...) was abundantly available at cheap rates, particularly in Asia.

Private equity funds appear in very diverse forms (see Vitols 2008 for a balanced account) and have a somewhat longer-term perspective than hedge funds. The latter are characterised by arbitrage strategies, a high turnover of assets and aggressive trading as well as managerial incentives to outperform financial benchmarks (Goyer 2006: 407). A recurring criticism is that they are 'milking' employees, society (because they receive tax relief for their leverage) and even shareholders (ITUC 2007). Whether or not this is true is not a topic to be discussed here. I will only mention the counterarguments: that these funds bring efficiency to sometimes ailing companies and that venture capital funds – a form of private equity – are often essential for start-ups.

A final change worth mentioning which at least indirectly indicates change in a liberal direction is the decline of the wage share – i.e. the income of labour (including that of self-employed persons) as a share of GDP (see Figure 1.4). This has been in decline since about 1975, particularly in Japan and Europe.[10] This development is partly due to the shrinking number of self-employed persons, the rising number of pensioners receiving a capital income and the fragile position of low-skilled workers in the context of global competition. Competitive wages for these workers are low wages (cf. IMF 2007: 171). And perhaps it is true that, before state redistribution, low wages, and, as a consequence, the wage share did decline more in Europe than in the US, where a considerable group of low-paid workers always existed.

Figure 1.4   Wage share of national income in the EU15, Japan and the US, 1970-2005
(Share of total wages and salaries in total value added[a], percentage)

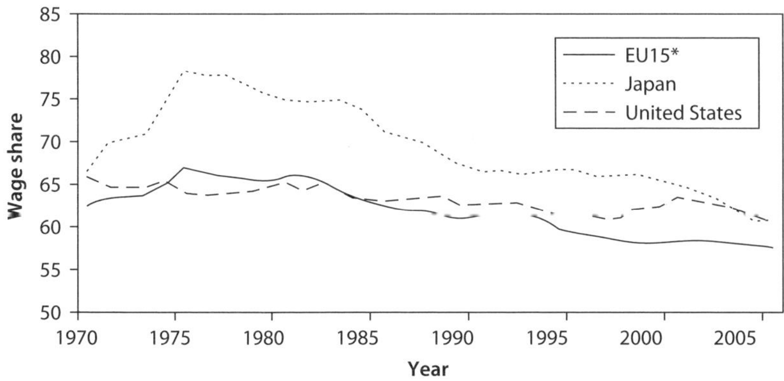

a) Total labour compensation, including employers' social security and pension contributions and imputed labour income for self-employed persons.
b) GDP-weighted average of the following countries: Austria, Belgium, Denmark, Finland, France, Germany, Ireland, Italy, the Netherlands, Spain, Sweden and the United Kingdom.
Source: OECD 2007: 117

The declining wage share moreover illustrates the changed power relationship between capital and labour. The bargaining position of capital vis-à-vis the unions has improved for a number of reasons: its increased mobility (or only its alleged mobility) and the related capacity to use the threat of exit; the discourse that in order to stay competitive, wage moderation is required; and the decline in union density. As a result, wages have trailed the rise in profits and productivity.

Beside these changes and partially related to them, change also occurred in the fields of employment protection, state expenditures, unemployment benefits, market capitalisation, collective bargaining coverage and the amount of temporary work. For these indicators, more detailed data are available. The next step is to calculate, as far as possible, how much they have changed from the mid-1990s to the mid-2000s.

Institutional change: an attempt to quantify it

In the previous section and in Figure 1.1, the institutional change in a liberal direction has roughly been indicated. To measure this change is tricky, however, because the *qualitative* indicators – capital-labour rela-

tions and state-market relations – will have to be *quantified* and both the qualitative as well as the quantitative ones will have to be *weighted*. The quantification of quality and the weighting (attaching scores to) of every indicator is not possible without some degree of arbitrariness and without violating the principle of precision. The *qualitative* indicators are the presence (or absence) and the strength of the institutional arrangements mentioned in the type descriptions. Examples of *quantitative* indicators are the level of:
– market capitalisation;
– wage bargaining coverage;
– social security and welfare benefits;
– temporary work;
– employment protection;
– product market regulation;
– public expenditures;
– tax progression;
– employee influence in companies;
– company protection (against hostile takeovers);
– privatisation of infrastructure;
– the average time and cost required to open a business.

Below, we will use the first seven of the quantitative indicators in order to roughly determine how much Western political economies have moved in a liberal direction. Apart from an indicative estimate, I will abstain from the too complicated and less precise attempt to quantify institutional change in terms of statism and corporatism which, together with liberalism, are relevant for our sample countries.

First and foremost, we have to recognise that we are in the realm of imprecision here. It is true that when producing statements about 'more' and 'less', 'higher' and 'lower', we are obliged to argue as exactly as possible. But because of measurement problems, a sophisticated rule of thumb might bring as much of an approximation to precision as advanced statistical methods do. 'Hard' computation becomes problematic when the empirical basis is soft. This is the case when comparisons are lopsided and basic data are only crude approximations of reality (examples include gross instead of net unemployment benefits, or benefits data without the related eligibility criteria), when not all data are available for all years, and when a number of factors possibly relevant for estimating overall institutional change are neglected because of a lack of comparative data. Examples of such factors are the influence of workers in companies (is there any co-determination; did it change?), the regulation of financial markets, tax progression, company protection against hostile takeovers, and the extent of red tape hampering start-ups. The transformation of quality into quantity is another source of imprecision. It renders the social sciences by definition less precise than the natural sciences. The transformation is regularly done by attaching quantitative scores to qualitative entities (e.g. job dismissal procedures). This is a tricky procedure as such, and the relative weighting of these scores is once again arbitrary.

The best that we can do, therefore, is to present a rough impression of change in the institutional dimensions mentioned (Tables 1.5a and 1.5b on pages 30-31). The chosen period is between the mid-1990s and the mid-2000s, and the method of measurement is a very simple one. Change is calculated first in percent per factor and second as average value. The latter is done by weighting the factors (see explanation in Table 1.5b).

What are the main and most remarkable results? What can be said with the cautiousness required because of the weak data basis? The strongest liberalisation has taken place in the fields of market capitalisation (up to the year 2000, stock prices exploded) and product market regulation (apart from specific national developments, the latter also reflects WTO agreements and EU activities). In the case of employment protection, the picture is somewhat mixed, and the same is true for unemployment benefits and temporary work. The least pronounced changes occurred in the coverage of collective bargaining (in nearly half the cases it was stable, in four it increased) and in public expenditures. The latter coincide with relatively stable tax receipts (OECD 2008a: 264). There has been a lot of discussion about a globalisation-forced tax race to the bottom, but income as well as corporate taxes have not changed much. Statutory corporate taxes have been lowered, but by broadening the tax base the effective rates remained relatively stable (cf. Genschel 2002: 250; Swank 2006). State income shrank primarily because of the privatisation of public companies, and so did state expenditures.

Overall, with the exception of Ireland, all political economies have changed in a liberal direction – the most liberal countries becoming even more liberal and the less liberal countries becoming less embedded (see Table 1.6). It also seems that a slight convergence has taken place between Australia, Britain and the US on the one hand and the average of the economies approximating non-liberal, embedded types on the other hand. Canada, Ireland, New Zealand and Switzerland on the liberal side and Denmark, France, Norway and Spain on the other side do not fit into this picture but in terms of inhabitants, these countries are clearly outnum-

Table 1.5a   Changes in the indicators of market orientation – Part I

	Product market regulation (index 0-5)			Employment protection (index 0-5)			Temporary work (% of full-time jobs)			Collective bargaining coverage (%)		
	1998	2003	**Change**	c1990	2003	**Change**	1994	2004	**Change**	1990	2000	**Change**
Australia	1,3	0,9	**-30**	0,9	1,2	**+33**	-	-	-	80	80	-
Austria	2,8	1,4	**-50**	2,2	1,9	**-14**	6,0	8,9	**+48**	95	95	-
Belgium	2,1	1,4	**-33**	3,2	2,2	**-31**	5,1	8,7	**+71**	90	90	-
Canada	1,4	1,2	**-14**	0,8	0,8	-	11,3	12,8	**+13**	38	32	**-16**
Denmark	1,5	1,1	**-27**	2,3	1,4	**-40**	12,0	9,8	**-19**	70	80	**+14**
Finland	2,1	1,3	**-38**	2,3	2,0	**-13**	18,3	16,2	**-11**	90	90	-
France	2,5	1,7	**-32**	2,7	3,0	**+10**	11,0	12,3	**+11**	90	90	-
Germany	1,9	1,4	**-26**	3,2	2,2	**-31**	10,3	12,2	**+19**	80	68	**-15**
Ireland	1,5	1,1	**-27**	0,9	1,1	**+22**	9,5	3,4	**-64**	70	70	-
Italy	2,8	1,9	**-32**	3,6	1,9	**-47**	7,3	11,9	**+63**	80	80	-
Japan	1,9	1,3	**-32**	2,1	1,8	**-14**	10,3	13,9	**+35**	20	15	**-25**
Netherlands	1,8	1,4	**-22**	2,7	2,1	**-22**	10,9	14,6	**+34**	70	80	**+14**
New Zealand	1,4	1,1	**-21**	-	1,5	-	-	-	-	60	25	**-58**
Norway	1,8	1,5	**-17**	2,9	2,6	**-10**	12,9	9,9	**-23**	70	70	-
Spain	2,3	1,6	**-30**	3,8	3,1	**-18**	33,7	30,4	**-10**	70	80	**+14**
Sweden	1,8	1,2	**-33**	3,5	2,2	**-37**	14,6	15,1	**+4**	80	90	**+13**
Switzerland	2,2	1,7	**-23**	1,1	1,1	-	12,9	12,3	**-5**	50	40	**-20**
UK	1,1	0,9	**-18**	0,6	0,7	**+17**	6,5	5,7	**-12**	40	30	**-25**
US	1,3	1,0	**-23**	0,2	0,2	-	-	4,0	-	18	14	**-22**

Sources: Conway et al. 2005: 59; OECD 2004b: 117; OECD database Temporary Work; Dice Report 2001: 2

Table 1.5b   Changes in the indicators of market orientation – Part II

	Market capitalisation			Unemployment benefits*			Total public expenditures			Weighted average**
	1990	2002	Change	1993	2003	Change	1994	2004	Change	
Australia	35,1	93,1	+165	27	22	-19	38,4	35,1	-9	6#
Austria	7,1	15,5	+118	27	32	+19	55,6	50,1	-10	11
Belgium	33,2	52,0	+57	40	42	+5	52,4	49,6	-5	20
Canada	42,1	80,5	+91	19	15	-25	49,7	39,9	-25	15
Denmark	29,3	44,4	+51	51	50	-2	60,4	54,8	-10	7
Finland	16,5	105,6	+540	38	36	-5	62,3	51,2	-18	13
France	25,6	67,6	+162	38	39	+3	54,2	53,7	-1	7
Germany	21,2	34,6	+63	28	29	+4	47,9	47,0	-2	14
Ireland	15,6	49,4	+217	31	32	+3	44,2	33,7	-24	-4
Italy	13,5	40,3	+199	17	34	+100	53,5	47,8	-11	16
Japan	95,6	53,2	-44	10	8	-20	35,6	37,3	+5	17
Netherlands	40,8	96,1	+136	53	53	-	51,7	46,6	-10	13
NewZealand	20,3	37,1	+83	30	28	-7	44,8	39,2	-13	21#
Norway	22,5	35,3	+57	39	34	-12	54,1	45,9	-15	5
Spain	21,8	70,7	+224	32	36	+12	46,4	38,8	-16	7
Sweden	39,3	73,7	+85	28	24	-13	70,3	56,7	-19	15
Switzerland	70,0	207,1	+196	30	33	+10	34,7	36,6	+5	6
UK	85,3	119,0	+39	19	13	-31	45,3	44,0	-3	7
US	53,2	106,4	+100	12	14	+17	37,0	36,4	-2	6

*'Average of gross unemployment benefit replacement rates, three family situation and three durations of unemployment'.

** With the exception of 'market capitalisation', the change of which was divided by a factor of 10,[11] all criteria were treated equally. Furthermore, minimal changes – Austrian market capitalisation moved only slightly from 7.1% to 15.5% – were given only one percentage point and changes from a very low start level have only received half point, e.g. in the case of the strong rise of unemployment benefits in Italy.

On the basis of only 6 and 5 (instead of 7) criteria respectively.

Sources: OECD n.a.; OECD 2006b: 189; Höpner 2005b: Table 2.

bered by Australia, the UK and the US as well as by Japan, Germany, Italy, the Netherlands, Belgium and Sweden. Taking this into consideration, the last decade differs from the previous one, as it was analysed – on the basis of somewhat different criteria – by Hall and Gingerich (2004), who did not detect changes worth mentioning. They are still right, however, to claim that the differences between e.g. Norway, Belgium and Sweden or France and Italy on the one hand and on the other hand the US are still large (see Figure 1.5).

Table 1.6   Degrees of institutional change on the axis between embedded and liberal capitalism, mid-1990s – mid-2005
(% change in parentheses)

Relatively High	Above Average	Average	Below Average	De-liberalisation
New Zealand (21)	Japan (17)	Austria (11)	Australia (6)	Ireland (-4)
Belgium (20)	Italy (16)		Denmark (7)	
	Sweden (16)		France (7)	
	Canada (15)		Spain (7)	
	Germany (14)		UK (7)	
	Netherlands (13)		Switzerland (6)	
	Finland (13)		US (6)	
			Norway (5)	

Looking at individual countries, the most striking case seems to be Ireland that did not liberalise at all. Product market regulation was loosened there, market capitalisation grew and state expenditures decreased, but employment protection and unemployment benefits increased. Of the sample countries, Belgium liberalised the most, followed by Sweden, the Netherlands and Finland (a remarkable case due to the explosive Nokia-related rise in market capitalisation). Japan's market capitalisation fell, reflecting the decline of this country's stock market, but whether or not Japan has considerably liberalised is a disputed question. Here, the indication of overall change is 'above average', which seems to be less than Ronal Dore asserts (2006/07: 22f) – he speaks of a 'shareholder revolution' since the 1990s – but perhaps more than Steven Vogel (2005: 162), who thinks that most change in Japan has been 'routine adjustment' and 'bounded innovation (...) shaped by pre-existing institutions'. Italy is worth mentioning because of the sharp rise in its unemployment benefits (from a pre-modern, non-liberal level to the Western average). Finally, one has to mention the significant increase in temporary jobs in countries where employment protection is still high – Belgium, Italy and the Netherlands are examples, while in Britain and the US the amount of temporary work is low and relatively stable (but this is not the case in Canada). In Scandinavia, it has declined with the exception of Sweden (a slight increase there).

What these changes show when plotted on the axis between pure liberal and embedded capitalism is roughly illustrated in Figure 1.5 for the sample countries, with the US as a contrasting case. This figure is based on the data from Tables 1.5a and 1.5b and a system of scores assigned to the items these tables contain (for details, see Becker 2009: 71f). It also reflects the fact that every capitalist political economy is basically liberal and therefore the continuum starts at the value of 13.[12] The most striking conclusion is perhaps that Switzerland, which is both highly corporatist and highly liberal, is in the vicinity of the US, while the other countries remain far, or even very far, from the US (the same could be said of France, Germany and Italy, while the remaining Anglo-Saxon countries would have to be located somewhere between Switzerland and the US).

Figure 1.5   Location of political economies on the axis between the ideal types of pure liberal and embedded capitalism in the mid-1990s and mid-2000s (T_1, grey) and (T_2, black)

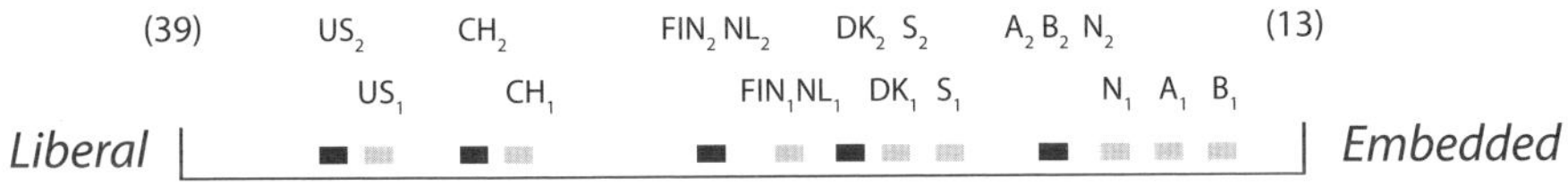

Changes in a liberal direction are not the only changes that have taken place. France has not liberalised much, but statism does seem to have declined (Hall 2007). Levy (2005: 123) states that only the statist policies and not the statist framework have been dismantled, and that statism became 'market-conforming' (ibid: 119). In some of the strongly corporatist countries analysed in this volume, by contrast, a specific movement in the opposite direction has occurred.

Due to shifting power relations between capital and labour, wage bargaining – known for its relatively centralised character – has changed in four of these countries: Austria, Denmark, the Netherlands and Sweden. Starting in the 1980s, bargaining patterns have shifted to a relatively decentralised level (a trend that also was visible in most other political economies; cf. OECD 2006a: 81). Although the move is in a liberal direction, it did not imply a fundamental weakening of corporatism – it only changed its face from directly to indirectly centralised corporatism (see Table 1.7[13]), sometimes with a brief period of decentralisation in between as in Denmark and Sweden.[14] In contrast to the four countries with changing corporatism, Belgium, Finland and Norway by and large maintained their centralism. And in Switzerland, which is both strongly corporatist as well as strongly liberal, wage bargaining is relatively decentralised by tradition (which is also due to the fragmented political structure of the country).

A key feature of indirect centralisation is the political discussion of wage guidelines for the negotiations at branch level, with the government, the peak organisations of capital and labour as well as expert bodies involved. The national discussion of bargaining guidelines is also the context of the typical corporatist exchanges of, for example, wage restraint against tax reduction or the maintenance of a given level of social security (the times that increased benefits could be negotiated are over). The remarkable aspect is that the state has taken the initiative in this context: decentralisation was, as Due et al. (1993: 146) call it, a process of centralised decentralisation. And in indirect centralisation, the government behaved as the 'competition state' that Cerny (2000) has described. As a result, the statist component in the countries approximating corporatism became somewhat strengthened in recent years.

Table 1.7   Measure of coordination in corporatist wage bargaining systems

	1970	1990	2000
Austria	Centralised	Indirectly centralised	Indirectly centralised
Belgium	Centralised	Centralised	Centralised
Denmark	Centralised	Decentralised	Indirectly centralised
Finland	Centralised	Centralised	Centralised
Netherlands	Centralised	Indirectly centralised	Indirectly centralised
Norway	Centralised	Centralised	Centralised
Sweden	Centralised	Decentralised	Indirectly centralised
Switzerland	Decentralised	Decentralised	Decentralised

In sum, in the (still) highly corporatist political economies we have had, in different degrees, decreasing corporatist coordination and statist regulation in certain fields, but in some of these political economies (Austria,

Denmark, the Netherlands and Sweden) we have also had an extension of the role of the state as a guide in wage bargaining. We do not (yet) have the instruments and data to determine and graphically illustrate these developments exactly. In order to quantitatively determine and distinguish corporatism and statism, quality has to be transformed into quantity. This is a particularly tricky affair. Future work in this area will have to bring more precision. In Figure 1.6, I have nonetheless done this quantification – in the form of a rough indication by taking over the liberal scores from Figure 1.5, distributing the corporatist and statist scores on the basis of Siaroff's corporatism scale (see Table 1.1), and taking into consideration whether corporatism is tripartite (with explicit state involvement) or bipartite and whether the state structure is unitarian or federal (for more details, see Becker 2009: 75ff).

Figure 1.6 illustrates the Swedish development in the field between the three relevant ideal types of liberalism, corporatism and statism. Sweden is chosen because of its prominent role in the international discussion and because this country has undergone marked changes in the period between the mid-1990s and mid-2000s. In the figure, every dimension is a continuum in itself that starts at 0. Together, the values a country scores must add up to 100%. Sweden's liberalism score has increased from about 40% to nearly 50%, while the score on corporatism – Swedish corporatism is bipartite – has declined from about 35% to 30%

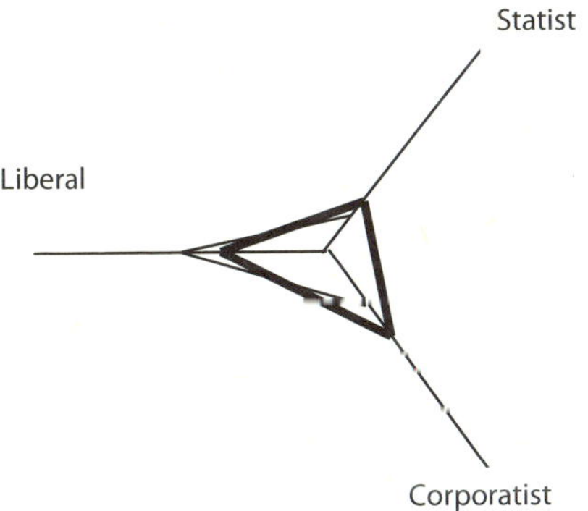

Figure 1.6   Rough indication of the Swedish case in the field between the statist, corporatist and liberal ideal types at T_1 (mid-1990s; fat line) and T_2 (mid-2000s; thin line)*

*Each of the three rays starts at a value of 0 at the centre of the web and has a maximum value of 100. The total of the spider web of the illustrated case must also add up to 100 (percent).

and the score on statism has slightly decreased from its mid-1990s level of about 25%. If we would have chosen Switzerland instead of Sweden, we would see an almost static picture – Switzerland moved only slightly– where the liberal dimension is more pronounced, the corporatist one less so and statism rather weak. As in Sweden, corporatism is bipartite, but in contrast to Sweden, the Swiss state structure is federal and contains many veto points. And the other countries would reveal different 'spider webs' again. Before plotting more cases, however, more precision must be brought into this work.

The contributions

The subsequent chapters analyse the recent politico-economic developments in four pairs of countries: Sweden and Finland, Denmark and Norway, Switzerland and Austria, and Belgium and the Netherlands. Taking two countries at a time gives a comparative dimension to the contribution and carves out the specific national trajectories with more clarity. All of these chapters deal with the same set of questions: What happened to the countries' welfare systems, corporate governance, labour market legislation and (corporatist) industrial relations? The country contributions also point out the relevant additional peculiarities of their cases – e.g. the special role of immigrant workers in the Swiss labour market or the conflict-ridden division between Flanders and Wallonia in Belgium. Each chapter has an individual character due to the emphasis on the common aspects of their subject in different degrees. In terms of the typology presented in this chapter, all case studies investigate the institutional movement in the field between the corporatist, statist and liberal types.

The first case study is that of Karl-Oskar Lindgren on Sweden and Finland. For decades, Sweden has been the Nordic model country par excellence. However, after its severe economic crisis in the early 1990s (along with Finland), it lost its model status. Since the 1980s it has been a hot discussion topic whether or not Swedish corporatism has seriously been weakened or only been changed by the retreat of the employers' association from centralised collective wage bargaining in the late 1980s. In the 2000s, the country regained its model status, joined this time by Finland, the 'Nokia model'. The author, who is particularly interested in the interplay between stability and change, sets out to answer the question how much these current 'Nordic' political economies differ from the earlier Swedish model.

Though under strain due to the decline in union membership by a few percentage points in recent years, Swedish corporatism has experienced a revival since the late 1990s, moving towards state-led indirect centralisation after the social democrats returned to power. This is an example of what Lindgren calls continuity through change – a subject he also presents brief theoretical ideas about. Change in Finland, where the social democrats were never as dominant as in Sweden, was rather moderate. Its corporatism is still centralised. Challenges, Lindgren adds, could stem from electoral shifts – since the mid-2000s, coalitions of centre and liberal parties govern in both countries (in Finland, the Greens are also involved) – if they turn out to be structural, as well as from Europeanisation, which poses a threat to the socio-economic peculiarities of Finland and Sweden (but also of other Nordic countries). Support for the welfare system is still strong, and the fundamentals appear to be quite stable, however.

The Danish and Norwegian capitalisms are examined in the next chapter by Mikkel Mailand. Because of its oil, Norway is the richest country in the world (apart from tiny Luxembourg). Nonetheless, the egalitarian social democrats are still the dominant government party. Relatively stable political relations (though the right wing has grown) correspond to a relatively stable, still centralised corporatism. Denmark, by contrast, has been governed by conservative-liberal coalitions from 1982 to 1993 and since 2003. In the 1990s, the country was considered an economic model because of its famous concept of 'flexicurity', which combines relatively weak dismissal protection with high public employment and a very high level of unemployment benefits. Mailand is critical of flexicurity and, in a reversal of Esping-Andersen's concept of 'decommodification of labour', he analyses it as a step towards 're-commodification'.

Overall, Mailand ends with similar conclusions as Lindgren in the previous chapter. He also identifies similar challenges. Denmark has, as Sweden, somewhat changed its institutional settings but without undermining corporatism, while Norway, as Finland, features a high degree of continuity. Not to forget, Norway is not an EU member state and therefore less affected by Europeanisation (although far from unaffected by it). This is probably one of the reasons that it has been less liberalised than Denmark, which after the early 1990s put emphasis on the competitiveness of its economy and deregulated it to some degree. Mailand puts his cases into historical perspective, and instead of naming them as approximately corporatist capitalisms he prefers the largely synonymous concept of 'negotiated economies'.

From the Nordic region, the book moves to the Alps for an analysis of Austria and Switzerland, countries that have not received the attention they deserve in comparative political economy. Switzerland has a very high employment rate and the reputation as a haven of financial and economic stability (as well as a haven for secret bank accounts), and Austria has been, almost unnoticed, one of the rising economic stars of the EU since its entry in 1995. The authors, André Mach and Alexandre Afonso, provide an overview of the developments in these countries' political economies over the last 20 years. First, they investigate socio-economic performance and, in a related thread, highlight the institutional foundations of economic governance in both countries. Thereafter, they outline continuity and change across the spheres of the political economy dealt with in all of the case studies. Throughout their text, they give particular attention to the power relations between state and economy as well as capital and labour.

As with the other authors, Mach and Afonso detect a general trend towards a more market-driven model that nonetheless did not undermine the established basic institutional structures. Furthermore, they write that patterns of change must be differentiated both between Austria and Switzerland as well as between spheres (for example, industrial relations or the welfare system), depending on power relationships and institutions governing separate economic spheres. In Austria, the state is considerably stronger than in hyper-decentralised Switzerland, and the same is true for its corporatism. In contrast to Austrian public intervention, Switzerland traditionally places a higher degree of emphasis on private initiative. It cannot compensate for the lower reform capacity that strong decentralisation brings about. Comparing these two different countries offers a nice illustration of path dependence.

The final pair of countries consists of Belgium and the Netherlands, the latter a distinctly service-led economy and the former still reliant on industry to a considerable degree. While the Netherlands in the late 1990s and early 2000s has been widely discussed as the Dutch 'delta' or 'polder' model (large parts of the country are in the Rhine delta and are below sea level on 'polders'), Belgium has, just as Austria, largely been ignored in international comparisons – an extra reason to include it here. The contribution of Hester Houwing and Kurt Vandaele shows that, despite the resilience of corporatist industrial relations and welfare institutions, socio-economic and employment policies changed since the 1990s towards activation and flexibility in order to raise the employment rates and maintain the sustainability of the welfare regime. As a consequence of the relative weakness of the unions and far-reaching financialisation (notably in the Netherlands), the authors indicate a shift in a liberal direction.

In the Netherlands, they observe a declining role of the social partners in the formulation of social policy, while the labour market has become more flexible. In Belgium, a certain etatisation accompanied liberalisation. Overall, Belgium is perhaps the more remarkable case. This might be because in the late 1990s it tried to copy the Dutch delta model, renaming it the 'belfry model' (after all the belfries in the old Flemish cities). It was not a success, however. The main reason, prominently outlined in Howing's and Vandaele's contribution, is the conflict-ridden relationship between Flanders and Wallonia. This relationship has undermined *Belgian* corporatism, enhanced the role of the state and triggered regional institutional separatism.

The final chapters by Schmidt and Becker/Van Kersbergen relate to the country studies but are of a different character and broaden the spectrum of the volume. In chapter 6, Vivien Schmidt puts the changes of the small corporatist countries in a European context and compares their development to that of a few bigger EU members, such as France and Germany. She also addresses the very important question what smallness means in the context of the topics discussed in this volume. Perhaps not everyone realises immediately how small some of the sample countries are. Only Belgium and the Netherlands have more than 10 million inhabitants – the Netherlands with 16 million inhabitants is the most populated. Denmark, Finland and Norway have slightly more than five million inhabitants. Many provinces of the bigger European countries (Bavaria and four other German states, Catalonia in Spain, Lombardy in Italy) are larger than these countries, let alone American states such as California and even European capitals such as London and Paris.

Is smallness an advantage? Politically it has been so in northwest Europe, Schmidt says, because smallness makes it easier to maintain corporatism and to build up effective decision-making (the Swiss political-institutional structure is very fragmented, however). The comparative analysis of the institutional structure of politics is therefore an important element of this chapter. The author's considerations on the process of Europeanisation directly relate to the theme of state capacity. For it appears that the small corporatist countries are more successful in following the EU criteria than the larger member states – a feature that appears not to be true for Ireland and the small southern European countries of Portugal and Greece. Economic openness and a pragmatic politico-ideological discourse about openness and globalisation are, together with national differences, further elements that, in Schmidt's view, can give a competitive edge to the 'smalls' discussed in this volume.

In the final chapter, Uwe Becker and Kees van Kersbergen begin with the fact that, despite the liberalisation described in the previous chapters, the sample countries are still highly corporatist and yet belong to the top performers in almost every respect. Therefore, Becker and Van Kersbergen ask whether corporatist capitalism is a specifically European socio-economic model. They not only look for a social model in the narrower sense of the welfare system but also for a social model in the comprehensive sense of a *socio-economic* model. They situate their contribution in the context of intensified global competition and the current economic crisis that has called the ongoing liberalisation of capitalism into question. Analysing socio-economic performances (inequality, poverty, care of the environment, but also innovative capacity), they find the sample countries among the best performers and the Scandinavian political economies even as the best of all. They conclude that there are good normative arguments to launch corporatist capitalism as a European socio-economic model. Becker and Van Kersbergen also address the question whether or not corporatist capitalism – or parts of it – can be realised in other EU countries.

Notes

*   For constructive criticisms I thank Daniel Mügge and Vivien Schmidt.

1   Prominent scholars arguing along similar lines are Schmidt (2002a: 107f) and Crouch (2005: 23, 62f).

2   Correspondingly, I generally prefer to talk in terms of political economies approximating ideal types like the liberal one instead of naming them liberal. When this is incidentally done – as in the title of chapter 7 – it is only for the sake of simplicity and with the meaning of approximating a certain type.

3   Take for example political economies that structurally reveal high or, on the opposite, low levels of state interventionism. These political economies include political cultures where state interventionism and state reluctance respectively are considered 'normal' by a relevant majority – even if the norm is contested. Or take corporatist capital – labour relations that not only, by definition, involve negotiations in terms of the common interest, but also a culture of consensualism. Culture as a structural property pointing to patterns of interaction among citizens (Thompson et al. 1990), but also, as in the examples, between organisations as well as between citizens and the state, is inherent to many (or most) politico-economic relations. As an integral part

of social relations, culture does not need to be mentioned as a separate criterion, however. Higher or just lower than average levels of risk-taking and of
individual independence, by contrast, are examples of relatively autonomous
cultural traits and therefore not a structural aspect of whatever capitalist
variety.

4   The names Nordic and Scandinavian are used synonymously in this volume,
    although Lindgren in chapter 2 prefers Nordic. These names do not have ex-
    actly the same meaning – strictly speaking Finland does not belong to Scan-
    dinavia – but it has largely become common to use them as synonyms.

5   Both may bring about generous welfare systems and redistribution. Of the
    strongly corporatist countries Scandinavia and continental examples most
    approximate this divide, while in the statist field French history has been
    one of social-democratisation (as well as recently of liberalisation). Because
    of the basic liberal – embedded distinction it makes no sense to construct a
    liberal sub-variety of statist and corporatist capitalism. Corporatist or statist
    elements and liberal elements come of course together and constitute spe-
    cific hybrids, simply because capitalism is basically liberal.

6   This trend is confirmed by a PEW (2007: 13) research on American attitudes
    to the 'poor and needy'. Seeing the American support for narrowing income
    differences growing one has to keep in mind, however, that the differences
    they accept are much larger than in Europe (cf. Table N.1) – even if they
    might have become smaller since 1992. A striking fact is again that West Ger-
    mans accept much larger income differences than Scandinavians and even
    the people in Canada and 'Down Under' do.

Table N.1   **Legitimate income differences in eight countries, unskilled factory
worker is 100**

	How much do you think a ... should earn		
	Unskilled factory worker	Doctor	Chairman of a large national company
Sweden	100	195	239
Norway	100	207	228
West Germany	100	384	711
Austria	100	438	615
Australia	100	326	480
N-Zealand	100	351	419
Canada	100	420	512
US	100	614	1114

Source: Svallfors 1997: 289

7   A relevant context is the state-socialist past of the East Germans raising their non-individualist attitudes above those of the Swedes.

8   One has to buy detailed data from advisory companies, and these data are very expensive.

9   According to Richard Sennett (2006: 40) pension funds keep stocks on average for no longer than 3.8 months (it is not clear whether he talks about American funds or pensions funds worldwide).

10   The usual calculation of the wage rate is not undisputed because it does not appropriately take into account elements such as transfer and property income and therefore is unable to distinguish between disposable income and employee compensation – according to *Wikipedia*. In an adjusted graph of the wage rate the decline is less pronounced.

11   The huge changes in market capitalisation – 540% in Finland – are impossible in the other fields where negotiation and struggle are important factors pushing or hampering change. By contrast, market capitalisation (if it is not that of former state-owned companies) is a process autonomously managed by companies. Moreover, it is strongly influenced by the ups and downs of the stock market.

12   The basis of the construction is a five-level scale that for every criterion runs from very low over low, intermediate and high to very high and attaching 1 point to every level (half a point in the case of temporary work though the minimum is also one), and giving six points extra to every national political economy because capitalism is basically liberal. Because every country gets at least one point for each of the seven criteria, the minimum level is 6 + 7 = 13 points. The maximum is 6 + 6 x 5 + 3 = 39.

13   Table 1.7 is taken from the *Final Report* of the 5th Framework project Small-cons (2006) and the information regarding Belgium and Norway is taken from the contributions of Houwing/Vandaele and Mailand to this volume. OECD data (in 2006a: 81) slightly differ from those in Table 1.7. They distinguish between centralisation and coordination and operate a five-level scale. They signal slight changes in the level of Swiss centralisation (from level 3 down to level 2) and do not see any change in Austria and the Netherlands in this respect (constantly level 3).

14   In Sweden this was largely due to the retreat of employers from any centralised bargaining in the late 1980s. In the changed context of 1997 they came back, however (cf. Elvander 2002b).

2 The Variety of Capitalism in Sweden and Finland
Continuity Through Change

Karl-Oskar Lindgren

In recent years, partly spurred by the failure of the globalisation thesis predicting rapid institutional and political convergence across countries (e.g. Lash & Urry 1987), we have witnessed an increased interest among comparative political economists in the distinctiveness and performance of various national economic systems.[1] The extensive literature on the "varieties of capitalism" that has evolved over the last decade provides a particularly prominent example of this current trend (Hall & Soskice 2001, Hancké et al. 2008).

Traditionally, the Varieties of Capitalism approach (VoC) holds that developed industrialised economies cluster into two distinct groups labelled Coordinated Market Economies and Liberal Market Economies (CMEs and LMEs). In most writings on the topic, these two varieties of capitalism are pictured as stable and durable equilibriums to a set of coordination problems facing economic actors in various spheres of the economy.

This account of contemporary capitalism has, however, been criticised on typological as well as more substantive grounds. First, a number of authors have argued that the liberal-coordinated dichotomy of the VoC approach does not adequately cover the fundamental differences existing in capitalist economies. For instance, in the introductory chapter of this book Uwe Becker argues that we are better advised to distinguish between five, rather than two, distinct ideal types of capitalism (see also Becker 2009). More precisely, Becker suggests that we draw a distinction between capitalism of the *liberal* type on the one hand, and four distinct forms of coordinated or embedded capitalism on the other hand – i.e., *statist, corporatist, patrimonial* and *meso-communitarian.*

Second, and of particular relevance for the present chapter, the VoC approach has been criticised for exaggerating the extent of institutional stability in many countries by portraying non-market coordination as a thing some countries have and others lack, when in reality, "coordination is a political process, and an outcome, that has to be actively sustained and nurtured" (Thelen 2001: 73). That is, every now and then we should expect important political and economic actors to assess whether the coordination practices inherent in the present national capitalist system actually serve their interests. And to the extent that this is not the case, we should expect these actors to try to change the institutional framework in a way that furthers their respective interests (Lindgren 2006; Hall & Thelen 2009). This is especially true in small open economies, since these countries are particularly vulnerable to the competitiveness problems associated with malfunctioning institutional frameworks (Katzenstein 1985; Elvander 2002).

Because support for the existing institutional framework within a country is always contingent upon actors' perceptions of the effects of this framework, institutional stability cannot be assumed but needs to be explained. Even more importantly, since stability and change are two sides of the same coin, we cannot understand institutional change without understanding institutional stability (cf. Hall & Thelen 2009). Consequently, if the VoC approach is to be anything more than a classification exercise, we need to pay greater attention to the dynamics of how distinct national capitalist systems evolve and endure over time.

Toward this end, this chapter studies the recent developments in the national capitalist systems of Sweden and Finland. In an international context, Sweden and Finland are interesting in that both countries are representatives of what is commonly referred to as the Nordic social model, which has enjoyed considerable attention among both scholars and politicians over the years. In the 1970s and 1980s, the Nordic model, characterised by a large welfare state and extensive non-market coordination (mainly of the corporatist type) was commonly hailed as the prototype of a well-functioning variety of capitalism that promoted equity as well as efficiency. But in the 1990s, and against the backdrop of the severe economic crisis hitting Sweden and Finland, the Nordic model fell into disarray, and many commentators predicted its imminent demise. Nonetheless, in the last few years the Nordic social model seems to have risen from the dead, and in many quarters the corporatist Nordic capitalism is once again pitted as a viable, or even superior, alternative to the Anglo-Saxon one (e.g. Sapir 2006).

This renewed interest in the Nordic political economy, however, raises at least two important questions. To what extent is the current Nordic model, as practised in Sweden and Finland, really the same as the celebrated Nordic model of the 1970s and 1980s? What explains the relative stability and change of different aspects of the national capitalist systems in Sweden and Finland over time? The aim of the present chapter is to answer these questions.

By raising and addressing these issues we move beyond the static account of capitalism still characterising much of the contemporary research on varieties of capitalism. Through its detailed account of the more recent developments in Sweden and Finland, the analysis of this chapter provides part of the information necessary to answer the question posed by Becker in the introduction of the book: i.e., whether and to what extent the capitalist systems of the small corporatist economies of Western Europe have experienced a move in a liberal direction as a result of the global politico-economic changes taking place in recent decades. Although merely descriptive, the analysis of the chapter also helps to identify important mechanisms of continuity and change within the capitalist systems of small open economies. In this respect, the present study contributes to ongoing attempts aimed at developing a more dynamic theory of capitalist diversity (cf. Deeg & Jackson 2007).

The rest of the chapter proceeds as follows. The first section deals with the economic and political impacts of the severe economic crisis hitting both Sweden and Finland in the early 1990s. The second traces institutional developments since the start of the economic recovery in the mid-1990s. The third assesses the relative stability and change of the national capitalist systems in Sweden and Finland over the last couple of decades, and discusses possible explanations for these developments. The fourth and final section concludes and points to some of the challenges currently facing the Swedish and Finnish varieties of capitalism.

The 1990s crisis: a moment for change

Economic development in Sweden and Finland during the 1970s and 1980s was marked by relative economic success, and many observers praised the Nordic model as a third way between socialism and capitalism. In the early 1990s, however, the third way seemed to come to an abrupt end when both Sweden and Finland experienced an economic downturn of a magnitude unseen since the Great Depression of the 1930s.

The origin of the 1990s crisis has been the subject of intense debate in both countries. But most commentators seem to agree – although they differ in their emphasis on the relative importance of various factors –

that the crisis was spurred by an unfortunate combination of bad policy decisions, unsolved structural problems and an international economic slump (Honkapohja & Koskela 1999; Hagberg et al. 2006). In Finland, the unexpected collapse of the Soviet Union further added to the economic problems.

Regardless of the exact reasons for the economic crisis, however, the consequences were severe, as can be seen in the figures displayed in Table 2.1. Both the Swedish and the Finnish economies experienced negative growth rates for three consecutive years from 1991 to 1993. Between 1990 and 1994, the Finnish unemployment rate rose from 3% to almost 17% – the second highest in the entire OECD area – and in Sweden, the unemployment rate more than quadrupled from 2% to 9% in the same period.

Table 2.1 Economic outcomes in Finland and Sweden, 1970-2004

	70-74	*75-79*	*80-84*	*85-89*	*90-94*	*95-99*	*00-04*
Finland							
Unemployment	2.9	5.7	5.8	5.0	10.9	12.9	9.1
Employment	69.0	69.6	72.0	72.8	65.9	63.3	67.6
Growth	5.6	2.4	3.1	4.0	-1.4	4.6	2.9
Inequality	26.7	21.4	20.5	20.0	20.3	23.4	25.8
Productivity	–	–	–	2.6	1.1	2.3	2.0
Sweden							
Unemployment	2.2	1.9	3.0	2.2	5.8	8.6	5.5
Employment	73.6	77.8	78.8	80.0	75.7	70.5	72.9
Growth	3.4	1.5	1.8	2.7	0.1	3.1	2.6
Inequality	–	21.1	20.3	21.2	24.5	26.4	28.6
Productivity	–	–	–	0.5	0.4	1.4	2.1

Note: See the appendix for a description of the variables.

As the table makes clear, the rise in unemployment was matched by a rapid decline in employment. During the first half of the 1990s, the employment rate decreased by more than 10 percentage points in both countries. And, in Sweden in particular, the economic crisis was accompanied by low productivity growth and rising income inequality. In both Sweden and Finland, the early 1990s was also characterised by falling disposable income and profitability.

According to the VoC literature, an external shock like an economic crisis is considered an important impetus for institutional and policy change (cf. Hall & Thelen 2009). In times of crisis, political actors are forced to reassess the benefits associated with existing institutions and policies, and contemplate available alternatives. The cases under consideration here are no exceptions to this general rule.

The early 1990s clearly constituted a moment for change in both Sweden and Finland. In particular, three different factors came together to create a golden window of opportunity for those wanting to liberalise the corporatist capitalist models of the two countries. The first was the growing influence of monetarist and market-liberal ideas in the policy debate, as described by Mark Blyth and others (Blyth 2002; see also Boréus 1994, Kauppinen 1994). From the market-liberal perspective, overly generous welfare policies and extensive product and labour market regulations were at the root of the economic crisis in both Sweden and Finland (e.g. Henrekson 1996; Lindbeck 1997). The way out of the crisis was therefore through welfare cuts and extensive deregulation of product and labour markets, since this would reduce the market power of wage-setters and thereby lower wage costs and increase employment and productivity, according to the market liberals. Second, skyrocketing public deficits in both countries made it increasingly difficult for the supporters of universal welfare provision to oppose public expenditure cuts aimed at balancing the economy. A third and final factor adding to the pressure on the Swedish and Finnish capitalist systems was the election of centre-right governments in both countries in 1991. These parties' support for universal welfare policies and market regulations was historically considerably more contingent, and less ideological, than that of the social democrats. The stage was thus set for a radical restructuring of the Swedish and Finnish capitalist systems.

In order to see whether and to what extent the national capitalist systems of Sweden and Finland were subject to change over the course of the 1990s, we will study the development in the four core areas of the capitalist system identified by Becker in his introduction, i.e., the areas of welfare benefits, labour market legislation, industrial relations and corporate governance.

Starting with the issue of welfare benefits, we may first consider the development of benefit generosity over time in three core welfare state programmes: unemployment insurance, sickness benefits and pensions. In a recent study, Scruggs & Allan (2006) report an aggregate generosity score – using a modified form of the procedure used by Esping-Andersen

(1990) in the construction of his famous decommodification index – for each of these programmes. In the cases of unemployment insurance and sickness benefits, the score includes net replacement rates, the coverage of the insurance, the duration of benefits, the length of the qualification period and the number of waiting days, whereas in the case of pensions, the score is composed of pension replacement rates for minimum and standard pensions, the pension take-up ratio, qualifying years for standard pension and the proportion of pension contributions paid by the employee. For each of the three programmes, a higher aggregate score indicates more generous entitlements. The scores for Sweden and Finland over the period 1970-2002 are displayed in Table 2.2.

Table 2.2 **Welfare benefits and taxes in Sweden and Finland, 1970-2004**

	70-74	*75-79*	*80-84*	*85-89*	*90-94*	*95-99*	*00-04*
Finland							
UB	4.2	4.9	5.2	8.1	9.2	9.1	8.5
Sickness	9.9	8.7	9.4	10.8	10.6	9.9	9.6
Pensions	10.8	12.9	15.3	16.3	14.6	13.4	12.5
Tax wedge	–	41.6	42.9	46.6	47.3	49.3	45.3
Sweden							
UB	7.5	9.1	9.9	11.0	11.8	10.9	10.4
Sickness	14.7	15.4	15.4	15.5	15.0	14.1	13.7
Pensions	13.0	15.6	18.5	18.1	16.0	14.8	11.8
Tax wedge	–	50.7	50.7	51.7	46.7	50.3	48.3

Note: See the appendix for a description of the variables. The time series for UB, sickness and pensions end in 2002, so for these variables the figures in the last column refer to the period 2000-2002.

As can be seen in the table, there was a trend toward less generous welfare benefits in both countries during the 1990s. In order to curb the rising public deficit in Finland at the beginning of the 1990s, the centre-right government found it necessary to impose cutbacks on most welfare entitlement programmes. As described by Uusitalo (1996:5), this was done by means of a number of different techniques: "indexed increases to benefits were cancelled, compensation levels of earnings-related unemployment, sickness and maternity benefits were lowered, and eligibility for some benefits was tightened." The greatest opposition to these cutbacks

came from the trade unions. In 1992, for instance, Finnish unions coun-
tered a governmental proposal of reduced unemployment benefits with
the threat of a general strike. The conflict remained unresolved until the
centre-right government "agreed not to reduce unemployment benefits,
and instead reluctantly accepted the union's demand for increased taxes"
(Sundberg 1993). A similar conflict occurred also in 1994 when the government, in the face of the threat of a general strike, was forced to give up
its plans for changed labour laws and unemployment benefit cuts (Bergholm 2007).

The development of welfare benefits in Sweden during the 1990s closely
mirrored that of Finland, as can be seen in Table 2.2. Under the shadow of
an exploding public deficit and aggressive speculative attacks against the
Swedish krona, the centre-right government implemented a number of
cuts in welfare benefits in 1992 and 1993, most of them with Social Democratic support. To take but a few examples, unemployment and sickness
benefits were reduced from 90% to 80% of previous earnings, basic pensions were adjusted downward by 2 percentage points, and the eligibility
conditions in many social insurance programmes were tightened (Huber
& Stephens 2001; Palme et al. 2002). As in Finland, the fiercest opposition
to the welfare cuts in Sweden came from the trade unions. In October
1992, the LO, the largest blue-collar confederation in Sweden, took a radical initiative, calling for massive political protests against the centre-right
government which mobilised tens of thousands of participants across the
country (Dagens Nyheter 1992). A similar protest, although of smaller
magnitude, was arranged by the LO the year after.

When discussing the development of welfare benefits, it seems conse-
quent to comment at least briefly on the closely related development of
the tax system. Turning to the development of taxes, we see in Table 2.2
that in Finland the average tax wedge – defined as income tax plus employee and employer social contributions less cash benefits as a percentage of labour costs – remained at a similar level in the early 1990s as in the
late 1980s. Looking at the annual figures, however, the tax wedge started
to increase in 1992 when Finnish taxes were increased in order to curb
rapidly rising public deficits.

In Sweden, on the other hand, taxes were drastically reduced in 1990,
i.e., before the onset of the economic crisis, when the Social Democratic
government implemented what in Sweden has been known as the "tax
reform of the century". Upon entering office in 1991, the centre-right government had plans to reduce Swedish taxes even further. But due to the
economic depression, the newly elected government had to give up most

of these plans and instead the Swedish tax wedge was kept at a constant level during the initial phase of the economic crisis.

As mentioned previously, market liberal ideas gained increased currency in policy debates in Sweden and Finland in the early 1990s. From this perspective, high taxes and overly generous welfare benefits were part of the structural problem of the Swedish and Finnish economies; the other problem was the excessive market power of wage-setters due to various types of imperfections in product and labour markets. To assess the impact of the 1990s crisis on the national capitalist systems of Sweden and Finland, we shall therefore also consider the developments with regard to the areas of *labour market legislation* and *industrial relations* in general, and the nature of competition in product and labour markets in particular. Toward this end, Table 2.3 provides data on four important and readily available indicators related to the workings of these markets: the extent of product market regulations (PMR), employment protection legislation (EPL), union density (UD) and the degree of coordination in wage bargaining (CWB).

Table 2.3 **Labour and product market regulations in Sweden and Finland, 1970-2003**

	70-74	75-79	80-84	85-89	90-94	95-99	00-03
Finland							
CWB	3.8	4.0	3.6	3.6	3.6	4.0	3.8
UD	58.6	66.9	68.8	71.0	76.0	78.5	77.4
EPL	1.0	1.4	1.9	2.2	2.3	2.3	2.3
PMR	–	5.5	5.4	4.9	4.2	2.8	2.5
Sweden							
CWB	5.0	5.0	4.4	3.8	3.8	3.0	3.8
UD	71.0	75.7	79.1	83.3	84.8	84.7	78.7
EPL	1.9	3.4	3.5	3.6	3.2	2.8	2.7
PMR	–	4.5	4.5	4.5	3.6	2.5	2.0

Note: See the appendix for a description of the variables.

Using the OECD's index of the strictness of product market regulations, we see that there has been a clear trend toward product market deregulation over time in both Finland and Sweden. (The index varies from 0 to 6, higher values indicating stricter regulations.) Although there are some signs of product market deregulation already in the late 1980s, at least in Finland, the process clearly gained momentum during the first half of the 1990s, when large-scale privatisation reforms were launched in both countries.

In order to describe the developments with regard to employment protection legislation, the summary score of Allard (2005) is used. Building on earlier work by the OECD, this measure assesses the strictness of the employment protection legislation on a scale from 0 to 5, with higher values indicating a higher degree of job security. As can be seen in Table 2.3, employment protection increased in both Sweden and Finland from the early 1970s to the late 1980s, but thereafter we see somewhat different developments in the two countries. Whereas employment protection legislation remained largely unchanged in Finland during the 1990s, in Sweden it was relaxed in the beginning of the decade at the hands of the centre-right government. Nonetheless, even after these reforms, Swedish employment protection legislation remained one of the strictest in the entire OECD area.

For a long time, Sweden and Finland, together with Denmark, have been the most unionised countries in the world. And as can be seen in the table, the direct effect of the 1990s crisis was to further increase union membership in both countries. At a time of crisis, even previously unorganised workers turn to unions for protection. Thus, in this regard the economic crisis in Sweden and Finland served to strengthen, at least temporarily, one of the defining characteristics of the traditional Nordic model.

Corporatist wage bargaining – i.e., centralised and highly coordinated wage bargaining run by strong and encompassing unions and employer organisations – was another salient feature of the traditional Nordic model. According to many economic observers of the 1980s, well-functioning wage bargaining was the main explanation for the good employment performance of the Nordic countries during the economic turbulence of the 1970s (Katzenstein 1985; Bruno & Sachs 1985). The reason corporatist wage bargaining is thought to be conducive to low unemployment is that it forces wage-setters to consider the macro-economic effects of their wage settlements, such as the effect on the general price level. Or, using economic parlance, under corporatist bargaining wage-setters are induced to internalise the negative externalities of high wage settlements.

As can be seen in Table 2.3, and as is well-documented in previous research, there was already a clear tendency toward less extensive wage coordination in both countries in the 1980s. (The index measuring the degree of coordination in wage bargaining varies from 1 to 5, with higher values indicating more extensive coordination.)

This tendency was most marked in Sweden, where the break away from centralised bargaining in 1983 by employers and unions in the manufacturing sector was a fundamental blow to the centralised wage bargaining system that had been in place in Sweden since the late 1950s. During the 1980s, a number of attempts were made to restore centralisation, and wage bargaining oscillated between central and industry levels. These attempts, however, finally came to an end when the Swedish Employers' Confederation (henceforth SAF) decided in 1990 – as a direct result of growing employer discontent with the outcomes of centralised bargaining – to resign from collective bargaining and closed down its bargaining and statistics department (Elvander 1988; Pontusson & Swenson 1996).

Developments in Finland were similar, although less dramatic. During the 1970s, following the pattern established by the famous Liinamaa Agreement in 1968, wage bargaining in Finland usually took the form of tripartite income policy agreements between the government, unions and employers. But in the 1980s the parties failed to reach such agreements on no less than three occasions, and there were clear signs of growing dissatisfaction with the centralised wage bargaining system, in particular among employers (cf. Lilja 1998).

The immediate impact of the economic crisis in the early 1990s, however, was to temporarily stall the move toward decentralised wage bargaining. In Sweden, against the threat of the approaching economic downturn, the Social Democratic government managed to push through a centralised stabilisation agreement in 1990 by appointing a "national mediation commission", the so-called Rehnberg commission, including representatives of the social partners. This agreement contained low nominal wage increases and a general ban on local negotiations for the next two years. And in Finland, in the aftermath of the devaluation of the markka in 1992, the social partners forged a central income policy agreement that delivered strictly zero wage increases for the next two years (Asplund 2007).

Although the advent of the economic recession served to temporarily silence employers' demands for the decentralisation of wage bargaining, the crisis did nothing to alter their basic views on this matter. On the contrary, employer resistance to centralised bargaining intensified in both Finland and Sweden during the early 1990s. In Finland, as Lilja describes, although the discussion on the need to decentralise wage bargaining had already started in the 1980s, it was "not until the start of the deep recession in the 1990s that the debate became urgent" (1998: 171). In Sweden, the controversy over the forms of wage bargaining was fuelled anew in 1992 when the Swedish Engineering Employers' Association (henceforth

VI), the leading employer organisation in the manufacturing sector, openly declared that the central (industry) agreements should regulate only the peace obligation and general conditions of employment, whereas wages should be negotiated at the local level. This statement was interpreted as a direct declaration of war by the manufacturing unions.

The employer offensive against centralised wage bargaining was further spurred by the election of non-socialist governments in both countries in 1991. Whereas the centre-right government in Finland explicitly expressed an intention "to diminish the role of trade unions and to get rid of the old corporatist wage bargaining system" (Kiander 2005: 100), the new Swedish government revealed its lukewarm attitude to centralised bargaining when refusing to reappoint the Rehnberg commission in 1993.

In Finland, the growing claims for decentralisation manifested themselves in the bargaining rounds of 1994-1995, which, at the initiative of employers and with the tacit support of the government, were conducted at the industry level in a fairly uncoordinated manner. The outcome, however, was not what the employers had hoped for. The bargaining rounds were fairly conflict ridden, and despite a record high unemployment rate the nominal wage increases were relatively high from an international perspective, which served to slow the economic recovery in Finland (Hagberg et al. 2006).

After some limited moves in a decentralised direction in the bargaining round of 1993, Swedish employers, led by the VI, intensified their efforts to decentralise bargaining in 1995. This resulted in one of the most decentralised and uncoordinated bargaining rounds since the end of the Second World War in Sweden. As in Finland, however, the experiment with uncoordinated bargaining turned out to be a rather unpleasant experience for the employers. After an early agreement by the parties in the highly profitable forest industry, employers in other sectors were forced to concede to similar wage increases that were high by international standards and considered severely detrimental to competitiveness by most employers outside the forest industry. Consequently, the bargaining round of 1995-1996, which was the most conflict ridden in Sweden since that of the "great conflict" in 1980, caused great discord within the employer collective and increased awareness of the risks associated with uncoordinated wage bargaining.

The fourth core area of a national capital system identified in the introduction of this book is the system of *corporate governance*. In the VoC literature, the corporate governance system of liberal market economies is typically said to be based on dispersed ownership, strong legal protection for minority shareholders, and large stock markets, whereas the corporate governance system of coordinated market economies is taken to be characterised by the opposite – i.e., concentrated ownership, weak protection for minority shareholders, and relatively small stock markets (Hall & Gingerich 2004: 12).

Traditionally, the corporate governance systems of Sweden and Finland have been of the latter type (see e.g. Carlsson 2007; Liljeblom & Löflund 2006). Already from the advent of industrialisation, the stock markets in both countries used to be characterised by powerful and committed owners and a rather high degree of ownership control. Different types of dual share systems, in which the voting rights differ across different types of shares, have also been in frequent use in both countries, which serve to further enhance the power of leading owners. For instance, in Sweden many large multinational companies such as ABB, Ericsson and SKF used to practice a differentiation of 1 : 1000 between A and B-class shares, and similar although somewhat less extreme systems were also common in Finland. This meant that the leading owners could remain in control over their companies even in a situation in which they no longer owned a majority of the total shares in the company (as long as they owned A-class shares).

Another distinctive, and inherently corporatistic, feature of the corporate governance systems of Sweden and Finland has been the practice of employee representation on the boards of large- and medium-sized firms. In Sweden, legislation concerning employee representation at the board level was passed already in the 1970s, granting employee representation on the boards of all firms with more than 25 employees. In contrast, employee representation at the board level in Finland remained voluntary for a long time, although the practice of employee board representation was rather widespread among Finnish firms from the late 1970s. In 1990, however, new legislation was passed in Finland stating that employees had the right to be represented on the boards of all firms with more than 150 employees.

Similar to the other core economic areas discussed above, the traditional corporate governance systems of Sweden and Finland came under increasing stress in the early 1990s. Most importantly, the combination of financial market liberalisation and currency devaluation spurred a sharp rise in foreign ownership in both Sweden and Finland during this time. As a direct result of this, old ownership structures were challenged and traditional corporate practices such as the dual share system and employee board representation came up for debate in both countries. According to critics of the traditional corporatistic corporate governance model practiced in Sweden and Finland, the differentiation of voting rights across different types of shares as well as the practice of board-level employee representation tended to favour conservative corporate strategies and make the necessary structural adjustments more difficult to achieve. In sum, the sharp rise in foreign ownership as well as the spread of liberal market ideas in the policy debate constituted important challenges for the corporate governance systems in Sweden and Finland during the economic crisis of the 1990s.

As is evident from the previous discussion, there were clear signs of a move in the liberal direction in both Sweden and Finland in the early 1990s. Social benefits were made less generous in order to curb skyrocketing budget deficits, old corporate practices were challenged due to the increase in foreign ownership, product markets were deregulated, and the coordinated wage bargaining systems of the two countries came under heavy pressure. Equally important, however, the early 1990s witnessed a sharp drop in intra-elite trust, which for a long time had been one of the hallmarks of the Nordic society. The political and economic events of the time brought to the fore increased tensions between the organisations of the labour markets – as seen in the heated controversy over the proper level of bargaining – as well as between the centre-right governments in each country and the unions. At odds with the traditional Nordic consensus political model, most cuts in social benefits over this period were implemented despite strong union opposition. It was thus not only the content but also the form of politics that took liberal turns in Sweden and Finland during the years of economic hardship in the early 1990s. We will now turn to developments since the mid-1990s.

Economic recovery and the revival of corporatist capitalism

In Finland as well as in Sweden, signs of economic recovery first became visible in the export sector in the aftermath of the large currency depreciations in both countries in 1992. But it was not until 1994 that the countries once again exhibited positive economic growth rates. After that, however, economic and productivity growth really took off in both countries. As can be seen in Table 2.1, during the second half of the 1990s, the yearly average rate of growth was 4.6% in Finland and 3.1% in Sweden, and average productivity growth rates were 2.3% and 1.4% respectively. These figures are very high both by international and historical standards; the Finnish and Swedish economies had not grown this quickly since the early 1970s. Further, economic and productivity growth continued to be high in both countries during the early 2000s. There was, however, a less dramatic recovery of employment in both countries in the latter half of the 1990s. In Finland, the unemployment rate peaked at nearly 17% in 1994 and has since then gradually lowered to a level of 7% to 8%. In Sweden, unemployment hit its peak of about 10% in 1997, and then fell to its current level of between 4% and 6%.

In both Finland and Sweden, the process of economic recovery coincided with the return to power of the Social Democrats. In neither country, however, did this imply a drastic change in economic policy. Upon re-election in 1994, the Swedish Social Democrats did undo some of the changes implemented by the earlier centre-right government, in particular with regard to the administration of unemployment benefits and employment protection legislation, but they also intensified efforts to improve public finances by implementing additional cost-savings measures in many welfare state programmes. For instance, the replacement rate in case of sickness or unemployment was further lowered to 75% (although a replacement rate of 80% was reinstated in 1997), the indexing of pensions was decreased, and both child and housing allowances were lowered. In Finland, the so-called rainbow coalition – headed by Social Democratic Prime Minister Pavo Lipponen – followed a similar course of action upon entering office in 1995, and imposed additional savings measures in many areas such as pensions, sickness benefits and unemployment insurance (Uusitalo 1996; Benner 2003).

Thus, the trend toward less generous social benefits continued in both countries in the late 1990s, as can be seen in Table 2.2. At the same time, taxes were increased as part of the far-reaching financial stabilisation programmes implemented in Sweden and Finland. In Table 2.2, we also see that the total tax wedge in Sweden had returned close to its pre-tax reform value by the late 1990s, whereas the Finnish tax wedge reached its all-time high in 1995-1996.

Judging from these figures, it was therefore not so much the content of politics as its form that was re-oriented once the Social Democrats returned to power in Finland and Sweden in the mid-1990s. Rather than striking a confrontational stance with the unions, as the centre-right governments of the early 1990s had done, the Social Democrats sought to implement their economic reforms in cooperation with, or at least with the tacit consent of, the unions. As a result, a revival of social concertation and partnership was seen in both countries during the latter part of the 1990s.

This development was particularly pronounced in Finland. One of the main priorities of the new Finnish government was to restore coordinated wage bargaining. In September 1995, in fact, the government managed to get unions and employers to sign a central income policy agreement governing the development of wages for the next two years in exchange for promised tax cuts. The agreement, which contained moderate nominal wage increases, was the most comprehensive income policy agreement since the Liinamaa agreement in 1968, and one of its initiators went so far as to describe it as "representing the peak in the history of Finnish incomes policy" (Pekkanen quoted in Rehn 1996: 268).

The income policy agreement of 1995 marked a return to centralised bargaining in Finland and was followed by similar agreements in 1997, 2001, 2003 and 2005. In fact, during the period 1995-2007, it was only in 2000 that wage bargaining was conducted at the industry level without a previous central agreement. So why did Finnish employers give up their principled resistance to centralised bargaining and agree to once again take part in tripartite income policy negotiations?

The first reason for the change in employer attitudes was no doubt the experience of the uncoordinated bargaining rounds of 1994 and 1995. Despite the widespread consciousness of the crisis in Finnish society and mass unemployment, it proved impossible to secure wage restraint and labour peace in uncoordinated bargaining at the industry level. With no prospect for any labour market reforms aimed at drastically lessening the bargaining power of workers, employers decided that, at least for the moment, the increased stability and predictability ensured by centralised bargaining was of higher value than the increased flexibility associated with decentralised bargaining.

Second, it should be noted that even in the early 1990s Finnish employers took a more pragmatic view than did their Swedish counterparts on the issue of centralised bargaining. Even though Finnish employers also stressed the need for increased flexibility in wage setting, they never "announced that centralised agreements would be completely ruled out in the future" (Niemelä 1999: 18). Instead, Finnish employers attempted to obtain increased room for local-level negotiations within the structure of centralised bargaining. To a large extent, this has been a successful strategy. Whereas *average wage* increases in Finland have been effectively regulated by the central agreements, decisions on *relative wages* have in the last decade been delegated to the local level to an increasing extent (Asplund 2007: 27). And even though there exists continued disagreement between unions and employers over the desirability of increased wage flexibility, recent survey evidence indicates that both parties "are reasonably satisfied with the existing framework of collective bargaining owing to its stabilising influence on labour market relations and overall wage developments" (Pekkarinen & Alho 2005: 83).

A third factor contributing to the revival of centralised wage bargaining in Finland in the mid-1990s was the decision to join the European Monetary Union (EMU). Both Finnish employers and unions have advanced centralised bargaining as an important means by which to safeguard against the types of adverse economic shock to which a small country like Finland may be subject within a monetary union (Pekkarinen & Alho 2005: 75).

Similar to developments in Finland, in Sweden the failure to secure wage moderation and labour peace in the uncoordinated bargaining rounds at the industry level in 1995 caused employers to start to reconsider their principled commitment to decentralised wage bargaining – despite skyrocketing budget deficits and mass unemployment. For instance, in a newspaper article in 1995, Göran Trogen, the managing director of the second largest employer organisation in the manufacturing sector, urged the parties of the labour market to leave the trenches and make efforts to re-establish mutual trust and confidence between employers and unions in the spirit of the famous Basic Agreement of 1938 (Trogen 1995).

Moreover, the VI came to the conclusion in 1996, after a thorough evaluation of available options with regard to wage bargaining, that the time was not yet ripe to push for a complete decentralisation of wage bargaining (Sandgren 2002: 25). Given the strength of their opponents, the VI considered wage negotiations at the local level without an accompanying peace obligation too risky. Moreover, during the bargaining rounds of 1993 and 1995, the manufacturing unions had made it crystal clear that they would never sign a central agreement containing a peace obligation if wages were to be decided at the local level. As Göran Johnsson, former chair of the largest manufacturing union, Metall, says, "I used to tell them [the employers] that of course we are very stupid sometimes, but we are not that bloody stupid" (Interview with Johnsson 2002).

At the same time, the Social Democratic government initiated a dialogue with the social partners about the future of collective bargaining in Sweden. In 1996, Swedish Prime Minister Göran Persson wrote an open letter to unions and employers asking for their views on the possibility of jointly finding new forms of wage bargaining that could bring down wage increases in Sweden to a sound European level. A few weeks later, this letter was followed up by a new letter, this time from the labour market minister, urging all parties involved to come up with proposals aimed at improving the Swedish wage bargaining system before the end of March the next year (Sandgren 2002: 29ff).

The parties of the labour market interpreted the government's initiative as a direct threat of state intervention should they be unable to come to a voluntary agreement for an improved structure for wage bargaining. And a shared and deep-seated distaste for governmental involvement in wage bargaining did indeed bring unions and employers together. The most important outcome of this process was the so-called Industrial Agreement, which was initiated by the trade unions and signed in March 1997 by the parties in the manufacturing sector, including the VI.

The two most important provisions of the Industrial Agreement were the declaration that wage increases in the manufacturing sector should set a pattern for wage increases in the rest of the economy, and the introduction of a completely new system for conflict resolution in the manufacturing sector. The Industrial Agreement has had a profound effect on the Swedish collective bargaining system in at least two regards. First, it largely inspired the governmental bill on a new mediation institute that was passed by parliament in 2000. Second, it has served as a model for similar agreements in other sectors of the economy (Elvander 2002: 130).

Moreover, by establishing the Industrial Agreement, unions and employers in the manufacturing sector came to a truce over wage bargaining levels. Particularly important was that the employers, by signing the agreement, at least temporarily decided to give up the push for decentralised bargaining. This should not, however, be interpreted as a fundamental shift in employer preferences on the issue. Rather, and as pointed out by one of the leaders on the employer side, it simply means that employers, by signing the Industrial Agreement, "chose to prioritise the cost development, to fight it, over the idea of decentralisation" (Interview with Trogen 2002). Former chief negotiator of the VI Anders Sandgren provides additional support for this interpretation when mentioning the return to power of the Social Democrats as an important factor for the organisation's decision to accept the Industrial Agreement:

> The problem with labour dispute measures was the decisive factor. The government had shown some intentions to come to grip with labour disputes, but all experience showed that a Social Democratic government was unable to make a decision that the LO opposed (2002: 44).

To a large extent, the pattern-setting function of the manufacturing sector has been respected by the other sectors in the bargaining rounds since 1998. This has meant a revival of wage coordination in Sweden. But unlike what was the case in Finland, coordination in Sweden was not restored by means of a re-establishment of centralised bargaining. Employer resistance to centralisation was far too strong for this to be possible, even though the LO did attempt (largely unsuccessfully) to regain a more important role in wage bargaining during the late 1990s. Instead, a pattern-setting system of the German type was established in Sweden by the hands of a cross-class coalition in the manufacturing sector.

The revival of coordinated bargaining in Finland and Sweden during the late 1990s described in this section and further illustrated in Table 2.3 indicates, at least partially, a return of coordinated capitalism in these countries. Another sign of this is that the relations between the trade unions and the government improved considerably in both countries once the Social Democrats returned to power in the mid-1990s. In line with the traditional mode of Nordic country decision-making, the Social Democrats took great care to implement savings measures in cooperation with, or at least with the tacit consent of, the unions (Anderson 2001; Uusitalo 1996). The return to importance of social concentration is also evident in the large pension reforms undertaken in Sweden and Finland in the last decade. Anderson, for instance, argues that the historical political compromise in the introduction of the new pension system in Sweden would not have been possible without the tacit agreement between employers and unions about the necessity of reform (2001: 1065). And in Finland the grand pension reform of 2005 was a direct result of a tripartite agreement between the social partners and the government (EIRO 2001).

No doubt the revival of coordinated capitalism in Sweden and Finland in the mid-1990s was most pronounced with respect to the reforms taken by politics. That said, however, there were also some indications in both countries of a reversal, or at least a significant weakening, of the liberalisation trend with respect to policy content in the early 2000s. In Sweden, unemployment benefits, sickness benefits and child allowances were all made more generous during the first half of the 2000s (although both unemployment and sickness benefits have, once again, been made less generous since the centre-right government took office in 2006). Similarly, changes were made in Finland in the early 2000s to mitigate some of the cuts implemented during the recession of the 1990s. These changes included increases in national pensions, a restoration of the minimum allowance in sickness insurance benefits and an increase in the earnings-related unemployment allowance (Niemelä & Salminen 2006). In Table 2.2 we can also see that taxes were lowered in both Finland and Sweden once public finances had recovered by the late 1990s. This development has been most marked in Finland, in which the tax wedge has been lowered to the level of the early 1980s. Yet, from an international perspective Sweden and Finland still stand out as high tax economies. So we should refrain from interpreting these tax cuts as clear signs of their capitalism moving in a liberal direction. Especially since recent tax cuts in Sweden and Finland were aimed to a large extent at bringing taxes back to their pre-crisis level.

There are, however, also areas in which the liberalisation trend is more visible. In particular, the deregulation of product markets continued in both countries in the late 1990s and early 2000s, as can be seen in Table 2.3. Moreover there are some, although not very strong, indications that the liberalisation of the corporate governance systems in Sweden and Finland that was initiated in the early 1990s has gained some momentum. For instance, the fraction of listed companies applying shares with differentiated voting rights has been declining in both Sweden and Finland over the last decade (OECD 2007: 22). Often this development has been a direct result of increased foreign ownership or international mergers. Obviously, the reduced importance of the dual share system has served to strengthen the position of minority shareholders, although from an international perspective, dual-class shares are still in rather wide use in Sweden and Finland. Some observers, especially trade union representatives, have also argued that the increased frequency of international mergers in Sweden and Finland has made the traditional system of employee representation at the board level more vulnerable, since when mergers take place employees risk being excluded from the various boards (see e.g. Kvam 2001).

At the same time, as in most other OECD countries, the stock market has grown rapidly in both countries in recent years. Today, both Sweden and Finland have well developed equity markets. Yet liberalisation has been slower with regard to the dispersion of ownership. From an international perspective, ownership is still rather concentrated in Sweden as well as in Finland, and in both countries family ownership continues to play an important role (Pedersen & Thomsen 1999; Faccio & Lang 2002). Thus, although there is a slight tendency of a move in a liberal direction of the corporate governance systems of Sweden and Finland over the last decades, the magnitude of this move should not be exaggerated. The corporate governance systems of Sweden and Finland still seem to be closer to the ideal type of corporatist capitalism than to that of liberal market capitalism.

Turning to the developments in the labour markets, the increase in union density experienced by both Sweden and Finland during the economic crisis was offset once the economy turned for the better in the latter half of the decade, as can be seen from Table 2.3. During the 2000s, unionisation was in decline in both countries, and although we lack reliable data for the most recent developments, this trend seems to be accentuating. It should be noted, however, that the decline is from a very high level and despite the recent drop in union density, Sweden and Finland still stand out as two of the most heavily unionised countries in the world. A fact that bears witness to the continued strength of the Swedish and Finnish unions is that employment protection legislation has been kept more or less intact (see Table 2.3) over the last decade even though many policy experts, national as well as international, have pointed to the need for liberalising reforms in this area.

Sources of stability and change

The fast economic recovery of Finland and Sweden in the late 1990s and early 2000s has, together with similar developments in Denmark (particularly its 'flexicurity'; see Mailand's contribution in this volume), inspired a renewed interest in the Nordic political economies, which is once again being portrayed as a viable alternative to Anglo-Saxon laissez faire capitalism. Some even speak of a Nordic miracle (Dutch Ministry of Finance 2005). This, however, raises the question of how Nordic the current Nordic model is.

Asking whether the contemporary Nordic model, as practiced in Finland and Sweden, is the same as the traditional one is like asking whether the glass is half empty or half full. The previous discussion has shown that there are important instances of both continuity and change in the two countries under study, and it is not obvious how to assess overall developments.

There is no doubt that welfare benefits became less generous in Sweden and Finland over the course of the 1990s. Yet, looking back on the 1990s crisis in Sweden, Palme et al. (2002: 137) summarise the welfare reforms in the following way: "On the whole, what marked the changes was that, on the one hand, they were very large in numbers and tended to limit generosity, but their magnitude, on the other hand, was small." Lindbom

(2001) makes a similar point when characterising the cutbacks in welfare in Sweden as a case of adjustment rather than of retrenchment. These descriptions also square nicely with Finnish developments over the same period, since as Benner (2003: 137) for instance notes, the 1990s welfare reforms in Finland were "more of a quantitative than a qualitative nature." In summary, although there was a tendency toward welfare state liberalisation in both Sweden and Finland during the 1990s, the core elements of the two welfare states appear to have survived the crisis.

The findings with respect to developments in the product and labour markets are likewise mixed. In both Sweden and Finland, we have observed a trend toward product market deregulation and liberalisation of corporate governance since the early 1990s. And after a temporary increase in union density at the height of the economic crisis in Finland and Sweden, unionisation has been on the decline in both countries. Equally important, however, is that both countries have witnessed a revival of coordinated wage bargaining, another hallmark of the traditional Nordic model, from the mid-1990s.

Given that the early 1990s constituted a golden window of opportunity for those wanting to liberalise the Swedish and Finnish variety of capitalism, in my view it is, however, not so much the traces of change as the traces of continuity that are in need of explanation. Starting with the question of welfare state change, we may ask why we did not see more radical welfare state reforms in Sweden and Finland during this period. It appears the relative stability of the Swedish and Finnish welfare states can be attributed to two main factors.

First, even in the midst of a severe economic crisis – and despite the prominence of monetarist and market liberal ideas in the policy debate – public support for a universalistic and generous welfare state remained very high in both Finland and Sweden. Regarding Finland, Sihvo and Uusitalo (1995: 257) show that for each of the five types of social benefits they investigated, the balance of opinion – i.e., the difference between the percentage of those who think more tax money should be spent on the benefit in question and the percentage of those who think less tax money should be spent on it – was still positive at the height of the economic downturn in 1993.[2] Svallfors (1995: 69) presents survey results indicating that public support for the welfare state in Sweden was as high in 1992 as in 1986. As Katzenstein (1985) and others have argued, strong welfare state support in small open economies such as Finland and Sweden may be explained by the need of individuals to shield against the vagaries of a globalised economy.

Although this strong support for welfare in Sweden and Finland did not preclude cuts in public expenditure to alleviate the economic crisis, the fact that public support for the welfare state remained high even in times of crisis no doubt had a restraining effect on the number and magnitude of welfare reforms implemented. A testimony to this is that Swedish and Finnish politicians took great care throughout the crisis to present welfare cuts as a means by which to maintain the universalistic welfare state, rather than as a way to abolish it.

A second factor contributing to the relative stability of the Swedish and Finnish welfare states during the 1990s crisis was heavy trade union opposition to cutbacks in social welfare. Several times the powerful Finnish unions managed to get the government to renounce planned welfare cuts by threatening general strikes. Similarly, Swedish unions mobilised, at least partly successfully, protests against proposed cutbacks in social benefits on several occasions during the 1990s. For instance, the decision to increase the replacement rate from 75% to 80% in unemployment and sickness insurance benefits in 1997 was a direct concession to LO demands (Scarbrough 2000; Edbalk 2007).

The strong position of the trade unions in Sweden and Finland also goes a long way toward explaining the revival of coordinated wage bargaining over the last decade. In a context like the Nordic one characterised by high union density, few restrictions on the use of industrial action, and generous welfare benefits that increased the bargaining position of the unions by decreasing competition from "outsiders", decentralised wage bargaining has entailed substantial risk for employers. The experiment with uncoordinated and fairly decentralised bargaining in Finland and Sweden during the mid-1990s made this abundantly clear. Furthermore, once the Social Democrats returned to power in Sweden and Finland, employers no longer saw any prospect for legislative reforms aimed at drastically lessening the bargaining power of unions. This induced employers to give up their principled demand for full-blooded decentralisation of wage bargaining. At the same time, the return to coordinated wage bargaining in the two countries helped to bring wage formation under control, which in turn lessened the demand for further liberalisation of welfare and labour market policies.

Consequently, and as I have argued in more detail elsewhere (Lindgren 2006), whereas the presence of large unions and generous welfare benefits serve to increase the gains associated with coordinated wage bargaining by increasing the amount of negative externalities that can be internalised, coordinated wage bargaining serves to increase the gains associated with strong unions and generous welfare benefits by weakening the link between social protection and unemployment. Thus we are here faced with an important instance of so-called institutional complementarity, i.e., a situation in which the co-existence of a particular set of institutions enhances the performance of each individual institution.

Although Deeg (2007) might be correct in suggesting that the relationship between institutional complementarities and institutional change is much more ambiguous and contingent than commonly thought, the institutional complementarities identified here clearly had a stabilising effect on developments in Sweden and Finland during the turbulent times of recent decades. That is to say, an important reason we did not see a more radical liberalisation of the Finnish and Swedish national capitalist systems during the 1990s was that such defenders of the traditional Nordic model as the unions managed to utilise the presence of institutional complementarities to their advantage.

Conclusion

No doubt the current Swedish and Finnish national capitalist systems depart in important respects from the capitalism that characterised these countries during the heyday of the traditional Nordic model. Yet it still seems justified to identify them as distinctively Nordic. This is because, recent changes notwithstanding, the current capitalist systems of Sweden and Finland much more closely resemble the type of capitalism practised in these countries in the 1970s and 1980s than the Anglo-Saxon capitalism of the 2000s or the Anglo-Saxon capitalism of the 1970s and 1980s for that matter.

Moreover, and as Hall and Thelen (2009) point out, it is important to distinguish the institutional changes that weaken the coordination capacities of coordinated market economies such as the strongly corporatist Nordic ones from those changes leaving these capacities intact. And, as has been shown in this chapter, many of the changes undertaken in Finland and Sweden since the early 1990s have been of the former type. Cutbacks in social welfare during the economic recession, for instance, were not so much driven by a wish to abolish the universalistic welfare state as by a wish to maintain its core elements through a period of extreme economic hardship. This interpretation is further substantiated by the fact that in both countries, cuts in welfare spending in the 1990s were accompanied by tax increases. If the intent had been to fundamentally change the national capital systems in Sweden and Finland, taxes should have been cut along with welfare benefits.

Similarly, changes to the wage bargaining systems during the latter half of the 1990s should be seen as an attempt to restore effective wage coordination in Finland and Sweden, which was one of the hallmarks of the traditional Nordic model. In Finland, as we have seen, wage coordination was restored through a series of centralised income policy agreements. But although the formal attributes of the old centralised bargaining system have largely been left intact, there is at the same time a clear trend toward the delegation of responsibilities to the local level. This is thus an example of how institutional change can be pursued through a reinterpretation of the meanings of old institutions (see Hall & Thelen 2009). In Sweden, however, employer antagonism toward centralised wage bargaining was too strong to make this type of institutional change possible. Instead, coordinated wage bargaining has been restored at the initiative of a cross-class alliance in the manufacturing sector, by means of the introduction of a new and regularised system for pattern-setting bargaining.

To a large extent, the recent transformation of the Swedish and Finnish capitalist systems can thus be seen as a way to maintain the basic functionality of their political economies in a period of immense external, as well as internal, pressure for change. The most suitable characterisation of the evolution of the national capitalist systems of Sweden and Finland over the last couple of decades, therefore, seems to be continuity through change.

This finding speaks to the close but often neglected connection between the concepts of continuity and change. Given that the external circumstances are changing, in politics the way to maintain things as they are is often through change, and not seldom maintaining things as they are is the most effective means to ensure fundamental change. Although intuitive, this observation has far-reaching implications for future research in the field. Most importantly, in order to construct a truly dynamic theory of capitalist diversity, we need to go beyond the traditional dichotomy of continuity and change and develop a more elaborated typology differentiating between various forms of continuity and change. In doing so, we ought to focus on the function of changing or not changing a particular policy over time.

The fact that the coordinated model in Sweden and Finland appears to have survived the immediate crisis of the economic downturn of the 1990s does not, however, mean the model is secured for eternity. As pointed out in the introduction, ultimately corporatist coordination of the type practised in Sweden and Finland is an outcome that has to be actively sustained and nurtured. The survival of the Nordic capitalism in these countries therefore hinges on the fact that the model can continue to serve the interest of powerful actors also in the future. It is not difficult to identify a number of contemporary challenges to the existing institutional frameworks in Sweden and Finland.

In Sweden, for instance, there is growing discontent with the new bargaining system among the non-manufacturing unions; they have threatened to disregard the pattern-setting function of the manufacturing sector in the next bargaining round if not granted greater influence over the determination of wages (LO-Tidningen 2007). At the same time, the centre-right government, elected in 2006, has come into open conflict with the unions over cuts and changes implemented in the unemployment and sickness insurance plans.

Likewise, there are indications of increased tension in the Finnish bargaining systems. Following the announcement by the influential Federation of Finnish Technology Industries that it would follow a decentralised approach in the bargaining round of 2008, a new central income policy agreement failed to materialise once the old agreement terminated at the end of 2007. The outcome of the sectoral bargaining round of 2008 was rather high nominal wage increases which have caused the Finnish government to stall planned tax decreases. The costliness of the agreements notwithstanding, Finnish employers report that they are satisfied with the sectoral bargaining round since it has delegated important decision-making powers to the local level (EIRO 2008a). It is still too early to tell whether the bargaining round of 2008 represents a new turning point with regard to collective bargaining in Finland, or whether it merely represents a means by which to temporarily relieve some of the pressure that has accumulated over the years of central income policy agreements.

Finally, two additional challenges of a more fundamental nature facing Finland and Sweden should be mentioned. The first is weakening unionisation. If the Swedish and Finnish unions continue to lose members at the current pace, the universalistic welfare state will eventually lose one of its strongest contenders, and at the same time employer incentives to participate in coordinated bargaining will lessen. In the long run, such a development will undermine the very institutional complementarities that helped maintain the Nordic model throughout the 1990s.

A second important challenge is the ruling in December 2007 by the EC court in the much discussed case of Laval concerning a trade union boycott of a Latvian building company operating in Sweden. The essence of the decision of the court was that the Swedish trade unions are restricted in their use of industrial action to force foreign companies to sign collective agreements when operating in Sweden (EIRO 2008b). According to the trade unions, this ruling constitutes a fundamental blow to the Nordic model of collective bargaining in which minimum protection standards are established in collective agreements rather than enshrined in law as in many other European countries. The more precise implications of the court's verdict are still a matter for debate, however, and it is still too early to determine the future importance of this ruling.

As pointed out in the introduction, an existing institutional framework can be sustained only as long as it serves the purpose of important economic actors. Today, Sweden's and Finland's Nordic capitalism still provides a viable alternative to the type of free market capitalism practised in Anglo-Saxon countries, but this will continue to be the case only to the extent that the Nordic model can adapt to meet the challenges it is currently facing. Historically, however, adaptability has been one of the trademarks of the Nordic countries.

Interviews

With G. Johnsson, Chairman Metall. Interview conducted on 6 May 2002.
With G. Trogen, Chairman Almega. Interview conducted on 5 April 2002.

Appendix: Measures and Data Sources

Wage Coordination (CWB). This measure of wage coordination is taken from Kenworthy (2001). The index ranges from 1 to 5, where 1 is the minimum coordination. Kenworthy's data covers only the period up to 2000 but has been extended for the period 2001-2003 by the present author.

Employment. Civilian employment as percentage of the population aged 15-64. The series builds on OECD data but was obtained from Armingeon et al. (2008).

Employment Protection Legislation (EPL). This is Allard's (2005) measure of job security. The indicator measures the strictness of employment protection legislation annually on a scale ranging from 1 to 5, higher values indicating stricter regulation (higher job security).

Growth. The annual growth rate of real GDP in percent. The data builds on data collected by the OECD but were obtained from Armingeon et al. (2008).

Inequality. The Gini coefficient of disposable income. The data are drawn from income surveys conducted at irregular intervals. The Swedish data are from Statistics Sweden and the Finnish data are from Statistics Finland. The data series for the two countries are not exactly comparable, since there are some slight differences in the official methods for calculating disposable income in Sweden and Finland.

Pensions. An index of the overall generosity of the pension system computed on the basis of pension replacement rates for minimum and standard pensions, the pension take-up ratio, qualifying years for standard pension, and the proportion of pension contributions paid by the employee. See Scruggs & Allan (2006) for computational details. Data are from Scruggs (2005).

Product market regulations (PMR). This is an OECD indicator of regulatory and market regulations in seven non-manufacturing industries. The industries are classified in each period along a scale from 0 to 6, from least to most restrictive, on five regulatory and market dimensions. The scores are then averaged across the industries to obtain an economy-wide measure. Data were obtained from OECD.Stat.

Productivity. Annual multi-factor productivity growth in percent. Data were obtained from OECD.Stat.

Unemployment benefits (UB). An index of the overall generosity of unemployment benefits computed on the basis of net replacement rates, the coverage of the insurance, the duration of benefits, the length of the qualification period, and the number of waiting days. See Scruggs & Allan (2006) for computational details. Data are from Scruggs (2005).

Union density (UD). Net union density in percent. Data were obtained from Nickell (2006).

Unemployment. Standardised unemployment rates. The series builds on OECD data but was obtained from Armingeon et al. (2008).

Sickness. An index of the overall generosity of sickness benefits computed on the basis of net replacement rates, the coverage of the insurance, the duration of benefits, the length of the qualification period, and the number of waiting days. See Scruggs & Allan (2006) for computational details. Data are from Scruggs (2005).

Tax wedge. This measure is defined as income tax plus employee and employer social contributions less cash benefits as a percentage of labour costs for an average production worker (AWP) in the manufacturing sector. Data are from the OECD database *Taxing Wages*.

Notes

1   The research for this chapter was funded by the Swedish Council for Working Life and Research as well as the Jan Wallander and Tom Hedelius Foundation.
2   The five types of social benefits investigated are: unemployment insurance, sickness insurance, national pensions, child allowance, and housing allowance.

3　Change and Continuity in Danish and Norwegian Capitalism: *Corporatism and Beyond*

Mikkel Mailand

Introduction

The literature on *varieties of capitalism* (VoC) (e.g. Hall & Soskice 2001; Rueda & Pontusson 2000; Hall & Gingerich 2004) has illuminated contemporary relations between state and social partners as well as between capital and labour in advanced economies. As stated in other chapters in this volume, the literature on VoC has largely focused on the larger industrial countries and ignored the small EU member states. This is also the case with the small Scandinavian countries. There are only a few exceptions (e.g. Campbell et al. 2006) within the VoC literature.

Relations between state, capital and labour are often presented in earlier studies in political economy and industrial relations – especially those found within the *studies of corporatism* –as one of the key issues to understand the dynamics of Scandinavian states. Cooperation and consensus-oriented relations between these actors – which in terms of power are more equal than in many other countries – have also been said to be an important factor in the economic success of these countries. Sweden became the prime example of Scandinavian corporatism and was often included in comparative studies (Korpi 1983; Katzenstein 1985; Rothstein 1992). Less attention was paid to labour market relations in the two other Scandinavian countries: Norway and Denmark.

Taking as its point of departure the premise that relations between state, capital and labour are of special importance in understanding the dynamics of capitalism in these small Scandinavian countries, the following analysis will pay special attention to corporatism in a wider empirical comparative analysis of the state and development of capitalism in Denmark and Norway. However, corporatism and the four other themes selected for the country-chapters in this volume – welfare state system, labour market legislation, corporate governance and tax regime – are closely connected, because corporatism should be seen as policy processes employed in relation to various economic and social issues, such as the four other areas. In the two small Scandinavian countries in focus, corporatism is especially relevant for the first two of the four areas, as will be illustrated by the analysis below. Hence, elements of corporatism will be found in sections other than the section on corporatism below.

This chapter argues that although Denmark and Norway can be seen as Coordinated Market Economies (CME) – one of the two types within the VoC approach – a more accurate description might be Negotiated Economies (NE; Pedersen 2006; Campbell & Pedersen 2007). NE is a more decentralised, network-based and learning-oriented version of a coordinated market economy and resembles the corporatist type that Becker proposes in the introduction to this volume. In this chapter I prefer the concept of the 'negotiated economy', however. In the period under investigation, NE has somewhat weakened in the two countries' political economy and given way to a move in a liberal direction. This change seems to have been stronger in Denmark than in Norway, but it has not meant that either of these countries closely approximates the ideal-typical Liberal Market Economy (LME).

The following section presents in brief the political and economic context in the two countries. The third section contains analyses of peak-level and meso-corporatism in Denmark and Norway. The following three sections briefly analyse developments in labour market legislation, the welfare state, corporate governance and the tax regime. The final section sums up similarities and differences between the two countries and briefly discusses the question of the most appropriate typology for describing the Danish and Norwegian developments in the five selected fields. Finally, the direction of reforms and other changes within the two countries are discussed.

The political and economic context of the two countries

In *Denmark,* industrialisation took place relatively late, whereas the institutionalisation of industrial relations took place relatively early. The September Compromise of 1899, in which the employers' organisations and the trade unions recognised each other, is usually seen as the heyday of organised industrial relations in Denmark. The sequence of industrialisation and the institutionalisation of industrial relations created an industrial relations system marked by craft divisions.

Since the 1930s, the Social Democratic Party has played an important role in the development of the Danish welfare state. But it has been less strong than in the other Scandinavian countries because when in government, it has often been in minority governments. The tradition of minority governments has continued into later decades, but in recent years the social democrats have repeatedly not been a part of the government: from 1982-1993 and again from 2001 until today, liberal and conservative parties have been in office. However, these governments have not seriously challenged the welfare state.

The changes in governments in recent decades have taken place more or less simultaneously with changes in the economic climate. Like many other European countries, Denmark experienced a period of nearly constant low growth and high unemployment from the 1970s to the early 1990s, but in the mid-1990s unemployment started to decrease rapidly.

Denmark was affected, but not hard-hit, by the international recession at the beginning of the present decade. With unemployment at around 3% in recent years, labour shortages have been felt in some sectors. However, it remains to be seen to what extent this positive state of the Danish economy will be influenced by the present financial crisis. In late 2008, Danish exports experienced their largest decline in the country's history. As in Norway, the migration of labourers from new EU member states was one of the ways in which the demand for labour was met, but in Denmark migration was slower to take off than in its northern neighbour.

Norway's industrialisation occurred late, was patchy and closely connected to its natural resources. This development has fostered diverse patterns of unionism and class coalitions – as in Denmark, but in contrast to Sweden. The Norwegian economy has for many years been heavily dependent on exports based on natural resources, especially oil.

As in Denmark, Norway's social democratic party has been in government for most of the period from the 1940s to the 1980s, but the party has been stronger and more dominant than in Denmark. However, in more recent decades, the social democrats have experienced long periods in opposition: between 1981 and 1986, between 1997 and 2000, and again from 2001 to 2005. The relationship between the biggest trade union confederation (LO) and the social democrats is still close, and contrary to the situation in Denmark there are also close formal links (Lismoen 2002).

The long-lasting economic boom – supported by revenues from oil and other natural resources – has increased the demand for labour. An inflow of a large number of migrant workers from the new EU member states has helped to satisfy this demand. Nevertheless, employers complain about labour shortages, and the unemployment rate in 2006 was as low as 3% (Dølvik 2007: 27).

Change and continuity in industrial relations and corporatism

This section focuses on industrial relations and peak-level corporatism in the two countries. So-called 'meso-level corporatism' – corporatism within specific policy areas – will be examined in the section on welfare regimes.

Peak-level corporatism in Denmark

Industrial relations in Denmark have been marked by relatively central-ised coordination and strong, consensus-oriented social partner organ-isations. However, in the late 1980s, a process was begun that ended up making sectoral framework agreements for company-level bargaining the norm – a system that has been described as centralised-decentralisation (Due et al. 1993). In spite of this, both the coverage of collective agree-ments and trade union organisational rates have remained high and have long stood at around 70 percent.

In general, the state's role in industrial relations has been shrinking. The role has primarily been restricted to arbitration and conciliation and rare interventions in collective bargaining rounds. Peak-level corpo-ratist arrangements regarding wages and income policy have been lim-ited. Hence, Denmark is not like other European member states, where governments and social partners signed 'social pacts' during the 1990s (Ebbinghaus & Hassel 1997; Fajertag & Pochet 2000; Bacarro 2003), and Denmark has never had a permanent general tripartite body, such as the socio-economic councils seen in Austria, the Netherlands, Portugal or Spain. However, there have been plenty of other national-level tripartite activities. This reflects the Danish model of industrial relations, where the core is a bipartite and relatively centralised system of collective bar-gaining between strong social partners, but where the social partners are involved in the formulation of legislation related to the labour market and in the administration of it (Due et al. 1993).

Nevertheless, in the 1990s there have been attempts to set up permanent general tripartite structures and to reach 'social pact'-like agreements. Al-though these attempts did not lead to any pacts or general tripartite bod-ies of the scope and scale known in a number of other EU countries, the so-called Tripartite Forum and its affiliated Statistical Committee did play some role for a short period in the late 1990s. Moreover, it could be argued that although no explicit social pacts were signed in the 1990s, the tripartite 'Common Declaration' from 1987 which prescribed wage restraint has been a 'functional equivalent' of the social pacts in other countries during the 1990s because it has been internalised to a very high degree the actions of the key societal actors. The Common Declaration terminated in 1998, but a new bipartite agreement on wage restraints was reached the same year in the form of the so-called Negotiation Climate Agreement (*Klimaaftalen*). With the Common Declaration's general agreement on wage restraint and with wages and employment conditions almost solely regulated by collective agreements, remaining issues to establish tripartite dialogues mainly concerned welfare issues. Due to a strong economy and labour shortages, wage restraint has been under heavy pressure both in the private and public sectors in recent years. However, labour migration and more recently the economic recession may have helped to keep wage demands down.

The decentralisation process of industrial relations, among other things, was made possible by the weakened power position of labour (Mailand 1996). Still, the Danish trade unions hold a relatively strong position and are from time to time able to challenge employers and government alike, as well as strike both bipartite and tripartite agreements – some of which will be presented below. To what extent this will continue remains to be seen. The strong consensus between the employers' associations and the trade unions have been weakened somewhat in the present decade, reducing the social partners' opportunities to set the scene, and the trade unions have started to lose members at a rapid pace.

Given the voluntaristic tradition of industrial relations in Denmark, we must question the adequacy of using the term 'corporatism' to describe the industrial relations system. Hence, few Danish industrial relations researchers do so. If one must talk about corporatism in Denmark it is more accurate to do so in relation to the formulation and administration of welfare-state policies than in relation to the regulation of wages and conditions at work (see below).

Peak-level corporatism in Norway

Norway has traditionally had one of the most centralised coordination of industrial relations in Europe, and the state also plays a strong role in wage setting in the private sector, in contrast to the situation in Denmark.

Union density is lower than in Denmark – around 53% – which might be because the trade unions do not administer the unemployment insurance funds as in Denmark.

From the 1970s, the dependence on natural resources led to larger fluctuations in the economy and more state intervention in wage setting than elsewhere. In response to the economic crisis, falling oil prices and industrial conflict, the main social partners agreed in 1987-88 in informal talks with the Labour government to break the inflationary wage-spiral and restore competitiveness by a combination of centralised income policies and austere economic policies.

The informal agreement of 1988 was codified in 1992 in the so-called Solidarity Alternative spelled out by a government-appointed tripartite body. The aim was to halve unemployment in five years and the tools were a combination of wage moderation, tax reform, review of public expenditure, expansion of active labour market policies (ALMP) and training, structural policy measures, and finally monetary policy, which aimed to achieve a stable exchange rate (Dølvik & Martin 2000: 280).

The Solidarity Alternative did not – in the short term at least – solve the problems of the economy. Unemployment rose to 9% and production in the private sector declined. However, facilitated by the revenues from oil exports and improvements in the international economy in 1993, the Norwegian economy started to recover.

Despite LO's commitment to continued wage moderation, the wage-restraint policy experienced a breakdown in 1998 after large-scale strikes had led to record-high wage increases far beyond inflation. The change from a Labour government to a centre-right government in 1997 contributed to the end of the Solidarity Alternative. The new government proposed the abolition of one holiday and suggested cuts in sick pay and other benefits as part of a crisis package, but this upset the trade union movement and led to the first strike ever in which all trade union confederations participated. The development illustrates, according to some observers, the inability of the Norwegian trade union movement to sustain wage moderation through an extended boom period (Dølvik & Martin 2000: 284-8).

Nevertheless, the government succeeded in getting the trade unions involved in yet another round of crisis management in late 1998. LO had never allowed the other trade union confederations to take part in income policy talks, but this time all confederations on both sides were invited to the table in a number of tripartite committees. The most important of these were the so-called Arntsen committee set up to prepare for the 1999 pay round. In the committee it was agreed that the forthcoming wage increase should be limited to 4%. LO managed to obtain an improvement in life-long training in exchange for its wage restraint promises (ibid.: 286).

Norway was hit hard by the international recession of the early 2000s when 25,000 jobs were eliminated. A new round of concerted income policy was initiated under the centre-right government that came to power in 2001 after just one year of social-democratic rule. The centre-right government attempted to liberalise the labour market, especially with regard to policies on temporary workers, but the Labour Party blocked these when it came into power again in 2005 (Dølvik 2007: 27).

Although power relations between labour and capital might have changed in favour of the latter due to the internationalisation of production, the ongoing process of individualisation and other pan-European developments, the trade unions and their social democratic allies have prevented large-scale transformations in a liberal direction.

As in Denmark, Norway has corporatist structures within specific policy areas – both in relation to formulating regulation and implementing the policy. These will be dealt with now.

Changes in labour market legislation

The voluntaristic industrial relations tradition in Denmark – which to some extent is also found in Norway – implies inter alia that labour market legislation is relatively limited and few important changes have taken place in this area in recent years. Nonetheless, some important changes in labour market regulation have been agreed upon between the social partners.

Denmark

Denmark has for some years now been considered the model country for flexicurity – the fashionable combination of flexibility and security in the labour market. The Danish flexicurity model has developed gradually over one hundred years and has often been said to include considerable flexibility through liberal rules for hire-and-fire, active labour market policy and generous social benefits, which together create an equilibrium leading to high mobility and high employment rates (e.g. Bredgaard et al. 2006).[1] The 'leg' of the triangle related to labour market regulation – the liberal hire-and-fire rules – were decided upon primarily by the social partners, since these matters are mainly regulated through the collective agreements.

In international comparative studies, the most widely used index for hire-and-fire rules is the OECD's employment protection legislation index (which also includes regulation by collective agreements). This index more or less confirms that employment protection in Denmark is liberal even though it is not among the most liberal countries: Denmark is only the tenth least strictly regulated out of 28 countries analysed. The development in Denmark has been in the direction of making regulation more liberal (OECD 2005; see also Table 1.6a in the introduction of this volume).

The increased role of sector-wide agreements seen in recent years has further developed and deepened flexicurity. Developments in the key bargaining sector – the manufacturing industry – can also be found in other sectors, where flexibility was extended to the organisation of work, overtime etc. Over the last ten years, the scope for shop stewards and management to draw up local agreements on working-time issues has been systematically expanded. As long as negotiations at the plant level take place within the framework agreements at the sector level, both employers and employees agreed to decentralise bargaining authority. This decentralisation is a precondition for the flexibility achieved in this area. The possibility of negotiating wages at the local level has existed in the metalworking industry ever since the start of its collective bargaining history. Hence, in the manufacturing sector the possibility of paying wages related to performance or results is, in principle, unchanged. But the scope for local wage negotiation has increased with the decentralisation of the bargaining system (Andersen & Mailand 2005).

The right to continuing training was introduced in Danish collective agreements in the early 1990s. This can be seen as a development contributing to functional flexibility, i.e. the potential for employees to perform several and various functions in the same enterprise. Provided the employees receive a sufficiently broad upgrading of skills, continuing training also helps to increase labour market mobility in general. The collective bargaining system also provides security. Since the late 1980s, it has been the declared goal of the social partners to secure both the competitiveness of enterprises and the employment of employees. For the trade unions, the order of priority at subsequent collective bargaining rounds has been 'job feast over wage feast.' As a consequence of the expanded scope of the bargaining agenda, other forms of security have been included in the collective agreements (ibid.). The result has been that the already flexible Danish labour market has become even more flexible.

However, it is not the case that legislation has had no role at all in the recent development of labour market regulation. Firstly, it is important to be aware that salaried employees' hire-and-fire is regulated by legislation that in general provides longer terms of notice than the collective agreements do. Secondly, until 1990, temporary employment was relatively strictly regulated. Special permission was required for actors other than the public employment service to act as temporary work agencies (Csonka 1992). The liberalisation of the employment service in 1990 contributed to bringing down the Danish employment protection (EPL) score.

Thirdly, since only around 70% of employees in Denmark are covered by collective agreements, the government has – on its own initiative or as a result from pressure from the EU – introduced so-called 'follow-up' legislation, which extends the regulation to those not covered by the collective agreements. This has been the case in relation to EU directives on part-time and temporary work, for instance. Fourthly, health and safety at work has primarily always been regulated by legislation in Denmark. Finally, the indirect politicisation of collective bargaining described in the section on corporatism can be seen as implementing legislation though 'the shadow of hierarchy.'

Norway

As indicated in the section on corporatism, Norway has more centralised industrial relations than Denmark, with a greater role for the state. However, when it comes to the strictness of employment protection legislation (which also includes rules deriving from collective agreements), the OECD finds that this is only somewhat stricter than in Denmark, and that it has changed less since the late 1980s than Danish regulation has (OECD 2005).

The legal regulation is stricter than in Denmark in at least three areas: working time, hire-and-fire rules in the public sector, and temporary work (Larsen 2006). However, regarding the use of temporary work, it was as late as 2006 that the first Norwegian collective agreement on temporary agency workers was signed (Lismoen 2007).

These rules have, however, not blocked a massive inflow of labour migrants especially from the new European member states, which first and foremost have been attracted by job opportunities and high wages. But the inflow has triggered further regulation. For instance, to avoid social dumping and the social exploitation of migrant workers, the collective agreements have been extended to all companies within certain sectors.

This has taken place in the construction sector and is also being considered in the metalworking industry (Lismoen 2008).

Changes in the welfare system

Both Denmark and Norway are universalistic, Scandinavian welfare state regimes according to Esping-Andersen's well-known typology which also includes the continental or corporatist welfare state regime and the liberal welfare state regime (Esping-Andersen 1990). Several important changes have taken place in recent decades, but here the focus will be on three issues all related to the labour market: the introduction of occupational pensions; activation policies – that is, the 'recommodification' or the transition from passive benefits to active measures; and further education and training. They cover only a minority of the relevant areas, but include some of the most important reforms in the recent development of work and welfare in the two countries. In this section the focus is mainly on policy content but it also includes information on policy processes, among them the issue-specific corporatism (meso-corporatism) mentioned above.

Denmark

As a universal Scandinavian welfare state, issues such as pensions have not traditionally been related to the individual's position in the labour market as in Denmark's southern neighbours. However, with the spread of *occupational pensions*, this has started to change.

The first occupational pension[2] fund was established in 1900, but no more than a third of employees were covered by the 1980s. Extensive tripartite work on pensions in the 1980s prepared the ground and established a consensus for a breakthrough in the collective bargaining round of 1991. In this round of bargaining, the sector federations played a stronger role than in previous negotiations. The sectoral pension funds took the form of investment companies with capital and labour equally represented in the board and a trade union chairmen – a bipartite construction that the employers could also accept.

The percentage of employees covered by occupational pensions, as well as the percentage of employees' income paid to the funds, have increased during the 1990s. In 2003, it was estimated that 92% of all employees were covered, although not to the same extent. Referring to these calculations, the social democratic government found no need to introduce additional legislation as promised by the previous government. This would have extended occupational pensions to all groups. Importantly, LO also accepted this decision.

An even more important change in Danish welfare policy was the gradual development of *activation policies*.[3] In the late 1980s and early 1990s, a marked shift from a predominantly passive policy to a more active policy took place. This transformation was supported by new discourses. The work capacity and work ethic of the unemployed were called into question, and structural unemployment (manpower shortage concurrent with high unemployment) was high on the political agenda. Increasingly policymakers did not think it possible to solve the problems of unemployment within the framework of the existing employment schemes and support systems. A consensus gradually developed that activation policy was part of the cure.

The newly elected Social Democratic government therefore introduced labour market reform in 1994 (which, however, mainly repeated the recommendations from a tripartite committee from the previous conservative-led government). This reform targeted the so-called uninsured unemployed, i.e. unemployed recipients of the unemployment benefit funds. The state-led Public Employment Service (PES) was responsible for their activation. From a period characterised by fiscal tightening and politically accepted high rates of unemployment, compensated by far-reaching protection systems (administered by the unions), a giant leap was made to an expansive fiscal policy, genuine and early individual education and training of the unemployed, plus new regionalised corporatist steering arrangements. Furthermore, the government gradually introduced shorter periods of eligibility for unemployment benefit (seven years in 1994, reduced to four years in 1999), tougher availability assessments and compulsory activation. The benefit level remained unchanged, but the right to unemployment benefit could no longer be regained via activation or employment schemes. The maximum period spent in the unemployment benefit system was capped at seven years, with the possibility of an extension of two years' leave. Moreover, leave schemes for up to one year on unemployment benefit were introduced for sabbaticals, childcare and training/education in order to reduce the labour supply. These rights applied to both the employed and the unemployed.[4]

This strategy seemed to be very successful: unemployment was halved in five years, without causing any significant bottleneck or inflationary problems. However, the 1994 reform was adjusted several times. Each adjustment enrolled more and more unemployed persons in activation programmes. This was done by progressively tightening the obligation to provide the unemployed with an activation offer, by restricting access to the unemployment benefit system, by reducing the total unemployment benefit period from seven to four years, and by tougher availability assessments generally. The local authorities' activation schemes targeting the uninsured unemployed developed partly along similar lines to the activation schemes of the public employment services (PES). That is, activation applied to nearly all uninsured unemployed. However, the local authorities' schemes still differed in terms of instruments and target groups.

The liberal-conservative government that came to office in late 2001 changed the content of activation policy by emphasising more assistance in job search and more stress on job training in the private sector, limiting the use of education as an activation tool. Moreover, after the reform introduced in 2002, social assistance and social insurance clients were brought under the same legislation, and the tri- and multipartite bodies at the central level were amalgamated. Finally, the reform led to the increased use of new private actors such as temporary work agencies, private training institutions and consultancies in delivering the activation measures. Yet reform measures in 2007 – this time of the local administrative structure – granted the municipalities greater responsibility for activation policy, merged the PES and the municipalities activation schemes, and reduced the role of social partners at the regional and local levels even more.

Another important dimension of the Danish welfare state is the voluminous *continuous training* system. Its development took off when labour market training centres – called AMUs – were established in the 1960s. Over the years, a range of continuing training courses have been developed, some more vocational than others. These numerous courses can be divided into vocational adult education and training (in which AMUs are one of the cornerstones), general adult education, and training and general education (*folkeoplysning*). Continuous training – including training for the employed – has been publicly financed to a larger extent than in most other EU countries and the level of training and education activities mentioned is the highest in the European Union. So-called 'occupational self-governance' has been the governance model, and bi- or tripartite bodies are found on all levels: an intersectoral council advising the minister, sector-based 'continuous training councils' as well as boards for the individual schools.

The latest continuous training reform in 2001 introduced the (tripartite) Board for the Labour Market Financing of Education and Training. As part of the reform's aims to concentrate public finances on the less skilled and on formal or recognised competences while including more companies in financing the activities, the board was asked to give advice on the total volume of continuous education, the financing of the activities and how the different activities should be weighted. If it is foreseen that the activities will exceed the budgetary limit, the board has the opportunity to request additional funding from employers. This is in line with another tendency to increase the role of the social partners in continuous training, namely the introduction or extension of employees' rights to take part in continuous training (Due et al. 2005).

The preparation of the 2001 reform took place without the participation of the social partners in the pre-legislative committee that concluded its work in 1999. However, the white paper was discussed in the 'Tripartite Forum' and its affiliated Statistical Committee (see above). During the negotiations, the social partners agreed with most elements of the reform as proposed in the white paper, including the guidelines for the Labour Market Financing of Education and Training, which later became one of the new features in the reform (Due et al. 2005). Hence, what started out as a process from which the social partners were excluded ended up as a concerted process. More recently in autumn 2004, civil servants published an in-depth study of continuous training in Denmark, which formed the starting point for tripartite negotiations in early 2006. These negotiations led to a tripartite declaration of intent that might again lead to an agreement on large-scale reform in this area in the coming years in order to have the social partners carry a greater part of the financial burden of continuous training. In the private sector, collective bargaining was established as planned in 2007. Since 2008, all employers in the manufacturing industry have been obliged to pay approximately 35 euros per employee to the fund annually – an amount to be doubled in 2009. From 2009, employees with more than nine months' seniority will be entitled to have up to two weeks of continuous training – of their own choice – financed from the funds. Agreements on higher contributions to the fund are expected in later bargaining rounds (Due & Madsen 2006; DI & CO-industri 2007; Mailand 2008).

Norway

Active social and labour market policy has not had such a strong profile in Norway as in Denmark, and in 2004 spending on active labour market policy stood at 0.4% of GDP and passive measures at 0.5% – the comparable figures for Denmark were 1.8 and 2.7% (OECD 2006: 271-274).[5] In Norway, the way to fulfil the aim of full employment was through regional policies and state funding of enterprises in difficulty combined with the income policy described above in the 1960s and 1970s, whereas active and passive labour market policies played a larger role in the Danish attempt to cope with their unemployment figures that were higher than in Norway (Halvorsen & Jensen 2004: 467).

Norway did, however, develop some active measures and when unemployment increased in the early 1980s, the maximum benefit period was increased. At the end of the 1980s, the discourse started to change and the 'work line' (*arbeidslinjen*) began to underline the incentives to work, rights and duty. At the same time, the obligation to work was strengthened and the maximum period for receiving unemployment benefit was reduced to three years in 1998 and to two years in 2003 (Arbeids- og Socialdepartementet 2005). Compared with Denmark's activation policy, in Norway more attention has been paid to letting the unemployed take part in training, subsidised employment and other 'second chances,' and more emphasis has been put on benefit sanctions, the tightening of eligibility rules and so on (see also Halvorsen & Jensen 2004: 474).

The role of the social partners in activation policy is not as developed as in Denmark, but nevertheless the social partners do have influence through a number of tripartite bodies at the national as well as local level.

One of these areas is *continuous training* (training of people in work). This area is covered by a corporatist tradition in that the social partners as a general rule are involved in policy formulation and – through their representation on boards – in policy implementation through the 130 local training centres (European Commission 2003). Moreover, training has become a bargaining issue for the social partners at the peak-level as well as at the sector level (Skule et al. 2002: 273).

The latest large-scale reform in the continuous training area is the Competence Reform of 1998. This reform cannot strictly be said to be sector-specific in that it was agreed upon in connection to an income policy agreement (see above). The initiative for the reform came from the trade union confederation LO, which had identified continuous training as one of its prime targets. The LO and NHO (the employers' confederation) had already agreed to add a separate chapter on continuous training in the 1994 Basic Agreement, and in 1996 the parliament called on the government to set up a committee to prepare reform measures for lifelong learning. Hence, the reform was prepared in the Buer committee set up with strong social partner representation. The committee's report from 1997 identified the workplace as the most important site for learning and called for, inter alia: a strong role for the social partners in the design of the coming reform, including the funding issue; recognition of informal competences; and the right for employees to take study leave (ibid.: 271).

The reform was passed by parliament and included the elements called for by the committee as well as tax exemption for employers financing education and other elements (European Commission 2003).

To support the implementation of the reform, the issue of continuous training became part of the following bargaining rounds. In the 1999 bargaining round, LO again agreed to exchange wage restraint for an improvement in continuous training. The government promised to spend 400 million NOK on a Competence Building Program. However, an agreement could not be reached on a model for financing educational leave. In the 2000 bargaining round, continuous training was again on the table. This time LO proposed that wage restraint should be traded off against the employers' financing of life subsistence during educational leave. But the parties did not agree on this, and the LO leaders' proposal was later turned down in a ballot of LO members. The members did not accept the idea of trading wages for continuous training – they preferred higher wages and longer holidays (Skule et al. 2002: 271).

As in Denmark, *occupational pensions* have become one of the recent decade's most controversial topics in the welfare and work area, but much later than in its southern neighbour. It is only within the last two or three years that a new pension system has crystallised.

Compared with the situation in Denmark, the reform of the occupational pension system in Norway has been much more integrated in an overall effort to recast all forms of pensions at once. In 2001, a pension committee was set up to consider 'the main objectives and principles of an integrated future pension system,' including a division of responsibility between the state and non-state pensions and the possibility of introducing a fund-based system. The committee – which had the participation of experts but not of the social partners – recommended a stronger employment-dependent element in the pension system (Neergaard 2004). In 2005, Parliament finally decided that all employees should have a statutory right to occupational pensions – in 2003 only an estimated 55% of all employees had obtained that right (Van het Kaar & Grünell 2004). The minimum contribution from companies was set at 2% of the salary.

Changes in corporate governance and the tax regime

As with the welfare system it is not possible to cover all aspects of corporate governance. Hence, the following will mostly focus on the presence and regulation of multinational corporations (MNCs) and corporate taxes. Since the issue of corporate governance partly overlaps with tax regimes, we will analyse these two under the same heading.

Denmark

Regarding the issue of *corporate governance*, it is notable that MNCs represent only around 1% of all private companies in Denmark but 16% of employees and 17% of turnover. Hence, they are much larger than the average Danish company. The average MNC has 74 employees, whereas the average Danish company has only four employees (Navrbjerg 2006).

Along with the other Nordic countries, Denmark is traditionally ranked among the top countries with the most competitive economies in the world. Most recently in the Global Competitiveness Report 2004-2005 released by the World Economic Forum, Denmark was ranked the fifth most competitive economy in the world. In 2005, corporate taxes were reduced to 28 % (Aarnsted & Koch 2005).

A special kind of MNC has attracted a great deal of attention in recent years – the private equity firm (*kapitalfonde*). It is usually understood to be a financial buyer that aims to buy a company with a view to selling it at a surplus.Private equity firms are feared as 'tough' employers without any interest in investing for the long term in the companies they buy. It is difficult to gauge how active this special form of MNC is in Denmark, but estimates of the amount involved were USD 112 million in 2007 and USD 192 million in 2008. Most of them are found within the manufacturing industry (Navrbjerg 2008).

From an international perspective, the Danish *tax regime* is characterised by a relatively heavy tax burden (approximately 50% of GDP) as well as a relatively high proportion of revenues from personal taxes and low proportion of revenues from property taxes and social security taxes. Moreover, as Table 3.1 indicates, tax revenues as a percentage of GDP have been increasing during the last 20 years – from 44.1% in 1985 to 50.3% in 2005. This level is one of the highest in the OECD countries (OECD 2007).

In 1987, the first of a number of tax reforms was introduced. Prior to the tax reform of 1987, the Danish tax system was characterised by high marginal tax rates with fairly narrow tax bases. Personal income taxation was based on a single income definition, taxable income, which included all types of income and deductions. In this system, negative capital income was taxed at the margin for all households, implying very low or negative real after-tax interest rates on household savings. The tax system also contained loopholes that narrowed the tax base, such as the tax exemption of certain capital gains on shares. The corresponding high marginal tax rates on wage income and very generous deductions for especially interest expenditures caused severe distortions in terms of low labour supply and low private sector financial savings. The 1987 reform involved a shift in the structure of taxation from labour income to the consumption of natural resources by lowering personal income taxation and increasing green taxes. The aim of lowering income taxation has, however, partly been offset by the gradual increase in local government tax rates during the period. The increase in corporate taxation in the reforms has been offset by other measures over the period, in particular a general decrease in the corporate tax rate from 50% in 1987 to 30% in 2001 (Jensen 2001). In order to make work pay, the 1990s also saw the introduction of a job allowance (tax deduction for earned income).

The cornerstone of the present Liberal-Conservative government's tax policies is a freeze on taxes that has been in effect since 2002. The tax freeze entails that a tax or duty may not increase, regardless of whether it is determined as a percentage or a nominal amount. However, income taxes are still relatively high. To support economic growth and to further expand the labour supply, the government will lower taxes on (earned) income. To improve work incentives and to make work pay, the job allowance was already raised from 2.5% to 4.25% of individual income, and the marginal tax rate was reduced by raising the income threshold for the 6% middle income tax (Regeringen 2007).

Norway[6]

In 2006, 17% of the employees in the private sector in Norway worked in foreign-owned enterprises – a figure similar to the Danish one.

In terms of the business environment, investment conditions in Norway are generally favourable. The country has an open, stable economy with no foreign exchange controls and a sound macroeconomic policy. The corporate tax rate is 28%, which is below the EU15 average of 31%. As a party to the European Economic Area (EEA) agreement and a member of international organisations such as the OECD, the WTO and the IMF, the country is firmly integrated into the international system of rules regulating investment and trade.

In accordance with the EEA agreement, foreign nationals and foreign-owned companies are free to acquire real estate in Norway as well as shares in Norwegian companies without any government interference.

This is, however, a fairly recent development. In 1995, the Law on Industrial Acquisitions (*Erhvervsloven*) replaced the relevant paragraphs in the Concession Law of 1917 (*Industrikonsesjonsloven*) under which foreign acquisitions of real estate or shares of companies holding rights to real estate in Norway required a government concession. Under the new law, the concession requirements were replaced by a reporting system which required any acquisition of more than one third of a Norwegian company – by foreign and Norwegian actors alike – to be reported to the government. The Law on Industrial Acquisitions was abolished in 2002. This means that general regulations on foreign industrial ownership in Norway no longer exist.

Fiscal incentives and tax breaks for FDI are currently absent from the Norwegian system. In terms of non-regulatory measures such as proactive investment promotion and facilitation along with targeted grants, Norway has taken a rather passive approach, and these measures do not feature in the current policy.

In terms of cultural attitudes vis-à-vis FDI, there seems to be some variation between public and political opinion. While the general public tends to view foreign ownership as a threat to national interests, policymakers are generally less categorical. The fear of losing control over national resources is no doubt present, but FDI is at the same time acknowledged as an important source for inflows of capital, technology and competence.

From an international perspective, the Norwegian *tax regime* is marked by a heavy tax burden with income tax as the most important source, but both the tax burden and the composition of the revenue is closer to the OECD average than the Danish equivalents (OECD 2004).

The most important of the recent tax reforms took place in 1992. The basic aim was to reduce tax-induced distortions by lowering statutory tax rates and to broaden the tax base, thereby making it revenue- and distribution-neutral. By broadening the tax base in the direction of a more accurate measurement of income, it was hoped that the differentials in the taxation of different activities would be reduced. The reform affected the taxation of wage earners, the self-employed and corporations. The maximum marginal tax rate on labour income was reduced from 57.8 to 49.5% (and from 64.9 to 52.4% for the self-employed), and the marginal tax rate on capital income was reduced from 40.5 to 28% (Aarbu & Thoresen 1997).

Since the 1992 reform, income tax has been levied on two different concepts of income: general income and personal income. In this dual income tax system, capital income earned by personal taxpayers is taxed as general income at a flat tax rate of 28%, while income derived from labour and pensions is taxed progressively as personal income (with the top rate at 64.7% in 2004). The flat 28% tax rate is also applied to the income of limited companies and other corporate taxpayers. To bridge the gap between the tax rates of general and personal income, the 1992 tax reform introduced a 'split model' in which a part of the taxable income of self-employed individuals was deemed to be capital income and subject to the 28% tax only and the residual income treated as personal income subject to progressive tax rates. This split model also applied to income earned by partnerships and limited companies where two-thirds or more of the partnership or company in question was owned by active partners or shareholders (Ministry of Finance 2007).

This split model did not work as was intended. Over the years, the rate differential between taxes on general and personal income increased significantly, from 28.1 percentage points in 1992 to 36.7 percentage points ten years later. In 2005 the centre-right government introduced yet another reform that, inter alia, saw a reduction of the marginal tax rates of labour income (personal income), and also made these rates applicable on profits exceeding risk-free returns in solely owned enterprises – i.e. self-employed individuals (ibid.). The present Labour government has introduced a tax ceiling similar to the Danish one, which has especially benefited homeowners because of increasing housing prices.

Table 3.1   Development of tax revenue in Denmark and Norway from 1985 to 2005, in percent

	1985	1995	2005
Denmark	44.1	48.8	50.3
Norway	42.7	40.9	43.7
OECD average	32.7	34.9	36.2

Source: OECD (2007e)

But there are still differences with the development in Denmark. The total tax revenue as a percentage of GDP has hardly increased during the last 20 years and is still around 43% – much lower than in Denmark (OECD 2007). Moreover, despite similarities in some ways, the tax revenue distribution between sources differs in that social security makes up a larger – and income tax a smaller – percentage of the total revenue in Norway than in Denmark.

Conclusions

Having described the development of the five selected features – corporatism, welfare state, labour market regulation, corporate governance and
tax regime – in Denmark and Norway, the state and development of these
features will now be compared in terms of the typology distinguishing a
liberal and a negotiated economy (NE). The latter should be understood
as a sub-type of the CME as it has been proposed by Pedersen (e.g. 2006)
and Campbell and Pedersen (2007). This type resembles the corporatist
type put forward in the introduction to this volume.

According to Campbell and Pedersen, not only Denmark and Norway
but also Finland and the Netherlands can be labelled an NE. An NE can be
specified with respect to at least three core features all related to corporatism:

1   Firstly, in an NE, corporatism is not necessarily centralised and thus
     can also take a decentralised form. This fits well the above descrip-
     tion that illustrated the importance of sub-national levels (the sec-
     toral level, the meso-level, the regional level and the firm level) for
     corporatism in Denmark and Norway.
2   Secondly, according to Campbell and Pedersen, the policy learning
     processes in these countries have included interests other than capital
     and labour. This has facilitated mobilisation of consensus around 'the
     national strategies for international competitiveness.' However, this
     statement only partly fits with the presentation of corporatism above.
     Apart from the social partners, it is mainly organisations of the local
     authorities that have been closely involved in the work and welfare re-
     lated areas presented – the involvement of NGOs and other interests
     has been modest. In most cases the social partners still have privi-
     leged access, even though it has been weakened to some extent. But
     in other areas such as environmental policies, housing policy, health
     policy and agricultural policy, other interest organisations than the
     social partners have a stronger say, at least in Denmark (e.g. Blom-
     Hansen & Daugbjerg 1999).
3   Thirdly, the traditional corporatist arrangement has developed into
     what – with inspiration from Visser & Hemerijck (1997), Traxler et al.
     (2001) and Molina & Rhodes (2002) – is called 'trimmed corporatism.'
     This form of corporatism includes four elements: an ideology empha-
     sising the importance of adapting to the international competition; a
     multilevel system of interest organisations involved in policymaking,
     policy implementation and 'policy fine tuning'; a collective system of

knowledge generation that supports the national consensus on a competitive strategy. Again, this description fits well with the developments described in Denmark and Norway.

In sum, the NE ideal type delivers a seemingly trustworthy third position to the two models included in the Varieties of Capitalism approach – even though the NE is a variant of the CME.

Policy process – corporatism

The emphasis in this contribution was put on *corporatism* which should be seen as a form of policy process – and less on the policy content in the four areas described.

It is possible to conclude that corporatism is still alive and kicking in both Denmark and Norway. The institutional set-up around industrial relations and the policy areas in focus have been restructured, but as a general rule the social partners have been involved both in the defining and restructuring processes and implementing them, even though in general their role has been reduced. Hence, the two countries are in this regard clearly still closer to the NE than to the LME model.

There are a large number of *similarities* between the two countries, both in the context of coporatist arrangements and corporatism itself. Firstly, the labour market parties are still relatively strong, both countries are consensus seeking and – after economic ups and downs – both have experienced more than ten years of employment growth. Secondly, the social democratic party has been a key player in both countries, and despite long periods in opposition in recent years, egalitarian norms are still dominant. The right-wing governments have not dismantled the welfare state. They have rightly restructured it, but so have the social democratic-led governments too – and they have been no less willing to include the social partners in the processes than the social democrats. Thirdly, corporatist arrangements in both countries are widespread in the three welfare-policy areas analysed, even though variations are found between areas, periods and between the two countries. Furthermore, it seems that the actors in both countries have addressed similar challenges in the three welfare areas in focus.

There are also a number of important *differences* in the regulation of the two countries and with regard to where corporatism is found. The state has played a much more active role in setting wages in Norway than in Denmark, and tripartite income-policy agreements are much more widespread in Norway. Hence, Norway seems to be a more 'traditional' corporatist country in that peak-level corporatism has remained strong decade after decade.

On the other hand, meso-level corporatism (corporatism related to specific policy areas or issues) seems to be weakened and weaker in the three selected areas in Norway than in Denmark. This finding is supported by a recent comparative analysis that shows that the number of boards and committees that involve social partners has decreased in Norway since the 1970s, which is not the case in Denmark (Christensen et al. 2008). Because Denmark combines voluntarism in industrial relations with neo-corporatism in welfare state issues (see also Mailand 2005), and meso-level corporatism has not weakened, Denmark represents weaker peak-level corporatism and stronger meso-level corporatism, whereas the opposite situation is the case in Norway.

Furthermore, there might be yet another difference related to the stronger involvement of the state in industrial relations in Norway. In Denmark, corporatism has a strong informal component (see e.g. Due & Madsen 1996; Pedersen 2006) meaning that bi- and tripartite coordination often takes place beyond formal corporatist bodies. The stronger state involvement in industrial relations and the more developed formal institutions for this in Norway might result in a different balance between formality and informality in Norwegian corporatism than in the Danish one. However, it is not possible from the descriptions above to tell if this is the case or not.

The question arises whether corporatism can be sustained in these two countries. Contrary to the ad hoc social pacts experienced since the 1990s in countries lacking strong social partners, it is difficult to imagine Scandinavian corporatism without strong social partner organisations. Membership is declining in both countries but is still high, and the social partners still have privileged access to the government in most policy areas, even in those areas where influence has been reduced. Moreover, the social partners' role in the regulation of wages and working conditions is not weaker now than in the past. Challenges such as offshoring, demographic changes, changes of governments, different forms of marketisation, fluctuating business cycles, and – especially in Denmark – pressure from companies to decentralise industrial relations have transformed the established models of regulation but have far from dismantled them. Furthermore, in recent years corporatist arrangements have been seen in new areas such as labour migration.

So, despite its partial dismantling, corporatism is still a relevant term for the regulation of work and welfare in Scandinavia. It is likely that there will be such a feature as Scandinavian corporatism, if not for another century, at least for the coming decade. However, if the present slow decline in the trade unions' organisational density in Denmark and Norway develops into rapid decline, the future for Scandinavian corporatism might seem more troubled.

Policy areas – labour market, welfare state, corporate governance and tax regime

The *labour market legislation* area is also marked by similarities with strong roles for the social partners. Legislation plays a stronger role in Norway, regulation is more centralised, and employment protection is a bit stricter and has moved less in a liberal direction than in Denmark. However, in neither country is the regulation among the most liberal in the OECD, despite Denmark's label as a 'flexicurity' best case. In sum, neither Denmark nor Norway present clear examples of NE or LME when it comes to labour market legislation. Denmark is in a middle position leaning towards the liberal ideal type, whereas Norway is in a middle position leaning towards the coordinated ideal type.

Regarding *welfare state* policy, only the development in social and labour market policies were analysed. Both countries are universalistic, social-democratic welfare states. However, decommodification in this area has been replaced by recommodification policies where citizen-based universal rights to social assistance as well as to social security have been modified by the right-and-responsibility turn. This development, which can be seen as a move in a liberal direction, has been more marked in Denmark than in Norway. However, the development in Denmark has more elements of providing the unemployed with new competences through the activation schemes, whereas the Norwegian schemes seems to be more of the 'work-first' type, which can also be seen as leaning more towards the LME.

There have not been substantial changes in relation to *corporate governance*. Both countries are relatively open to foreign direct investment, but neither offer tax breaks or other special economic incentives to foreign investors. It is not all status quo, however. In Denmark, a high tax country, there has been a rising awareness of multinational companies' attempts to reduce their tax burden through 'creative financial management', but at the same time corporate tax has been reduced. Moreover, both countries have witnessed an increase in FDI. The *tax regime* in both countries is characterised by an above-average tax burden. The burden is highest in Denmark and builds more on income tax and less on social contributions than in Norway. Again, the countries seem to be situated within the NE type. Reforms have also taken place in Denmark in order to 'make work pay', and the income tax dimension has been reduced by introducing green taxes, among others. In sum, recent changes in the tax regime in Denmark can be seen as a modest step in the direction of the liberal type, whereas the changes in Norway do not represent important changes.

The developments in these five areas are summarised in Table 3.2. It shows that although both Denmark and Norway both fall within the NE model, features that have similarities with the liberal market economy have existed for years and changes that can be seen as taking these capitalist economies closer to the LME have taken place during the last 20 years – but maybe more so in Denmark than in Norway.

Table 3.2 Varieties of capitalism, state and development in Denmark and Norway

	Denmark	*Norway*
Corporatism	NE (→ LME)	NE (→ LME)
Labour market legislation	LME/NE (→in most regards LME)	NE/LME
Welfare state	NE → LME	NE → LME
Corporate governance and tax regime	NE (→ LME)	NE

( ) = limited development

What neither the VoC nor the NE approach tells us, though, is why there have been changes in the two Scandinavian countries in a more 'liberal' direction and why these changes seem to have been stronger in Denmark than in Norway – at least in relation to the dimensions presented here. These changes towards 'liberalisation' have been noticed in other recent studies of European political economies (Streeck 2008; Howell 2003; Coates 2005; Hall & Thelen 2009). Some of these authors, however, discuss to what extent it really is the same path that is followed and whether the directions of change and the destinations are the same. In the case of Denmark and Norway, it is certain that the changes in a liberal direction have not transformed the two countries into liberal market economies.

Notes

1   In some newer publications well developed lifelong learning is added as a fourth leg of the Danish flexicurity model.
2   The section on occupation pensions builds on Due & Madsen (2004).
3   Where nothing else is stated the source of this section is Larsen & Mailand (2007).
4   The favourable conditions for taking leave were reduced significantly during the 1990s, and sabbatical leave has now been abolished.
5   2004 is the latest year with comparable figures between these two countries.
6   The source of the following presentation of corporate governance in Norway is Aanstad & Koch (2005).

4 Coming Together But Staying Apart
Continuity and Change in the Austrian and Swiss Varieties of Capitalism

Alexandre Afonso and André Mach

Introduction[1]

Austria and Switzerland are two small open European economies that share many similarities but also significant differences in their structures of economic governance. Both can be considered as strongly corporatist, since major aspects of their economic regulation rely upon a system of organised cooperation between labour and capital, but their respective positions on the "liberal" and "statist" axis (see Becker, this volume) vary to an important extent.

On the one hand, Austria and Switzerland have most commonly been identified as political economies where cooperation between economic actors has prevailed over arms-length competition. According to Katzenstein (1984; 1985), the dual strategy of external laissez-faire and domestic interventionism pursued by small European states was made possible by the co-operative stance prevailing among political and economic elites. Similarly, in the classification scheme of the varieties of capitalism approach (Hall & Soskice 2001), both countries are labelled coordinated market economies (CMEs), where non-market mechanisms of coordination play a crucial role in the setup of relations between economic actors. Aspects particularly worth mentioning are highly coordinated industrial relations, corporatist institutions (Katzenstein 1985) as well as a high degree of cartelisation in the domestic product market (Schröter 1999) and in the rules governing corporate governance (David & Mach 2004). In this perspective, both Austria and Switzerland are good examples of political economies where cooperative mechanisms of coordination have played a central role in the organisation of production processes.

On the other hand, the Austrian and Swiss political economies also display important differences in their underlying institutional arrangements and power relationships. Most importantly, market mechanisms and private solutions have played a more privileged role in Switzerland than in Austria, where political control over the economy has been greater. Along this latter line, Katzenstein (1984; 1985) already made a distinction between the *liberal* variant (Switzerland, the Netherlands and Belgium) and the *social* variant (Austria, Denmark, Norway) of democratic corporatism. These two variants differed in the respective strengths of their employer and labour organisations. Switzerland was considered the most liberal example, with weak trade unions, well organised and strongly export-oriented employers, and essentially private adaptation strategies designed within strongly cohesive business organisations. Austria, known for its "Austro-Keynesianism" combining fiscal, monetary and incomes policy throughout the post-war decades (Scharpf 1991), appeared to be the foremost example of social corporatism, with strong trade unions entertaining close ties with a dominant social-democratic party, weaker business associations dominated by SMEs, and public adaptation strategies. In Austria, the state has traditionally played a predominant role in shaping economic change, notably through an important industrial sector under public control. By contrast, in Switzerland, a much less interventionist central state combined with a powerful coordination potential among business interests has been a dominant feature in the organisation of the political economy.

This chapter assesses institutional continuity and change in these two countries. In the face of growing internationalisation, budgetary constraints and European integration, continuity and change have been determined by prevailing interest configurations and institutional limits in terms of public intervention and private governance. Hence, the dominance of private employers in Switzerland has fostered rapid change in areas where private regulation prevailed, such as corporate governance, whereas institutional veto points have strongly limited change in areas where public intervention was necessary. By contrast, the larger scope of public intervention in Austria and its more majoritarian features have allowed more space for change in welfare reforms, while the strong institutionalisation of corporatist institutions in labour market governance, for instance, has made it more resilient to change than Switzerland. In this respect, Austria and Switzerland provide good examples of how institutional change is dependent on the respective share of public regulation and private governance.

This chapter is structured as follows. We first briefly outline economic performance and macro-institutional frameworks in both countries. The next sections assess the dynamics of continuity and change in the different spheres of their political economies: corporate governance and economic regulation, labour market and industrial relations, and the welfare state. For each sphere, we assess the extent and type of change in a comparative perspective.

Performance and institutional regime

Austria and Switzerland have displayed fairly similar positive results in terms of macroeconomic performance (see Table 4.1). Besides high employment ratios, especially for Switzerland, unemployment has never exceeded 5% during the last thirty years. In the case of Switzerland, economic growth remained modest during the 1990s in comparison with other European countries (for more details, see Bonoli & Mach 2000; Hemerijck et al. 2000; Merrien & Becker 2005). By contrast, this was compensated to some extent in Austria by its entry into the EU in 1995 and the opening of new markets in Central and Southeastern Europe. Concerning their employment structure, the proportion of industrial jobs has declined but remains above the OECD average. Both economies also became much more dependent on their external economic environment, with a steady increase in exports as a share of GDP and the increasing importance of outward foreign direct investment, particularly in the Swiss case (see Table 4.2 below).

Table 4.1   Macroeconomic performance

	Austria			Switzerland		
	1980s	1990s	2000s	1980s	1990s	2000s
1. Real GDP growth (%)	2.0	2.7	2.0	2.3	1.1	1.9
2. Inflation (%)	3.8	2.4	2.0	3.3	2.3	1.0
1. Employment ratio (%)	63.8	67.3	68.2	76.7	84.0	84.0
2. Unemployment (%)	3.3	3.8	4.4	0.6	3.0	3.5

Sources: Armingeon et al. (2007)

Structuring factors in political economies can be grasped through the macro-institutional regime – the political system and the main political players including those of capital and labour – and the sectoral regimes governing specific spheres such as corporate governance, industrial relations and the welfare state. The first factor strongly determines the level of public intervention and tripartite corporatism possible in a political economy. Austria and Switzerland are very different in this respect, which accounts to a great extent for the divergent paths of development in their varieties of capitalism. In a nutshell, the differences can be summarised as *fragmented state, constrained executive power* and *bourgeois dominance* in Switzerland, and *centralised state, stronger executive power* and *strong labour* in Austria.

The great number of institutional barriers to state action in Switzerland has fostered extensive private self-regulation strategies in the economic sphere, whereas state intervention and public regulations have played a more important role in Austria. First, both countries are formally federalist, but Swiss cantons enjoy many more competences (in domains such as health/welfare, education and justice/police) than Austrian *Länder*, which has limited the potential for centralised macroeconomic management in Switzerland (Lijphart 1999: 189). Second, due to perfect bicameralism and direct democracy, executive power in Switzerland is much more constrained than in Austria, which features a more typical parliamentary democracy with a weak second chamber. Switzerland, by contrast, has been governed by grand coalitions with identical party compositions since 1959.

Given the low level of party discipline, majorities must be built up depending on the issue, which pushes Swiss governments into constant negotiations with parliamentary factions in a similar fashion to the system in the US. On top of this, laws are subjected to a referendum if 50,000 voters request it. In practice, this gives a veto power to any interest group able to gather those signatures. Finally, Austria and Switzerland have diverged significantly with regard to power relations between political forces. While in Austria social democracy has taken part in government on an equal or dominant basis vis-à-vis the right for 52 years between 1945 and 2008 (Pelinka 2008: 434), Swiss social democrats have always (continuously since 1943) participated on a *minority* basis in coalitions dominated by centre-right parties. The Swiss labour movement has been structurally weaker because of a number of adverse factors: a decentralised economic structure, the dominance of small firms, linguistic and religious cleavages and the continuous presence of a large foreign workforce – about a quarter of the active population – not endowed with electoral rights.

At the same time, for its part, Swiss business organised effectively early on under the leadership of export industries, finance and banking. In comparison, Austrian business has historically been weaker, mainly as a result of political alliances favouring the preservation of agriculture and handicraft at the expense of big business, and a large state sector allowing little room for the emergence of private business power (Traxler 1998: 240). These political constellations have strongly conditioned the priorities of policymaking. Austria carried out a form of centralised macroeconomic management ("Austro-Keynesianism") until the 1980s. This proved fairly successful in managing the oil shocks before being progressively abandoned from the 1980s onwards, along with the substantial privatisation of a hitherto large public industrial sector. Over this period, unemployment rose to about 5% and the government started to implement budgetary discipline and to move to a partial retrenchment of social benefits (Obinger & Talos 2009). The choice to join the EU in 1995 accelerated the reforms toward privatisation and liberalisation; it also implied conforming to the Maastricht criteria concerning public finances and prompted austerity measures.

By contrast, Switzerland never relied on a Keynesian approach to macroeconomic coordination and has favoured private adaptation strategies instead, thereby illustrating the adjustment pattern of "liberal" corporatism as outlined earlier by Katzenstein. Since World War II, Switzerland has notably relied on the massive presence of foreign workers with precarious work permits that have continuously constituted a significant part of the workforce (from 15% to 25%) and allowed for the adjustment of the supply of foreign labour to economic conditions up until the 1990s (Afonso 2005; Fluckiger 1998). Piotet (1987) characterised this pattern of adjustment as "selective corporatism". Foreign and female workers mainly bore the costs of economic downturns, whereas the Swiss male "core" workforce remained rather unaffected. In part because of the degree of flexibility of the labour market, substantial policy and economic changes did not take place in the 1980s. This changed with the recession at the beginning of the 1990s, which constituted a turning point in the economic evolution of the post-war period (for more details, see Bonoli & Mach 2000; Merrien & Becker 2005).

For the first time since the 1930s, unemployment increased sharply, reaching more than 4% in 1994, and public debt rose, partially due to slow GDP growth. The 1990s were also marked by important debates concerning Switzerland's relationship to the EU (rejection of the proposal to enter the European Economic Area in a referendum in 1992). Within this context, in the early 1990s there was a shift in the political orientation of the business community, especially its export-oriented sector. The initiative originated within an informal group of representatives of Switzerland's largest companies, along with several neo-liberal academic economists. Switzerland's competitiveness, they argued, was endangered by regulations and non-competitive arrangements making products and services too expensive (for more details, see Mach 2006). Even though the group's proposals were not fully implemented, they largely inspired the orientation of the social and economic policy reforms during the 1990s and 2000s. This constituted the general framework in which the changes in the different spheres of the economy outlined below took place.

Corporate governance and economic regulation

The increasing liberalisation of product and financial markets at the international level during the last thirty years has represented a profound change in the economic environment of small European states. Even if they could be expected to be less vulnerable to economic globalisation because of their longstanding integration in world markets, these dynamics nevertheless represented a profound change in the nature of external constraints they had to deal with. They fostered important reforms in the field of corporate governance and, more generally, in the nature and scope of economic regulation in both countries.

Here, we focus our analysis on two dimensions. First, we examine the reforms of the national corporate governance system in the two countries which plays a crucial role in how companies are controlled and financed. Second, we look more broadly at product market regulation, including the liberalisation policies carried out by the two countries during the 1990s.

Whereas Katzenstein (1985) underlined the importance of corporatist institutions and domestic compensation in the strategy of small European states to cope with the pressures of international markets, one can also identify specific characteristics in their corporate governance systems. Two elements are particularly important: the high degree of cohesion of the business community and the combination of free trade policies with elements of "selective protectionism" (for more details, see David & Mach 2004). Small European states are generally characterised by dense inter-firm networks, cohesive business elites and the prevalence of regulations designed to preserve national control over large companies in company law and financial rules. This applies fairly well to Austria and Switzerland, even though the instruments whereby this control was exerted were quite different. In the Swiss case, a highly cohesive business community was the major architect of the functioning of the corporate governance system. In Austria by contrast, control over the largest companies was essentially exercised by the state through state-owned banks and holdings.

Despite its high degree of internationalisation, the Swiss business community has maintained significant leeway in its corporate governance – in terms of power of decision and control over shareholding – while leading positions were kept in the hands of Swiss citizens. Three central elements were at the heart of this policy: a high concentration of ownership; a high density of interlocking directorates, especially the close relations between banks and industry; and the existence of specific protectionist regulations (laid down in company law) that allowed for the preservation of domestic corporate control in the hands of a small group of insiders (large historical shareholders, managers and bank directors).

Switzerland was often dubbed the "fortress of the Alps" by the international financial community (David & Mach 2004; Schnyder et al. 2005). With the liberalisation of financial markets since the 1980s and the opening up of new opportunities for investment, the financial sector has gained increasing importance. This change has favoured the emergence of new actors (particularly institutional investors) that imposed new constraints on large Swiss companies by developing aggressive strategies to increase returns on the equity of their portfolio investments. Moreover, it also induced "traditional" actors (notably the large banks) to change their preferences and strategies. The liberalisation of financial markets and the increasing influence of investors emphasising financial liquidity, shareholder protection and accounting transparency put increasing pressure on the Swiss corporate governance system. Its traditional functioning was affected on two dimensions: a profound change in the mechanisms of control of Swiss companies and the reform of the regulatory framework.

First, under pressure from new institutional investors, a gradual disappearance of the traditional mechanisms of control among the largest Swiss companies from the end of the 1980s could be observed. Most large companies progressively abandoned their protectionist mechanisms (such as voting right distortions) through the simplification of their capital structure.[2] The sharp growth of market capitalisation (see Table 4.3) also indicates the increasing importance of stock markets as capital providers for companies, and the growing role of institutional investors in corporate control. We can also identify a clear breakdown of the Swiss intercompany network (interlocking directorates) during the 1990s (Schnyder et al. 2005). This is especially true for the traditionally close ties between large banks and non-financial companies. This change is related to the shift in strategy of the largest Swiss banks, whose revenues increasingly stemmed from investment banking activities rather than traditional credit practices (see Schnyder et al. 2005).

Second, and alongside the changing practices of the largest companies, the regulatory framework was profoundly reformed during the 1990s with the reform of company law (1992) and the adoption of a new stock exchange law (1996). Even if these did not represent a brutal change and were the result of compromises between the decisive actors, the new regulations imposed changes in traditional corporate governance practices towards more transparency in disclosure rules and accounting presentation (Mach et al. 2007).

Changes in the mechanisms of control and the regulatory framework led to new strategies among the largest Swiss companies, which were much more exposed to the pressure of stock market evaluation and to the critical appreciation of institutional investors focusing on the promotion of shareholder value. The sharp increase in the amount of profits redistributed to shareholders (through dividend payouts and share buybacks) was an important feature of the new strategic orientation of firms during the second half of the 1990s. The increase in mergers and acquisitions also resulted in huge mergers between some of the largest Swiss multinationals, threatened by potential foreign acquisitions: Ciba and Sandoz into Novartis in 1996, UBS and SBS in 1998, Crédit Suisse and Winterthur insurance in 1999.

Many restructurings of major industrial companies also took place. These restructurings were generally motivated by the will to concentrate the activities of the companies on their core business and to abandon less profitable segments. This was the case for ABB, Sulzer or Algroup, some of the largest Swiss industrial firms, and also others in the chemical and pharmaceutical sectors. These changes were completely in line with those who advocate a more "shareholder value" oriented strategy of the companies (for more details, Schnyder et al. 2005). With respect to the longstanding patterns mentioned above, it is also worth mentioning that some important Swiss companies are now controlled by foreign companies: this is the case for Swiss (the national airline company controlled by Lufthansa), Winterthur insurance, Sulzer, Algroup and Serono, which are among the most well-known examples. At the same time, Swiss multinational companies saw a strong expansion abroad, which is illustrated by the sharp increase in the total outward FDI stocks during the 1990s (see Table 4.2).

Table 4.2	Outward and inward foreign direct investment, 1985-2007 (% of GDP)									
	1985		*1990*		*1995*		*2000*		*2007*	
	Out	*In*	*Out*	*In*	*Out*	*In*	*Out*	*In*	*Out*	*In*
Austria	2.0	5.7	2.7	6.2	5.1	7.6	12.9	15.7	34.0	34.0
Switzerland	27.0	10.8	28.9	15.0	46.3	18.6	92.9	34.7	142.6	65.7

Source: UNCTAD 2008 World Investment Report

Table 4.3	Evolution of market capitalisation, 1975-2005 (% of GDP)									
	1975	*1980*	*1985*	*1990*	*1995*	*1996*	*1997*	*1998*	*2000*	*2005*
Austria	9	3	7	17	14	15	18	17	14	41
Switzerland	30	42	91	69	130	136	225	260	322	256

Source: OECD Financial Market Trends (various issues)

In Austria, the issues surrounding the debates on corporate governance have been different. The major topic has been the privatisation of the large state-owned companies since the mid-1980s. Large Austrian companies are much less internationalised than their Swiss counterparts. This is mainly due to the central role of the state, which held controlling majorities of votes in most large firms (Kurzer 1993: 95) and thus prevented Austrian companies from expanding abroad (see Table 4.2 on FDI). This central position of the Austrian state in the control and strategy of the largest companies goes back to the Nationalisation Acts of 1946 and 1947. In 1989, the Austrian state was the largest domestic shareholder of the corporations listed on the stock exchange, holding 37.3% of the shares (Gugler et al. 2001; Jud 1994: 473).

The banking sector, which entertains close connections with Austrian governmental institutions, is another major actor in the corporate governance of large firms. Interlocking directorates are also very common in Austria, as many executives of banks are represented on various supervisory boards (Jud 1994: 483ff). The predominance of the state was not challenged until the end of the 1980s. Since state-owned firms produced mainly raw materials and some heavy machinery, they posed no direct threat to small firms, dominated by family ownership, specialised in the production of consumer goods and politically close to the ÖVP. There was even a degree of complementarity, small firms being supplied by large ones in cheap energy, building materials, iron and steel, and essential equipment. For the social-democratic party and the trade unions, this system was a way of exerting control over Austrian industry (Kurzer

1993: 102-103). It is thus not surprising that, in contrast to Switzerland, employee representation has played an important role in Austria, organised along the lines of the German co-determination system (Jud 1994: 467).

Similar to Switzerland, the concentration of ownership was particularly strong in Austria. By international standards, Austria seems to be the European country with the highest ownership concentration (Gugler et al. 2001). This concentration was strengthened by the existence of the state-owned holding (OIAG created in 1970) and the practice of "pyramiding" (mainly by banks), which allowed for the extension of control at a relatively low cost (Kurzer 1993: chap. 4; Gugler et al. 2001). In its heyday in 1975, the OIAG group counted 120,000 employees (approximately 18% of all persons employed in industry). Twenty years later, the situation had changed dramatically: in 1993, the state holding company has been transformed into a privatisation agency with the objective of relinquishing its majority stakes. The number of employees of the state holding fell to 4,800 as a result of the privatisation programme launched by the government during the 1990s. Even if efficiency increases in the privatised companies were officially mentioned as the main objective – especially after losses incurred by the nationalised industrial firms during the weak growth period of the 1980s – another major reason for this extensive privatisation programme was to increase public revenues through sellouts in order to reduce public deficits (Aiginger 1999; Nowotny 1998).

In many ways, the privatisations and the disappearance of the state holding represented a profound change in the Austrian corporate governance system. However, even if the maximising of revenue was a central criteria for choosing among the potential buyers, a second criteria was also introduced: the continuing operation in Austria of the privatised firms. The strategic goal was to keep these companies under Austrian influence and to make sure that headquarter functions and the resulting qualified employment opportunities would be located in Austria. For example, AMAG was sold in 1996 at a negative price to a joint venture consisting of the management and a large, private Austrian company. A kind of "national preference clause" was thus granted (Aiginger 1999: 265). In parallel with the privatisation programme and in the context of EU membership, several regulatory reforms concerning financial markets and the stock exchange were also adopted during the 1990s. The main objectives of these new regulations were to favour the transparency of companies, to facilitate financial transactions and to promote the traditionally underdeveloped Austrian stock exchange.

Starting from a very different initial configuration (the presence of large multinational companies in Switzerland and the traditional dominance of nationalised state-owned companies in Austria), both countries followed a more liberal market driven policy in the field of corporate governance. This was done through a policy of privatisation and of state withdrawal from the major companies in Austria. In Switzerland, the changes were mainly the results of the changing strategies of the largest Swiss companies which progressively abandoned their traditional mechanisms of control in a new international economic context. Large companies have become much more trans-nationalised and subject to the pressure of financial markets, Austria to a much lesser extent than Switzerland.

Product market regulation has also been the subject of important reforms since the beginning of the 1990s; both countries followed liberalisation policies in order to promote competition in their domestic markets. In Austria, as a member of the EU, these liberalisation policies were mostly underpinned by the implementation of European directives, whereas in Switzerland, domestic impulses were more important. In both countries, the different indicators measuring the degree of product market regulations distorting the functioning of competition decreased substantially from the beginning of the 1990s.

Despite the emphasis usually put on its liberal character and openness, the exposure of the Swiss economy to international markets has been significantly mitigated by different measures, such as subsidies (for agriculture), public regulations or private cartels, all of which have facilitated non-competitive behaviour while protecting domestic markets from international competition. Several studies emphasised how almost two thirds of domestic prices were either administered, strongly regulated or fixed by private cartels, which helped to explain the high level of domestic prices (Hauser & Bradke 1992). Because of changes in the international environment during the early 1990s (GATT agreements and European economic integration), and because of internal demands to promote competition, heavy pressure was finally applied to a domestic sector increasingly regarded as a "rent-seeking", non-competitive and structurally weak part of the economy. Because of the dual structure of its economy, characterised by the existence of "selective protectionist" mechanisms aimed at protecting domestic sectors, liberalisation policies in the domestic market took a particularly important place in Switzerland during the 1990s.

After the negative result of the referendum on entry into the EEA in December 1992, the government launched a programme of "economic revitalisation" whose main objective was to reduce production costs in the domestic sectors and enhance competition in the internal market; its leitmotiv was: "competitiveness abroad through increasing competition on domestic markets" (Mach 2006). One of the key elements of the revitalisation programme and inspired by European regulations were reforms of the "cartel law" in 1995 and 2003. Although the new law did not formally forbid cartels, it provided clearer guidelines and gave more power to antitrust authorities to combat anticompetitive practices. This reform faced strong opposition from the Small Business Association (USAM), which initially threatened to challenge the new law with a referendum but eventually accepted it. The revitalisation programme also included a new federal law on the internal market, which was expected to facilitate the free movement of goods, services and persons in the Swiss territory, and thus to reduce market segmentation across cantons.

Liberalisation measures further concerned the reform of agricultural policy and regulations of public procurement in the context of the GATT agreements. Such measures did generate some opposition among organised interests representing domestic economic sectors. Like all other European states, though with some delay, Switzerland also decided to liberalise its telecommunications sector (with a partial privatisation of the public operator) and, to a lesser extent, postal services before the first of January 1998, when the European directive on liberalising telecommunications came into force.[3] However, a first proposal to liberalise the electricity market was refused in a popular vote in 2002 after an optional referendum launched by the trade unions and the social democratic party (for more details, see Maggetti et al. 2010).

In Austria, the first state-owned companies that were privatised at the end of the 1980s were not natural monopolies in network industries but touched mainly the manufacturing and banking sectors. With the adhesion to the EU in 1995 and the need to comply with its directives, further privatisation and liberalisation measures concerned the telecommunications, postal services and electricity sectors. The general competition legislation was also strengthened during the 2000s, with the creation of a new independent federal competition authority in 2002.

Labour market and industrial relations

In Austria and Switzerland, labour market governance relies heavily on a system of cooperation between trade unions and employers, even if the extent of this coordination differs between the two countries: strong corporatism in Austria, and "lean" corporatism in Switzerland. By any standards, Austria is the corporatist country *par excellence*. It ranks first – ahead of Norway – in all 23 rankings of corporatism in the literature reviewed by Siaroff (1999: 184). Even in the case of collective bargaining at the sectoral level, organised interests are highly centralised, and the outcomes of bargaining apply to the whole economy. Switzerland, for its part, has been considered a more ambiguous case as regards its degree of corporatism, particularly in terms of the centralisation of interest groups (more fragmented on the side of labour) and wage bargaining.[4]

Reflecting the different balance of power between business and labour in the two countries, the scope of public regulation of employment relationships is also less extensive in Switzerland than in Austria. Labour law in Switzerland has been mostly limited to issues of health and safety at work, leaving the central points of employment relationships to collective bargaining and collective labour agreement (CLAs); legal constraints on hiring and firing have been low in comparative perspective (cf. Becker in this volume, Table 1.5a). The degree of public regulation is somewhat higher in Austria, but collective bargaining is still the central regulation mode, which is reflected in the absence of a statutory minimum wage in both countries.[5] Social partners have traditionally played a predominant role in core areas such as wage setting, the joint elaboration of governmental policy proposals, or vocational education. In this latter domain, both countries have a system of dual apprenticeship training (schooling and professional practice) involving both public authorities and companies. Similar to Germany, the system of apprenticeship ensures a smooth transition between school and employment through the acquisition of specific skills, thereby ensuring low youth unemployment rates in comparative perspective (Culpepper 2007; Trampusch 2008a).

The Austrian system of industrial relations, built after World War II, is exceptional in many respects with regards to its structure and institutional anchorage. In its heyday in the 1960s, both prices and wages were coordinated in a corporatist fashion through the so-called parity commission, until price control lost its effectiveness in the late 1970s along with the increase in imports. It was only formally abandoned in 1994 (Traxler 1998: 246). Nowadays, despite the international (notably the entry in the EMU) and structural pressures that have challenged corporatism elsewhere in Europe, industrial relations in Austria have remained remarkably stable in recent decades, mainly thanks to deeply rooted institutional structures (Traxler 1998: 239). One of these central features is compulsory membership of all companies, farmers and wage earners in the system of *Chambers*, designed as official semi-public bodies of interest representation.

On the employers' side, the Economic Chamber (WKO) and its regional affiliates have a monopoly of representation for all companies for both wage bargaining and consultation on draft legislation and administrative orders. On the workers' side, there is a division of tasks between the Chamber of Labour (BAK – *Bundesarbeitskammer*), which officially represents workers' interests in public policymaking, and the ÖGB (*Österreichischer Gewerkschaftsbund*) which takes part in collective bargaining. In contrast to the *Arbeitskammer*, membership in the ÖGB is not compulsory. The relations between them are based on an informal division of tasks rather than competition. Collective bargaining in Austria is conducted almost exclusively at the sectoral level, with a high level of co-ordination between sectors. The metalworking sector traditionally opens the bargaining round and sets the standard for other sectors.

The statutory membership of all employers in the Economic Chamber is the main mechanism that explains the coverage rates approaching 100% that have persisted until now (EIRO 2005; Traxler 1998). Since all companies are members of the Economic Chamber, they are all bound by the collective agreements negotiated by the peak organisation. This in turn extends to all workers independent of whether they are trade union members or not. Hence, even if union membership has declined steadily since the 1960s (see Table 4.4), this has not had any effect on the level of coverage of collective bargaining. However, despite this institutional stability, the Austrian system is also faced with a trend of "organised decentralisation" whereby specific elements are shifted to lower bargaining levels to allow for more flexibility across firms (Traxler 1995). For instance, the WKO has recently been calling for the suppression of productivity as a key pay-setting criterion in collective bargaining, and for the introduction of profit-sharing schemes at the firm level instead, so that wage increases would be more closely linked to the performance of individual firms (EIRO 2008). Despite the high degree of coordination of the system, wage inequalities have also been fairly important across sectors, gender and employee status.

In contrast to the relative stability in collective bargaining, fairly radical changes have been observed in the influence of social partners in policymaking in Austria. As argued above, the social partners (BAK and WKO) played a predominant role in the formulation of policies. They had a legal right to be consulted on any policy proposal through the *Begutachtungsverfahren* (consultation procedure). Policy deals were usually struck behind closed doors between the peak associations in close interaction with ruling parties, and parliament was usually a mere rubber-stamping institution for corporatist deals. In recent years, however, this system has been challenged by the erosion of the electoral base of the two traditional parties and the emergence of new parties hostile to corporatism, notably the populist FPÖ and the Green Party (Crepaz 1994; Traxler 1998: 258-259).

The accession to power of a new "black and blue" (ÖVP/FPÖ) coalition in 2000 after nearly thirty years of social-democratic presence in government has constituted a turning point in this process. Ruling parties have increasingly sought to bypass the veto power of social partners by marginalising them in policy procedures, and parliament (as a locus of power for ruling parties rather than of social partners) seems to have gained in importance as an agenda-setting arena during this period (Obinger & Talos 2006; Pelinka 2008). Many reforms inspired by a pro-market agenda have been brought forward against their will. Some of these reforms, notably in public pensions, were met by protest strikes, which partly accounts for the increase of industrial action in the 2000s (see Table 4.4). Besides this, the corporatist system has been faced with increasing legitimacy problems reflected by declining membership. The influence of social partners, however, seems to have been restored with the return of a grand coalition in 2006 (Afonso 2010b).

In historical terms, Swiss industrial relations have displayed much more liberal features and a lesser degree of coordination than in Austria, notably with regard to the centralisation of wage bargaining (Fluder & Hotz-Hart 1998: 274). Switzerland has been a contested case of corporatism precisely because of its fragmented organisational base. Traditionally, corporatism in Switzerland has been strong with regard to social partner involvement in policymaking and somewhat weak with regard to wage bargaining as such (Oesch 2007: 339). Even if the Swiss system of industrial relations can be considered a corporatist/coordinated model, it has always been a light/liberal variant of it from its early times of development. To some extent, it constituted a forerunner of what is now termed "competitive" or "supply-side" corporatism, in the sense that labour acquiescence has never been traded with expansionary economic policies but rather with more immaterial compensations, like participation rights in policymaking (Traxler 2001). Industrial peace was presented as a *sine qua non* for competitiveness in a strongly export-oriented economy.

Collective bargaining in Switzerland also takes place essentially at the sectoral level, while some collective labour agreements are negotiated at the company level for big companies such as major retailers Migros and Coop. The coverage of collective bargaining is fairly low in comparative terms and covers slightly less than half of the workforce (see Table 4.4). The outcomes of collective bargaining may be extended beyond signing parties, and made legally enforceable by public authorities if they gather more than half of the workers and half of the companies in any given sector; this has traditionally been the case in the construction sector. Similarly to Austria, though in a much more informal way, the coordination of wages across economic sectors mainly takes place through highly organised sectoral employer organisations (under the umbrella of the peak level employer association, *Schweizerische Arbeitgeberverband* – SAV) (Oesch 2007: 338; Soskice 1990: 41). In Switzerland, the trade union movement has been much more fragmented along religious or occupational lines. In 2000, the biggest trade union Confederation, the *Schweizerischer Gewerkschaftsbund* (SGB), only gathered about 50% of all trade union members. Besides the SGB, there are a number of other smaller trade union confederations, notably for white-collar workers, the Christian federation CNG, or specific professions like teachers, police officers or nurses (Mach & Oesch 2003: 164).

Table 4.4   Labour market and wage bargaining indicators (decade averages)

	Austria			Switzerland		
	1980s	1990s	2000s	1980s	1990s	2000s
1. Coverage of collective bargaining (%)	96.0	99.0	99.0	50.0	47.4	44.8
2. Trade union density (%)	52.1	41.7	34.4	27.9	22.6	20.0
3. Centralisation of wage bargaining index (0-1)*	0.917	0.895	0.777	0.385	0.392	0.409
4. Index of strike activity (working days lost per 1000 workers)	2.0	3.5	50.0	0.4	1.4	3.4

Source: Visser (2009) and own calculations based on Armingeon et al. (2007)
*With 1 indicating high centralisation and 0 indicating low centralisation.

Despite its already fairly liberal nature, the Swiss system of industrial relations was challenged in the 1990s by the abrupt change in economic conditions outlined above, marked by economic stagnation and the rise of unemployment to unprecedented levels (Mach 2006). In some sectors, like the machine industry, employment shrank by a third. Until then, the

Swiss labour market had remained virtually untouched by international crises due to the high level of flexibility in the labour supply provided by foreign workers (see above). During the 1980s, Switzerland was in a situation of full employment that could not be found elsewhere in Europe. Things changed radically in the 1990s, when unemployment could no longer be "exported" due to the stabilisation of the legal situation of foreign workers, who were now entitled to unemployment benefits (Afonso 2005). Changing labour market conditions but also international pressures on the Swiss economy created opportunities for substantial changes in the Swiss system of industrial relations and labour market governance in general.

First, there was a decentralisation "offensive" by employers, who asked for substantial issues of collective bargaining to be shifted from the sectoral to the company or plant level. Between 1991 and 1996, the number of CLAs concluded at the firm level increased by 11.5%, whereas the number of sectoral CLAs declined by 2.5%. Since the late 1990s, wage setting and working time regulation has been decentralised to the company level in important industries such as chemicals, clothing, banking, media printing and, to a lesser extent, watch-making (Mach & Oesch 2003: 166). This furthers weakens the position of labour, also because work councils only play a marginal role in the Swiss economy.

Second, besides changes in the level of bargaining, certain changes also took place in its material content. On the one hand, automatic compensation of inflation was removed from many major sectoral agreements at the beginning of the 1990s. On the other hand, a growing number of CLAs provided for individual rather than general wages increases. This, combined with higher unemployment among low-skilled workers, contributed not only to a significant amount of wage restraint in the 1990s but also to a rise in wage inequalities. General wage increases have almost systematically been below inflation, so that actual real incomes have even declined during the decade. This has been especially the case for low-skilled workers, since individual wage increases mainly benefit skilled workers. These evolutions have, however, followed different paths across sectors, depending on the amount of skill required and their exposure to international competition (Mach & Oesch 2003). On the trade union side, this changing environment has been met with new strategies, notably trade union mergers, an increase in industrial action or a more frequent resort to the political sphere (popular initiatives, referendums or legislative proposals) to compensate for losing ground in the sphere of collective bargaining (see for instance Trampusch 2008b; Widmer 2007).

With regard to the traditionally very important role of foreign labour, the old system of immigration quotas which theoretically allowed public authorities to control the supply of foreign workers and adjust it to economic conditions was progressively abandoned for EU workers and replaced by free movement as part of a series of bilateral agreements with the EU (Afonso 2007; Fischer et al. 2002). This opening up induced massive potential changes in the Swiss labour market due to persisting wage differentials between Switzerland and neighbouring countries. In order to prevent wage dumping, trade unions asked for a package of "flanking measures" involving the facilitated extension of collective bargaining, the possibility of introducing minimum wages and increased labour market control in the case of "observed abuse". This package was reluctantly accepted by employers' associations and right-wing parties. Hence, despite a decentralisation and deregulation trend that started at the beginning of the 1990s, there has also been some extension of coordination later on in some economic sectors in relation to these "flanking measures". For instance, the number of collective agreements that have been extended and made legally binding by the state has increased in recent years. In the face of increased competition from EU member states, notably through the posting of workers, the protection of existing standards through legally binding CLAs has been perceived by some employers, mainly in the construction sector, as a means to protect their market shares (Oesch 2007: 348).

There has also been evolution with regard to the other side of corporatism, namely social partner participation in policymaking. Corporatist policymaking seems to have been on the decline due to a number of factors: increased ideological polarisation also favoured by a more right-wing composition of parliament, retrenchment pressures on the welfare state, the mediatisation of politics, and the difficulties of traditional social partners to represent post-materialist values such as gender equality (Häusermann et al. 2004). It has been more difficult for social partners to reach compromises on issues of social and economic policy, so that after the failure of corporatist talks, the reform of pensions or unemployment benefits have been ultimately struck in parliament rather than in corporatist arenas. On the other hand, social partners have played a central role in very important recent policymaking processes for the Swiss economy, such as the opening up of the labour market to EU workers mentioned above (Afonso 2010). Contrary to Austria, the actual veto power given to interest groups by the institution of directed democracy has made it difficult to leave them aside, although patterns may vary across sectors and issues (see for instance Mach et al. 2003).

As a general picture, changes in the two countries in the sphere of industrial relations display diverging trends with regard to collective bargaining and participation in policy formulation. The already decentralised system of collective bargaining in Switzerland underwent a further decentralisation trend, whereas the highly coordinated Austrian system displayed relative continuity. On the other hand, whereas a right-wing coalition in Austria marginalised corporatist actors in policymaking, the veto power conferred to organised interests by direct democracy hampered this phenomenon in Switzerland, even if the capacity to strike corporatist deals has indeed been challenged.

Welfare state

Both Austria and Switzerland display the ideal-typical characteristics of Bismarckian welfare states, namely eligibility conditioned by labour market participation, earnings-related benefits, a system of funding based on contributions from wages rather than taxes, and devolved and decentralised policy management (Häusermann 2009; Obinger & Talos 2009). In both cases, its functioning tends to favour income compensation rather than redistribution as such, and the setting up of funding and benefits has been guided by the male breadwinner model. However, due to the differences in power configurations and institutional veto points outlined above, their welfare states have also displayed significant differences in their expansion and timing of development. On the one hand, because of the great number of veto points (mainly federalism and direct democracy), the Swiss welfare state has displayed an important delay vis-à-vis Austria with regard to the introduction of its core welfare programmes.[6] On the other hand, this institutional context has also slowed down retrenchment trends over the last two decades in Switzerland. By contrast, the welfare state in Austria has expanded more quickly, but has also recently undergone slightly more important changes because of the lighter institutional vetoes on policy change as well as the advent of a new right-wing ruling coalition in 2000.

Just like in Germany, the first social security measures (in particular social assistance, unemployment benefits, pensions) were introduced in Austria in order to pacify an insurgent working class in the second half of the nineteenth century, under the Habsburg monarchy and in the interwar period (Obinger & Talos 2006: 51ff.). During the *Trente Glorieuses*, the social security net underwent a considerable expansion under the influence of a progressive consensus between social democrats and conservatives, as well as a powerful labour movement: compulsory social protection included an ever greater proportion of workers, notably self-employed workers. The level of allowances also increased with the expansion of living standards. Between 1955 and 1985, social expenses increased from 15.9% to 27% of GDP. These measures not only included passive measures of protection but also active measures, such as active labour market policy, introduced in 1968 (Obinger & Talos 2006: 53). By international standards, Austria has displayed an above-average level of social spending over the twentieth century.

The trajectory of welfare state expansion in Switzerland has been significantly different. First, decentralised political structures and the power of business interests opposed to state intervention have fostered a fragmented, heterogeneous and layered system of social protection mixing private, public and semi-public service providers: private companies, trade unions, communes and cantons. Welfare state expansion has been a "pragmatic bricolage" of different existing social protection schemes rather than a real "government masterplan" (Häusermann 2009: 2; see also Leimgruber 2008). Until 1945, federal money was only spent in the form of subsidies to those different kinds of institutions in the domain of health, accident and unemployment. As argued above, the transfer of competences from cantons to the federal state was faced with the constraints set by federalism and direct democracy, so that the establishment of a nationwide system of welfare provision has been very difficult to achieve (Obinger 1998).[7]

Several measures of expansion have been refused by a majority of citizens in referendums over the twentieth century (see the example of health insurance in Immergut 1992). A major difference between Austria and Switzerland has also been the balance between public, semi-public and private carriers of social protection. This difference is especially observable in the domains of pensions and health: whereas about 80% of the Swiss workforce was covered by occupational pension plans in 2000, this proportion was only about 16% in Austria (Url 2003). The Swiss "three-pillar" system, which combines a system of pay-as-you-go public pensions, occupational pensions based on capitalisation, and optional individual savings accounts, has been praised as the way to follow for many countries (Leimgruber 2008). Health insurance in Switzerland is also exclusively carried out by private companies, and contribution levels are not based on incomes; low incomes received public subsidies. Accordingly, the Swiss welfare state is one of the least redistributive in the

OECD, inclusive of the liberal states (Iversen & Stephens 2008: 603; see also Häusermann 2009).

If the institutional framework has influenced the patterns of development of the welfare state, it has also conditioned patterns of continuity and change over the last two decades. Hence, the extent of changes can be considered more important in Austria than in Switzerland, even if the direction of changes has shown many similarities. As elsewhere, the ageing of societies, transformations in the structure of employment and financial difficulties have put welfare states under pressure for reform. Faced with rising public deficits and debts caused by problems in large parts of state-owned industries in the mid-1980s, the SPÖ/ÖVP coalition that came to power in 1987 implemented a programme of cost containment that resulted in several measures of welfare retrenchment (for instance in eligibility for early retirement) and increased contributions (Obinger & Talos 2009: 9).

In labour market policy, a combination of benefit cutbacks and increased control over the unemployed towards activation was put in place. Besides these retrenchment measures, however, a series of new benefits in care or health insurance were introduced, and the Austrian welfare state did not depart from its central characteristics during this period. The real breakthrough may have come in 2000 with the accession to power of the right-wing ÖVP/FPÖ coalition, that carried out a series of reforms along a neoliberal agenda – that is, a paradigm shift with regard to Austrian "social corporatism". A series of cutbacks in unemployment benefits (lower replacement rate, the end of indexation of benefits to inflation and wages) was carried out. A contested reform of pensions providing for the abolition of early retirement schemes and an increased length of contribution was met by the largest strike movement in Austrian history.

Interestingly, in the long run, the aim was to depart from a pay-as-you-go system and move more towards a three-pillar system as found in Switzerland. These reforms were met with considerable protest from trade unions in 2003, especially because the new coalition tried to implement the reforms by bypassing the traditional role of social partners in social policies (Obinger & Talos 2006). In sum, a series of retrenchment measures did take place in Austria, which is reflected to some extent in the evolution of social expenditures that slightly decreased between 1995 and 2003 (see Table 4.5).

	Austria			Switzerland		
	1985	1995	2003	1985	1995	2003
Total public social expenditures	23.9	26.6	26.1	14.8	17.5	20.5
Pensions	11.0	12.3	12.8	5.8	6.5	6.8
Health	4.9	5.9	5.1	3.9	4.7	6.0
Family policy	2.9	3.1	3.1	1.0	1.2	1.5
Disability benefits	2.8	2.8	2.6	2.2	2.5	3.3
Unemployment: passive measures	0.9	1.3	1.0	0.3	1.1	1.0
Unemployment: active measures	0.3	0.4	0.6	0.2	0.5	0.7

Source: Armingeon et al. (2007)

Even though it was faced with fairly similar challenges, the Swiss welfare state did not undergo such radical changes as early as in Austria, at least in terms of retrenchment. On the economic side, Switzerland was not faced with major disturbances on the labour market until the beginning of the 1990s, so that major pressures for welfare state reform came later than in most other countries. Besides this, because of its late institutionalisation, the costs of welfare were still at a low level by international standards when the Swiss economy was hit by economic unrest in the 1990s (Häusermann 2009). On the political side, even though a number of reforms have been implemented, rapid retrenchment measures have been slowed down by the many veto points of the political system (especially the optional referendum, which allows opponents to call for a popular vote on any reform adopted by parliament), and change has tended to be of an incremental nature. Interestingly, while the referendum was used by conservative political forces to oppose welfare state expansion up to the 1980s, it has since been used by social democrats and trade unions to oppose its cutback in the 1990s and 2000s. Direct democracy implies a strong political bias towards the status quo.

In general, reform dynamics have been guided by *retrenchment and financial consolidation* on the one hand, and *recalibration* to take into account new social needs and demands on the other (Häusermann 2009). In many reforms, given the veto institutional constraints outlined above, recalibration (valued by the left and progressive strands within the right) has been used as a *quid pro quo* for retrenchment (championed by the conservative right) (Bonoli 1999; Häusermann et al. 2004). However, patterns of change have varied across areas of social protection. In *pen-*

sions, an important reform was achieved in the mid-1990s that provided for an increase in the age of retirement for women but also introduced a "splitting system" whereby the contributions of both spouses would be added, divided by two and counted separately, as well as pension credits for mothers. Both measures improved the benefits of women, especially non-working women.

The last attempt at reform, which included unilateral retrenchment measures, such as cutbacks for widows or a further rise in the retirement age for women, was rejected in a popular referendum in 2003. In *unemployment insurance*, a series of urgent measures were carried out by decree in the 1990s to cope with the important increase in unemployment: the maximum period of entitlement was increased to two years, but the replacement rate was lowered from 80% to 70%. Another important reform introduced a set of activation measures whereby resources devoted to active labour market policies were multiplied by 6; at the same time, increased control and possible sanctions were introduced for the unemployed not "actively seeking work" (Bertozzi et al. 2005). In 2002, citizens accepted another reform measure providing for a toughening of conditions of entitlement and a shortening of the maximum period of allowances (Afonso 2010). In general, it has proven easier to carry out retrenchment in domains that concern a fringe of the population – like unemployment or disability policy – than in pensions, where cuts potentially affect everyone. Partly because existing schemes were so weakly developed in comparison with other countries, expansion measures have been achieved in *family policy*, with the introduction of a maternity insurance in 2005, and a harmonisation of family allowances in 2006. Confronted with important cost increases, the domain of *health insurance* has been a constant issue of debates over the last decade, and has remained in a deadlock so far. Both attempts to increase the role of the state and restrict reimbursements have been rejected so far.

Generally speaking, the constraining institutional framework in Switzerland has fostered more incremental reforms than in Austria, especially when the latter was governed by a right-wing coalition from 2000 to 2006. It must be kept in mind, however, that Swiss welfare programmes have remained at a lower level in terms of the array of social risks covered by law. In some ways, the wider heterogeneity of welfare provision (private/public mix) has also fostered a more flexible evolution because of the wider array of tools available, and an already greater importance of market-based schemes of social provision. As argued above, the Swiss "three-pillar" pension system (combining public, occupational and private schemes) has been considered – at least until the 2008 financial crisis – more ready for population ageing than strictly public schemes like the Austrian one (Leimgruber 2008). However, the great fragmentation of welfare provision, for instance in the domain of health, has led to lower costs in Austria than in Switzerland, where both the overall cost of the health system and the individual cost burden for patients is among the highest in the OECD.

Conclusion

Patterns of change and continuity in the Austrian and Swiss varieties of capitalism display an overall trend towards a more market-driven orientation, but prevailing institutional and coalitional determinants have strongly influenced the extent and direction of change across the different spheres of economic governance (industrial relations, corporate governance, welfare state). The trajectory and scope of change, as summarised in Table 4.6, vary both between the countries and between the spheres, depending on the interaction between power configurations and the institutional regimes governing the different spheres. With its weak trade unions, strong business and lean welfare state, the Swiss political economy seemed generally more readily adaptable to the constraints of a new international environment focusing on markets as the dominant mode of regulation. However, if change has been fairly swift in domains where private employer governance was the dominant mode of regulation – such as corporate governance and industrial relations – pressures for change have been faced with powerful institutional barriers (most notably direct democracy) in domains where institutional change required political intervention. In Austria, by way of contrast, the extensive role of the state in the political economy has made political intervention more important in triggering economic change, whereas the nature of the power configuration within private organised interests was not particularly favourable to enhanced market solutions. In Switzerland, substantial change still essentially takes place through private employer coordination, whereas in Austria change is mainly triggered by public intervention, as shown by the scope of welfare state reforms carried out by the conservative coalition that came to power in 2000 (Obinger & Talos 2006).

Table 4.6   Summary of continuity and change

	Austria	*Switzerland*
Political framework and power relationships	Centralised federalism; employers dominated by SMEs, strong labour; policy capacity dependent on coalitions.	Decentralised federalism; strong export-oriented business, weak labour; policy capacity constrained by various institutional veto points.
Corporate governance and economic regulation	Important changes in corporate control through privatisation and liberalisation, especially since EU-adhesion; promotion of competition.	Important changes in corporate control, market-driven reforms of corporate governance; new public regulations to promote competition.
Industrial relations and labour market	Continuity in collective bargaining despite organised decentralisation; marginalisation trend of social partners in policymaking.	Decentralisation trend; no marginalisation due to veto power conferred by direct democracy, but declining capacity to strike deals.
Welfare state	Acceleration of retrenchment reforms under black-blue coalition.	Retrenchment hindered in some domains by direct democracy; recalibration.

In the framework adopted here, longstanding institutional arrangements and power configurations continue to determine continuity and change both at the macro- and sectoral level. The constant defiance of Swiss dominant economic interests towards state intervention has favoured a relatively high level of private flexibility in the face of changing economic conditions. On the other hand, to the extent that public decisions are needed, Austria has probably displayed a higher reform capacity, for better or for worse. In this respect, longstanding distributions of power to public and private actors continue to determine patterns of continuity and change in their varieties of capitalism.

Notes

1   For useful comments on the chapter, we are very thankful to Uwe Becker, Pepper Culpepper, Silja Häusermann, Hanspeter Kriesi, Daniel Oesch, Yannis Papadopoulos, Raphael Ramuz and Christine Trampusch. Alexandre Afonso acknowledges the financial support of the NCCR Democracy and the Swiss National Fund for Scientific Research, as well as the Amsterdam Institute for Advanced Labour Studies of the University of Amsterdam.

2   The largest companies introduced a "single share", which reduces the possibility to control the composition of the shareholders. In 1989, only 13.1% of the companies listed at the Stock Exchange had a "single share"; in 2001, this proportion reached 70.7% (out of 198 companies). This does not mean, however, the end of family ownership and the victory of minority shareholders. There are still other measures, which allow Swiss corporations to channel the evolution of their shareholding structure: they may fix ceilings for voting rights at shareholders' meetings or introduce a percentage limit for each individual shareholding.

3   The Swiss Confederation remains, however, the majority owner in Swisscom (the biggest phone and internet provider) and in Swiss Post.

4   In Siaroff's (1999) indicator of corporatism termed "integration" understood as "a long-term co-operative pattern of shared economic management involving the social partners and existing at various levels such as plant-level management, sectoral wage bargaining, and joint shaping of national policies in competitiveness-related matters (education, social policy, etc.)", Austria ranked first with 4.625 out of 5, whereas Switzerland ranked seventh with 4.375 in the mid 1990s.

5   However, an agreement on an intersectoral minimum wage has been reached by Austrian social partners in 2007 (EIRO 2007).

6   For example: accident insurance (1888 in Austria vs. 1918 in Switzerland), mandatory unemployment insurance (1920 vs. 1982), old age pensions (1927 vs. 1948), mandatory health insurance (1955 vs. 1994) or maternity insurance (1955 vs. 2005) (Obinger and Talos 2008, 51ff; Leimgruber 2008, 5).

7   The time gap between the adoption of a constitutional principle and its coming into effect into a law has been extremely large: 106 years for health insurance (1890 vs. 1996), 60 years for maternity insurance (1945 vs. 2005) and 23 years for state pensions (1925 vs. 1948) (Häusermann 2009).

5 Liberal Convergence, Growing Outcome Divergence?

Institutional Continuity and Changing Trajectories in the 'Low Countries'

Hester Houwing and Kurt Vandaele

Introduction: historical similarities and differences

Belgium and the Netherlands, with respectively 10 and 16 million inhabitants, have several similarities in the cultural, political and economic spheres. Belgian and Dutch societies have often been described as 'consociational democracies' because of the existence of competing 'pillars' (groups) organised along ideological, notably religious, lines but with overarching institutions for facilitating negotiation and compromise by elites. Since the 1960s the consociational formula has been eroded by the continuing process of 'depillarisation', which in itself was caused by changing social values such as rising secularism. Nevertheless, the present opportunity structure for influence is still based on a proportional electoral system and party coalitions and hence, changes in socio-economic policy take place incrementally rather than in sharp swings.

Both countries are also small in an economic sense: given their narrow domestic market, they are economically dependent upon access to world markets but unable to influence world market prices. Due to this, economic vulnerability is a widespread assumption among the political-economic elite and much attention is paid to the competitiveness of companies. While regional economic integration is promoted to pro-actively avoid the need for economic adjustment, corporatist arrangements are adopted reactively for facilitating rapid adjustment with a minimum of social conflict (Jones 2008). Both countries have been promoting social partnership by setting up corporatist institutions at different levels of the economy. Representatives of both sides of industry – i.e. employers' associations and trade unions – have also been involved in the administration and management of the welfare system, the design and development of which is strongly shaped by Christian democratic and social democratic views on social policy.

Given a political system historically based on consensus, a regulated market regime and a Bismarckian continental welfare system, it comes as no surprise that both Belgium and the Netherlands have been identified as corporatist sub-varieties of coordinated market economies (Bruff 2008) or as straight cases approximating the corporatist capitalism type (see Becker in this volume). Apart from the similarities, there has been also a burgeoning body of literature in recent years pointing to profound historical differences in the economic structure, state tradition and labour-capital relations of both countries and stressing the path-dependent trajectories of the Belgian and Dutch corporatist institutional complex (Arnoldus 2007; Vercauteren 2007). Moreover, new comparative studies give evidence to different policy dynamics causing dissimilar socio-economic outcomes that have become particularly apparent since the 1990s (Hemerijck & Marx 2010; Kuipers 2006; Van Gyes et al. 2009).

Another striking finding from recent international studies (often not including the Belgian case) is that the Netherlands is often grouped within the cluster of Scandinavian countries with regards to labour market regulation (EC 2007), possibly shifting away from its southern neighbour. Taking those recent studies into account and based on our reading of secondary literature, we find indications that, while the institutional corporatist configuration remains largely intact, Belgium and the Netherlands are moving in the same broad direction today, i.e. leaving non-liberal capitalism, but at the same time their socio-economic outcomes seem to show more dissimilarities in comparison with previous decades.

This chapter is divided into six sections. Section 2 describes the institutional framework and the organisational structure of the main interest associations in the socio-economic sphere, highlighting the growing regional differences in Belgium. In subsequent sections we delve further into the dynamics of industrial relations since the late 1990s. Section 3 focuses on corporate governance practices, section 4 analyses the degree of wage coordination and deals with the main developments in labour market regulation. Section 5 looks at the welfare and tax regimes, and section 6 concludes this chapter.

Industrial relations: changing yet continued social partnership

The Netherlands has traditionally been a traders' country which in the 17th century was the centre of the commercial world. It industrialised in the 19th century, but it never developed a strong industry-based economy.

Belgium has even older roots in trade, but for its current outfit it is more important that it is the oldest industrial site on the European continent. Until the 1960s, it had a strong position in the production of coal, steel and related industrial products. Since its inception, uneven regional economic development was a significant feature of its economic space. It became particularly apparent in the 1960s when the coal and steel industries in French-speaking Wallonia declined while Dutch-speaking Flanders diversified and extended its industrial structure through foreign investment from notably the automotive and petrochemical branches. Since then, the divide between the two parts of the country has deepened. In 1994 it became pronounced by the establishment of a federal structure separating Flanders, Wallonia and Brussels, the bilingual capital. Today, Flemish and Wallonian varieties exist for nearly all the nationwide operating organisations – e.g. parties, unions and employer associations.

As in many other countries, the past forty years have been marked by deindustrialisation and an increased openness to international trade. Figure 5.1 illustrates these developments and shows that deindustrialisation

Figure 5.1 Deindustrialisation and trade in the Low Countries, 1970-2008/9

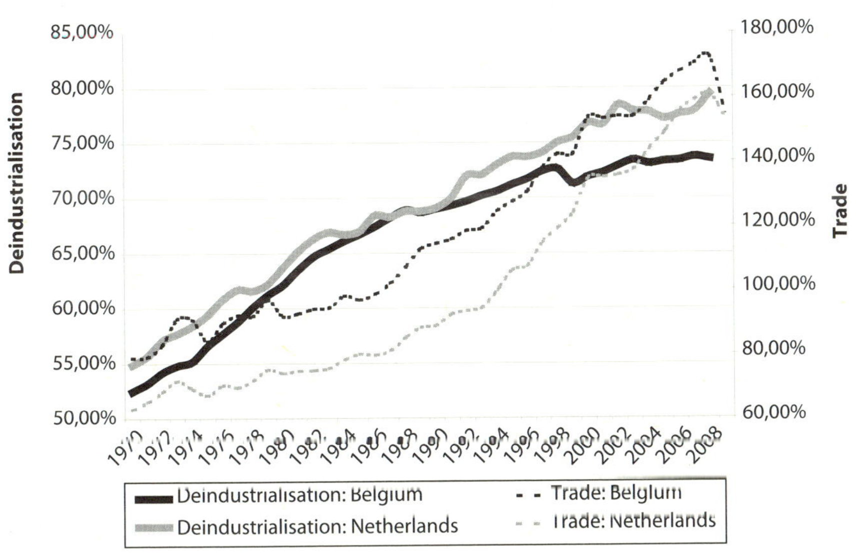

Source: stats.OECD.org

Note: Deindustrialisation: 100 minus the sum of civilian employment in agriculture and industry as a percentage of the working age population. Trade: trade-to-GDP ratio at constant prices and constant exchange rates (base year is 2000).

flattened somewhat after the mid-1980s, particularly in Belgium, while trade accelerated after the mid-1990s. The service sector did not compensate for the job losses in industry. As a result, structural unemployment rose, particularly in Belgium which was hit from time to time by sudden massive layoffs in the automobile industry (Renault, Opel and VW closed factories). However, industry still accounts for a significant part of Belgian exports (CRB 2008: 192-5) while the Dutch economy is mainly based on transportation and logistics, international finance, business services and agro-industry.

Both Belgium and the Netherlands have an industrial relations system with a strong role for the so-called 'social partners' in various corporatist institutions at the national, regional, sectoral and company level. The central Association of Belgian Employers (VBO/FEB) represents private sector companies, notably the medium-sized and larger ones, both nationally and across sectors. Its organisation rate is traditionally high and complements the relatively high union density rate. Small companies have (Flemish and Wallonian) associations of their own. The regionalisation is pronounced by the existence of purely regional associations that gain influence and increasingly act as a strong competitor to the national but fragmented VBO/FEB.

The merged Dutch Business Association/Dutch Christian Entrepreneurs (VNO-NCW) is the main employers' organisation in the Netherlands. Worth mentioning is also the association of SMEs known as MKB (the literal translation of SME). The overall organisation rate of the employers is about 85%. The main players on the union side are the socialist Federation of Dutch Unions (FNV), the Dutch Christian Unions (CNV) and the smaller union for medium- and higher-skilled employees (De Unie/MHP). Collective bargaining coverage is about 80%. Dutch union density dropped to 22% in 2006, while it rose to about 55% in Belgium (cf. introduction, Table 1.2) where the coverage rate is about 90% (Bocksteins 2006: 77-80).

In Belgium there are Catholic (ACV/CSC) and socialist (ABVV/FGTB) union federations that, following the general pattern, are regionally divided. The former is the largest and particularly strong in Flanders. While the Netherlands has a rather weak system of workers' representation through works councils, in Belgium only union members can be a member of these councils. Union involvement in social security management, the so-called 'Ghent system', further explains Belgium's relatively high union density.

The main corporatist institutions in the Netherlands are the bipartite Labour Foundation and the tripartite Social and Economic Council. Both institutions give advice to the government on socio-economic policymaking and legislation. These institutions and the 1982 Wassenaar Agreement, whereby social partners agreed on wage moderation in exchange for the reduction of working hours, reflect the Dutch tradition of consensualism, often denoted by the term 'polder model'. Trying to radiate a similar formula, the Flemish political-economic elite promoted the 'belfry model' at the end of the 1990s in a reference to the consensual character of industrial relations at the Flemish level (Arnoldus et al. 2004: 77).[1] But its use has hardly been taken up in the discourse. One of the reasons has probably been that in Belgium, industrial relations tend to be more adversarial than in the Netherlands (Table 5.1).

Table 5.1   **Days not worked due to strikes per 1000 employees in the Low Countries (six-year averages), 1990-2007**

	1990-95	*1996-01*	*2002-07*
Belgium*	132**	71	63
Netherlands	33	5	9

Source: *Days not worked*: for Belgium, Vandaele (2007) and Brochure (RSZ/ONEM); for the Netherlands, CBS. *Employees in employment*: stats.OECD.org.
*Strikes in the public sector are not included.
**Year 1990 is missing.

In contrast to the Netherlands, economic and social matters in Belgium were for a long time institutionally separated, because unions were worried that macroeconomic criteria would condition social demands. The 1996 law on the Promotion of Employment and the Preventive Safeguarding of Competitiveness marked a turning point, since it institutionalised wage moderation and calculated social benefits and employment conditions on the basis of macroeconomic criteria. The corporatist institution for negotiations between capital labour and the state is the Central Economic Council (*Centrale Raad voor het Bedrijfsleven/Conseil Central de l'Économie*, CRB/CCE).

Corporate governance: shareholder influence becomes strengthened

The large share of foreign companies in Belgium is not much lower than that in the Netherlands, but foreign companies determine the economic picture much more in Belgium because of the near absence of 'national champions'. The Belgian holding-type ownership pattern explains this. Despite Belgian businesses performing well financially, firms seem to have insufficient strategic dynamics to develop into multinationals. Management strategies tend to focus on profit rather than on growth through diversification and expansion (Daems 1998). Since the late 1980s, when multinationals increasingly pursued international expansion through acquisitions and takeovers, a considerable number of Belgian industrial companies owned by holdings were sold to foreign investors, purely because it was profitable. This weakened the Belgian business networks and gave rise to the 'anchoring debate' on the best strategy to maintain economic decision-making power in Belgium (Oosterlynck 2006).

Leaving apart foreign-owned companies, only a small but shrinking number of families still controls the largest Belgian companies, with business networks reproduced by elite clubs, elite management schools and 'inside' marriages (Puype 2004). As a result, the shareholders of family-based but listed companies lost their majority voting blocs to institutional investors and international competitors such as Anglo-Saxon investment funds. This decline came to a halt in 2007, however, when a new takeover law was implemented establishing a threshold of 30% to launch a mandatory takeover offer. In this new context, family shareholders quickly increased their share to a level just exceeding the threshold in order to keep de facto control over 'their' companies.

The financial crisis of 2008 caused a further weakening of Belgium's industrial-financial structure. Fortis, the largest Belgian bank, was split into a Dutch, nationalised part and a larger Belgian part that was sold to the French BNP Paribas. Other banks and insurance companies (Dexia, Ethias and KBC Bank) that were trading so-called 'toxic derivatives' also applied for regional and federal government bailouts.

In the Netherlands, the Ministry of Economic Affairs implemented a series of measures in the early 1990s aimed at privatising, liberalising and deregulating certain segments of the economy. Given the large Dutch banking sector and the huge pension funds, these developments led to the doubling of market capitalisation. Indeed, as a ratio of GDP, the market capitalisation of the Netherlands in the 2000s ranked among the highest in the OECD countries (see Table 1.5b in the introduction to this volume and Engelen et al. 2008: 17). This implied a shift of corporate governance to (institutional) shareholders (Delsen 2002: 20). FDI flows in and out of the Netherlands also more than doubled during this period. Additionally, large Dutch banks strove to increase their role in global financial markets and to make Amsterdam a financial hub via takeovers and mergers. The financial-economic crisis since the fall of 2008, which hit large Dutch banks very hard, has put these aims into question, however.

The corporate governance code in both countries is based on the flexible 'comply or explain' rule: the code has the character of a recommendation but companies have to explain when they fail to comply to any of the code's principles. In Belgium, the debate on corporate governance was already begun in the mid-1990s, but it was only in 2004, after the financial scandals in the US and Europe (with Enron as the best known example; speech-recognition technology company Lernout & Hauspie was a Belgian case), that the government installed a Corporate Governance Committee for preparing a comprehensive code. The Committee advocated acknowledging the 'Belgian context' – i.e. the typical owner structure with holdings and preferential shareholders. This code pays particular attention to an appropriate disclosure of a company's corporate governance framework, including the board's composition. This was in line with the 2003 European Commission's Action Plan on Modernising Company Law and Enhancing Corporate Governance in the European Union and intended as a framework for all Belgian listed companies. Furthermore, in 2005 another less detailed code was put into practice which set recommendations for non-listed companies.

Most of the listed companies have a corporate governance charter including the required information in their annual report. But information identifying the most important shareholders and the shareholder structure is notably missing (Van der Elst 2008: 29). Since only listed companies are expected to adhere to the code, its application is rather limited and most of the listed companies complying to the code do not meet all of its requirements (ibid.: 12, 30). The centrality of the principle of self-regulation allows for this (Corporate Governance Committee 2009). Nonetheless, with the code Belgium has developed in the direction of the Anglo-Saxon model, and its corporate governance rating (by rating agencies such as Moody's and Standard & Poors) has improved. At 47%, however, it is still below the European average (56%) and significantly lower than the Dutch rating (71%; Heidrick & Struggles 2009). The higher the rating, the better shareholder rights are served.

In the Netherlands, a commission was installed in December 2004 to further the usefulness and to secure the observance of the Dutch corporate governance code. The commission drafted a code in accordance with existing legislation governing firm-firm and intra-firm relations of listed companies (Corporate Governance Committee 2003). The code positions the rights of 'financial stakeholders' – i.e. shareholders and banks (in their roles other than shareholders) – at the centre, does not set aside a role for labour (co-determination) in corporate governance, and is based on the principle of self-regulation (Poutsma & Braam 2005: 171f), which makes it liberal. One non-liberal regulatory element is that in the case of hostile takeovers, the influence of shareholders is curbed. This is done by: a) the issuing of special priority shares and preference shares, and b) the use of a two-tier board system with a supervisory board and a management board ensuring the separation between shareholders and management decision-making (ibid: 157).

The legitimacy of priority and preference shares is increasingly disputed (e.g. by the European Commission), as was highlighted in 2007 when a private equity firm tried to take over Dutch toolmaker Stork but was blocked by the preference shares controlled by the supervisory board. A court forbade Stork to issue preference shares because this would prevent an agreement between corporate management and the shareholders. Also, the raison d'être of the two-tier regime has increasingly been disputed: a new law expected to become effective in 2010 or 2011 will permit a one-tier board system in large companies. Such a system would integrate direction and supervision, in line with the Anglo-Saxon practice and would strengthen the liberal component. The absence of legislation to hamper activist investors such as private equity funds is another illustration of this. And until mid-2010, the government parties did not intend to enact such legislation (Engelen et al. 2008: 12).

Corporatism and competitiveness: centralised wage coordination versus indirect decentralisation

Since the end of the 1970s, Dutch corporatism has been relatively stable. This can be explained by the commitment of employers, the institutionalised routine of dialogue, and the broad acceptance of wage restraint as key to enhancing competitiveness (Hendriks 2005). The unions' legitimacy is sometimes questioned because of their low organisation level, but peak-level negotiation on wage guidelines with union federations still provides valuable outcomes for employers, particularly in terms of social peace. The unions also strengthened their position when they mobilised a large number of people in 2004 to demonstrate against policy proposals to abolish the early retirement scheme (Mujagic & Zweers 2004) – a scheme employers used to replace older and expensive employees with younger and cheaper ones.

The Dutch social dialogue is facilitated by dense, small and often personal networks enabling trust (Hendriks 2005: 55). The Social and Economic Council and the Labour Foundation also play an important role in these networks. However, the policy of wage moderation did not occur solely in a context of trust and deliberated consensus. It was also a matter of ideological dominance of the wage restraint formula since the 1950s, facilitated by the eminent role of the Central Planning Bureau (an advisory agency of the government) in Dutch economic policy. And it was due to the position of the unions which deteriorated when membership since the 1970s decreased and power relations turned to the advantage of capital that, in the context of accelerating globalisation, became increasingly mobile. Against this background, more than moderate wage demands quickly became stigmatised as 'irresponsible' (Becker & Hendriks 2008).

In the 1980s and 1990s, the role of the central corporatist institutions gradually changed. The legal obligation of the government to seek the advice of the Social and Economic Council in economic and social policy matters was formally abolished in 1994, though in practice the advisory role of the social partners did not disappear. A more important change therefore was the decentralisation (and 'flexibilisation') process of wage bargaining that had already started in the late 1970s and that became embodied in the 1993 document "A New Course" by the Labour Foundation (Visser & Van der Meer 1998). This process was, however, accompanied by a turn to indirect centralisation: the 'wage space' became a topic of an annual government-induced discussion that results in non-binding but strongly recommended guidelines of the Social and Economic Council and the Labour Foundation for wage bargaining at the branch- and sometimes company-level. For example, during the 2002-2004 economic downturn, the guideline was a 'zero line', while in November 2008 the emphasis was on the need to stabilise wages to retain a reasonable level of consumer spending.

The government recognises collective agreements by using the instrument of general extension – i.e. the Ministry of Social Affairs and Employment declares an agreement is binding for an entire sector, whether or not firms are members of the sector's employers' association. This extension procedure was the subject of a heated debate in 2004, when the government urged the social partners to agree on a wage freeze to combat unemployment in a period of economic downturn. When they could not reach an agreement, the government threatened to no longer extend collective agreements containing wage increases. Although the government eventually withdrew this threat, it was an obvious attempt to regain some of its power in the collective bargaining process. In the literature, this type of state involvement is sometimes referred to as 'shadow of the state' (introduced by Scharpf 1993).

Belgium differs from the Netherlands in the way it has maintained centralised wage setting in the entire period under consideration (see the overview in Table 5.2). Remarkable is the salient role the state plays in this process, which since 1996 has shifted back and forth between government-sponsored and government-imposed solutions. Because of regional divisions, capital-labour negotiations have failed to realise agreements at the national level in these years. Based on a comparison of the wage costs per hour worked in three reference states (France, Germany and the Netherlands), a small expert group in the Central Economic Council is responsible for proposing an ex ante wage norm for the two-year duration of the next inter-sectoral agreement. If the social partners reach no agreement about the precise norm, the federal government proposes a compromise or corrects for this coordination deficit by unilaterally setting the wage norm. In this process, the Federal Planning Bureau (FPB/BFB) has an advisory task. From 1998 onwards, the wage norm has been interpreted as indicative instead of imperative but, all in all, by stipulating the biennial bargaining length, the competitiveness law contributed to a stronger hierarchical sequence at the lower collective bargaining levels. At these lower

Table 5.2   Wage setting in the Low Countries since the mid-1990s

	Belgium	*Netherlands*
Involved institutions	Central Economic Council proposes wage norm; advisory role for the Federal Planning Bureau; sectoral associations of capital and labour as bargaining agents	Labour Foundation and Social and Economic Council propose wage guidelines; strong advisory role for the Central Planning Bureau; bargaining agents are sectoral unions and employers' associations
Role of the state	Initiates discussion on wage norms and, if required, sets norms as framework for sectoral bargaining	Initiates discussion on guidelines; sporadic intervention threats ('shadow of the state')
Contextual target	International competitiveness (France, Germany and the Netherlands as reference states)	International competitiveness
Periodicity	Every two years	Twice a year (spring and fall)
Overall characterisation	Centralised	Indirectly centralised

levels, sectors and even companies have a bigger say in issues other than wages or employment terms such as lower pay and employment standards (Bocksteins 2006: 81-84; Van Ruysseveldt 2000: 208-212)

Business did not try to dismantle the centralised bargaining system in Belgium, not even in times when, as was the case recently, it effectively ceased to work. Business no longer passively complies with union demands as in the 1960s and makes use of the judicial system in case of strikes with increasing frequency (Vandaele 2007: 198-199). The overarching business association VBO/FEB conducts a pro-active media strategy by putting de-regulation, flexibility and wage moderation on the agenda of public discussion. But corporatist collective bargaining has a long tradition and the social partners frequently meet formally and informally in various forums in the socio-economic policy field (Luyten 2006: 392). Moreover, a good understanding between capital and labour has always been appreciated by employers. The initiative to weaken corporatism and enhance statism came from the government, particularly the so-called 'purple-green' co-alition (1999-2003) consisting of the liberal, socialist and green political parties. This coalition emphasised the 'primacy of politics' – though it did not intend to abolish corporatism. This would have caused upheaval and would not have been smart because without corporatist negotiations a politics of blame avoidance in socio-economic affairs would no longer have been an option for the government.

Towards more flexible labour markets

With an overall employment rate of just above 60% in 2007, the Belgian rate is significantly behind the Dutch rate and among the lowest in the OECD countries (see Table 7.2 in the final chapter). In Flanders, the rate is about 66%, while in Wallonia with its old industrial base it is 10 percentage points lower. As a consequence, unemployment is twice as high there. A specific problem is youth unemployment, though this is even higher in the Brussels region (Van Rie 2008: 7; this author presents much data on Belgium – Flanders, Wallonia, Brussels – and the Netherlands). At 74% in 2007, the Dutch employment rate is similar to the Scandinavian level. Looking at full-time equivalents (FTEs), however, the gap between Belgium and the Netherlands disappears. This can be explained by the much higher rate of part-time employment in the Netherlands, particularly among women (60% in the Netherlands versus 33% in Belgium in 2007) and juveniles 15-24 years of age (65% in the Netherlands versus 27%

in Belgium). Those in the latter group – largely consisting of pupils and students earning some additional income – often have jobs of only a few hours a week and for a limited time. The percentage of temporary jobs, although increasing in both countries, is also almost twice as high in the Netherlands than in Belgium (cf. Van Rie 2008 and Table 7.3 in the final chapter).

These differences need to be put into their specific institutional contexts. In the Netherlands, part-time and temporary work started to grow in the early 1980s, while in Belgium this development only became worth mentioning from around the mid-1990s. This was the time of the deregulation of work agencies, of the liberalisation of fixed-term contracts in 1994 as well as of the effective promotion of a career break scheme since 1996 (Vander Steene et al. 2002a). This scheme, already existing somewhat unnoticed since 1985, provided employees with the possibility to leave their jobs temporarily – full-time or on a part-time basis and for a number of reasons: parental, medical, educative – while maintaining some income out of the unemployment benefits fund. The conditions attached to this were that the employees had to have occupied their jobs for at least six months prior to applying for the career break scheme and that they could temporarily be replaced by unemployed people. Only in the latter case would the measure have an employment effect.

The late 1990s generally were a period of socio-economic change and change in the ideologies accompanying it. In 1999, the government adjusted its policy discourse and put socio-economic policy measures in the context of the 'active welfare state', i.e. a political economy based on the active individual responsibility of labour market participants, but also providing for adequate social protection. Employment growth was emphasised as the key issue of welfare state reform. At the same time it was acknowledged that workers would need a tool to adapt working time to their needs, in particular to be able to reconcile work, family and private life.

The social partners went along with the new discourse by introducing the so-called 'time credit scheme' in the inter-sectoral agreement of 2000. In this scheme, which had to improve on the older career break scheme and which was enacted into law in early 2002, taking leave was no longer dependent on the employer's permission but became a right for (almost) every worker. It brought about flexicurity 'made in Belgium' – labour market flexibility at a relatively low employment rate. Contrary to most existing leave schemes, one does not need a specific reason to take up time credit. Minimal standards of the system – such as the payment of €400 when uninterrupted work experience was less than five years and €500 when it was more – are stipulated by federal law. Specific modalities are filled in by collective labour agreements negotiated at the sectoral level or sometimes the firm level. In addition to possible intersectoral variations with respect to the maximum duration of the time credit (one year), various policy levels promote the time credit system in specific cases (e.g. called 'care credit' or 'study credit') through supplemental benefits in addition to the benefit paid out by the unemployment insurance.

The time credit scheme has become the most important leave scheme within the Belgian welfare regime (Debacker et al. 2004). Repeatedly, it was criticised by the employers' organisations which argued that it results in a loss of productivity and which accused certain workers on the scheme of misusing the system. As a concession to the employers' demands, the possibilities to modulate working time over an employee's life course have been restricted. Because time credits first had to be earned for employers, the scheme should primarily be seen as an incentive for employees to work longer in order to stimulate the employment rate (Vanderweyden 2002). Or the scheme should be understood, as in the view of notably larger service firms, as a temporary measure in times of economic difficulty – a measure that has, for example, been used to prevent dismissals in the economic downturn since 2008. On balance, the time credit scheme indicates a shift from the redistribution of labour within the full employment framework to the improvement of the work-life balance in addition to an employment enhancing tool and the flexibilisation of the labour market.

The Netherlands does not have a comparable leave scheme. But its developmental trend in the years under consideration resembles the Belgian one. In accordance with the general Western trend, Dutch employers asked for more labour market flexibility in the early 1990s to better align the supply and demand for labour and to remain competitive in the global market. Furthermore, the labour market participation of women, which had strongly risen since the early 1980s, led to a demand to combine working time with time to care for the family. While these new employees requested flexibility in the form of flexible hours, employers mostly requested flexibility by means of temporary contracts and a decrease in dismissal protection.

Dismissal protection has for decades been an issue in the Dutch debate on labour market flexibility. The score of the Dutch employment protection legislation (EPL) was 2.1 in 2003 (down from 2.7 in 1990 on a scale of 0 to 5, with higher scores indicating stricter regulation), which is close to the European average and also to the Belgium level of 2.2 (down from 3.2; see Table 1.5a in the introduction of this volume) and is still considered rigid by employers and liberal critics. For regular employment ,the score is even somewhat higher, while it is lower for temporary jobs – a difference that doesn't exist in Belgium.

When they want to fire regular employees, Dutch employers need a permit from the semi-governmental employment centre (the name of which recently changed from the Centre for Work and Income, or CWI, to Administrative Authority for Employee Insurances, or UWV Werkbedrijf). In 85-90% of all cases, the permit is given, whereas special clauses for older workers and in case of sickness may create considerable delay. Since the 1990s, the permit system has been increasingly criticised and circumvented by means of a route via the lower district courts, which established the practice of dissolving contracts quicker by imposing a severance payment on employers. While in 1986 the ratio of permits filed compared with court settlements was 14 to 1 (Wilthagen 1998: 9), both 'routes' are currently used to a more or less equal extent (WRR 2007a: 125). However, during recessions the permit route is more popular as it is cheaper and most requests are honoured due to economic necessity.

Attempts to abolish the permit system have been undertaken since 1993, when the Minister of Social Affairs and Employment announced he would do so. However, responding to union pressure, his successor withdrew the proposal and instead wrote a memorandum in 1995 titled Flexibility and Security, calling for a new balance between flexible and regular employment and asking the social partners to find a compromise. They responded by negotiating an agreement in 1996 that became the basis for the Flexibility and Security Law, implemented in 1999. The 1996 Agreement was a package deal. The unions wanted to preserve the system of preventive checks on dismissals of regular contracts by the governmental employment centre. The employers accepted this in exchange for greater flexibility in fixed-term contracts. Also, dismissal procedures were simplified and somewhat shortened (mainly for older workers). The modification of dismissal procedures and the flexibilisation of temporary employment entailed a loosening of employment protection legislation. At the same time, social security increased for people on small, flexible, on-call contracts, mainly consisting of temporary agency workers. Here, a Dutch variety of flexicurity emerged. Worth mentioning is moreover that the Flexibility and Security Law contains many provisions that are '3/4 mandatory law'. This means that derogation from the law is possible within a collective labour agreement. At the sectoral level, this regularly turns into more emphasis on flexibility rather than security as the more immediate day-to-day concerns of the workfloor become more prominent (Houwing 2010).

Many economists, lawyers and employers still argue that the Dutch system for dismissal based on two routes is unnecessarily complicated (Houwing et al. 2007) and discussions again culminated in the fall of 2007, when Christian Democrats and Social Democrats in the centre-left coalition failed to reach an agreement. To prevent a cabinet crisis, a commission was installed which presented its advice in June 2008. It stated that in the case of dismissal, employers should continue payment to the worker and assist him or her in finding a new job. The social partners swept the commission's advice aside, however, in their 2008 autumn negotiations. New proposals to render the labour market more flexible by reforming the dismissal law and the duration of unemployment benefits have been launched by almost all political parties in the light of the recent elections in June 2010. We will have to wait and see what will happen next.

Two measures on working hours meant to enhance flexibility have been introduced recently: the 2000 Law to Adjust Working Hours, giving employees more rights to work longer or shorter hours and the 2007 Law on Working Hours (a new adjustment) that enables employers to extend, within specific limits, working times. This move is intended to affect wage costs, as the extension of working time entails less overtime premiums to be paid by employers. A time saving system, whereby workers can save up overtime and holidays or a part of their wages to take time off at a later moment in their career, has also been introduced in recent years. A similar individualised system has not (yet) been introduced in Belgium. As with the time-credit system, the Belgian debate focuses more on internal forms of flexible labour through shift work and the deregulation of overtime work (CRB 2008: 92-6). In the car industry, however, an agreement on working time flexibility was reached in 2006, whereby working hours may be varied over a six-year reference period. In order to cope with production fluctuations, flexible working time arrangements have been further promoted in the inter-sectoral agreement of 2004 as well as follow-up agreements, cutting the cost of overtime work or reducing the employers' payroll taxes in case of shift and night work (ibid: 153).

Nevertheless, whereas at the end of the 1990s Belgium was still making significantly more use of shift work and overtime work than the Netherlands, this situation has now altered. Another specifically Belgian form of flexibility is the scheme of temporary unemployment, introduced in 1978, whereby blue-collar workers are entitled to unemployment benefits for a certain period of time during which the employment contract (and thus the payment of wages) is not terminated but partly or wholly suspended on a temporary basis. This temporary unemployment scheme might partially explain why temporary employment is less well developed in Belgium: the scheme reduces the need for temporary (agency) work and might therefore be considered as important as dismissal regulation for influencing job security – at least for blue-collar workers (Sels & Van Hootegem 2001: 340-343).

Its use shows a strong correlation with the business cycle and adds a particular dimension of flexibility, especially in the construction sector and industrial sectors. In response to the economic downturn since 2008, the scope of the system of temporary unemployment has been extended to agency workers and workers on fixed-term employment contracts, i.e. providing them with more job security; a related, albeit temporary, arrangement has also been put in place for white-collar workers since 2009 (Vandaele 2009: 589-592). A similar but far less popular temporary unemployment scheme in the Netherlands was abolished in 2006, though a temporary crisis-related scheme has been introduced in 2009 in the light of the crisis.

The main developments of the Belgian and Dutch labour markets are summarised in Table 5.3:

Table 5.3   Main features and trends of the labour market, 1990s-2000s

	Belgium	*Netherlands*
Relative level of part-time work	About EU average; increasing	Twice as high as the EU average; increasing
Relative level of temporary work	About EU average; increased by > 50%	High level; increased by c. 30%
Peculiarities of the labour market	Leave schemes ("time credit schemes")	-
Overall level of employment protection (EPL)	High; has decreased	Moderate; has decreased, particularly EPL temporary work
Peculiarities dismissal jurisdiction	-	Regular dismissal procedure often circumvented via court and severance payment
General trend	Flexibilisation/liberalisation	Flexibilisation/liberalisation

Dynamics in the welfare regime: from passive to active

In recent decades, Belgium and the Netherlands have both shifted away from passive income-protection measures, have embarked on more supply-side activation programmes on the labour market, and have tightened the eligibility conditions for unemployment benefits (De Beer & Schils 2009: 215). Originally targeted at the male breadwinner, the Belgian and Dutch welfare regimes are rooted in the principle of industrial insurance against occupational risks, financed by social contributions from workers and employers and much less through taxation. As is the case with many other welfare states across Europe, they have both been experiencing internal and external pressures up until the present day. Internal pressures include an ageing population, increasing (long-term) unemployment, and the shift to a service economy, while external pressures include increasing international competition through economic globalisation. Private social expenditure has been rising in both countries, but in contrast to the Netherlands, public expenditure (as a percentage of GDP) in Belgium has increased as well since the mid-1990s. While the Dutch poverty rate (7.7% in the mid-2000s) is well below the European average, Belgium (8.8%; see Table 7.3 in the final chapter of this volume) is around the average, with the poverty rate in Flanders at the same level as in the Netherlands but with a significantly higher rate in Wallonia (Hemerijck & Marx 2010).

In the Netherlands, several changes were implemented in the field of social policy after the country underwent a deep economic and public finance crisis as a result of the two oil crises in the 1970s. From the late 1970s to 1982, the unemployment rate rose to 15%, and in the 1980s and 1990s more than 10% of the labour force were recipients of the disability scheme; in the early 1990s almost a million people. The number of unemployed persons sextupled between 1980 and 1994. Between 1970 and 1985, the total number of welfare beneficiaries had doubled from 1.6 million to 3.2 million (Visser & Hemerijck 1997: 128), though this was also due to the large groups of (married) women that had entered the labour market for part-time work since the late 1970s, causing the female employment rate to rise. To fight the budget deficit and to curb employment eligibility, the criteria for unemployment and disability benefits were tightened in the course of the 1980s, minimum wages were frozen for several years and in the late 1980s unemployment benefits were lowered from 80% to 70% of previous earnings (see the detailed overview in Van Gestel et al. 2009). Starting in the second half of the 1980s, the labour market and the economy recovered but it is difficult (and not part of our remit) to estimate to what extent this was caused by the reforms in preceding years.

These reforms have been part of a general shift in emphasis from welfare and income to work – from welfare to workfare, as it is sometimes called. The incentives to go for jobs had to be strengthened, and activation measures for those receiving benefits had to be intensified. Since then, activating policies particularly aimed at the prevention of unemployment and inactivity and at the reintegration of people into the labour market have become central (Van Gerven 2008). Today, this is still the key focus of the Dutch system of social security; only when claimants seriously fail to obtain income through work does the system provide income security.

Workers of 55 or more years of age are a second group towards whom measures to increase participation are targeted. These measures focus on the 'pay-as-you-go' scheme, which is the basic, tax-financed tier of the Dutch pension system. Every Dutch citizen (as well as permanent foreign inhabitants in proportion to their years of residence) has the right to obtain a pension from this tier. The second tier is a contribution-financed pension that is organised by branch-related funds that invest in the capital markets. With the rise in life expectancy of recent decades, the entire scheme has become more costly. As elsewhere, the preferred remedy is to require people to work longer and/or to cut or freeze pension benefits. Reform plans for the state-sponsored first-tier pension therefore entail a rise in the retirement age from 65 to 67 to be implemented in two steps: in 2020 from 65 to 66 and five years later from 66 to 67. The second tier would adapt to these changes. During and after the national elections in June 2010, however, this plan was discussed again, and at the time of writing it is not clear whether and when the envisaged changes will indeed be legislated.

In Belgium, the economic crises in the late 1970s triggered, just as in the Netherlands, discussions on the limitation of social expenditure and the search for a new financial balance within the social security system (Reman & Pochet 2005). Statutory social security benefits are automatically linked to the level of the cost of living, but during the 1980s and 1990s the link was broken under pressure of a worsening of the public finances. And the principle that social security benefits have to follow wage increases was abandoned in 1982. In order to reduce the gap between benefits and wages, however, it was restored in 2006. Generally, the insurance character of the social security system has been eroded in the past decades, and emphasis has shifted to universal coverage and minimum income protection, with space for private insurers to organise an additional benefit system. This has caused a growing duality between those solely relying on the social security system and those that can also afford private schemes (Hemerijck & Marx 2010).

Since the 1990s, labour supply reduction policies came under pressure due to their failure to counter the rise in unemployment and due to Belgium's sharply rising public deficit and state debt. In order to ease the employers' burden in the social security system and to make labour cheaper, the system has increasingly been financed via income from VAT and via state subsidies since then. Consequently, in 1995 the government restricted the responsibility of the social partners for maintaining a financially balanced social security system and increased its own role. Furthermore, governments attempted to reform welfare via social pacts with unions and employers in order to meet the core convergence criteria of the Maastricht Treaty for joining the EMU. Other aspirant EMU member states with similar economic pressures and budgetary problems also started attempts to build social pacts. While these attempts in other EU states succeeded, their defeat in Belgium in 1993 and in 1996 illustrated that the consensus required for their realisation was lower in this country. This development gave way to a stronger role of the state. Eased by the economic upturn in the late 1990s and at the beginning of the twenty-first century, the budget deficit and public debt was finally reduced, until the financial crisis caused them to rise again.

The liberal-left government of 1999-2003 redefined the welfare state without dismantling it. The Belgian interpretation of the Third Way – in vogue in those years of the social democratic Blair and Schröder governments in Britain and Germany – was synthesised into the Active Welfare State as a consensus between liberals and socialists. It did not entail a clear rupture with the past. The role of institutional veto players such as labour and capital remained unchanged but social security policy was launched under the heading of individual responsibility and became oriented towards increasing the employment rate and guaranteeing social protection for everybody (Reman & Pochet 2005).

In the field of pensions, in 2001 the government created the Silver Fund in order to save for future public pension expenditures looming as a result of the coming retirement of the baby boom generation. On the condition that government debt is less than 60% of GDP by 2015, the fund is intended to cushion expenditure increases in the period between 2010 and 2030. The year 2015 is still ahead of us but the silver fund strategy has already run into trouble in the first decade of the new millennium when government debt increased instead of shrinking. As an alternative, and consistent with the emphasis on individual responsibility, individual life insurance and pensions schemes are stimulated through tax advantages for workers. This is in addition to the sectoral pension plans, legally supported since 2004, which covered more than two million workers in the private sector in 2007.

In order to deal with the ageing of the population, the liberal-left government put the issue of early retirement on the political agenda in 2004. In Belgium, early exit and leave arrangements, sometimes with individual firms offering additional supplements, became a widely adopted measure from the mid-1970s onwards. Rising productivity in Belgian industry resulted in a decline of adult men in employment, as was the case in other advanced capitalist economies. In the passive welfare systems on the European continent, of which Belgium was one, early exit was chosen as a way out. In the 1990s, however, with costs rising immeasurably and the growing dominance of market-conform strategies, passive welfare systems tended to become active ones and to withdraw from early exit schemes. The Belgian government also tried to scale down early retirement schemes. In 2005, after numerous formal and informal tripartite negotiations between the government and social partners, and large-scale protests of the unions but no agreement, the government imposed the Solidarity Pact between the Generations on the social partners (Vandaele 2007: 215). The word 'pact' is a euphemism in this context; it reflects the difficulty of reaching agreement in the political climate in Belgium during the 1990s and 2000s. Employment among elderly people has, by the way, been rising in the last decade, although it remains low from a European perspective (see Table 7.2).

The trend towards more market conformity and the emphasis on employment is also visible in tax policy. In Belgium, personal income taxes were raised in the early 1990s by the suspension of the indexation of tax brackets to inflation and the introduction of a variety of supplementary contributions. Fiscal consolidation was needed to reduce the budget deficit to below the threshold of 3% by 1997 for EMU entry. Facilitated by the beneficial economic environment, the full indexation of tax brackets was restored after 1999 by the liberal-left government, and the crisis surcharge was also phased out between 1999 and 2002 (OECD 2004). Until now, the overall impact of these reforms on the redistributive effect has been rather ambiguous.

As part of the tax reform and inspired by similar measures in the UK and the US, a low-wage tax credit was introduced in 2002 as a measure against the only small gap between income from work and social security benefits. The tax credit was intended to make accepting a job more attractive than benefit dependency. The Belgian tax credit did not take family income as a frame of reference but rather low-earning individuals (Verbist et al. 2007). Due to this universal character, the credit was less beneficial to one-breadwinner families such as single parents and couples, particularly those who had children. Since the financial advantage of low-paid jobs remained small, the tax credits contributed very little to employment growth. As a consequence, the tax credit was abolished in 2005. It was replaced by a so-called 'work bonus' in the form of a bigger reduction on social security contributions of low wage earners. The activation policy was further elaborated in 2004 when vouchers aimed to create jobs were introduced for unemployed people performing labour in the black market. The vouchers, given to potential private 'employers', made it possible to combine unemployment benefits with a low-paid job in the care sector (child, elderly or household care). Because of the tax relief on the wage costs incurred by the employer, this voucher system has been a success.

Despite all reforms of the tax system to enhance employment and economic activity – including tax reductions on employers' social security contributions – Belgium has still the highest tax wedge in the OECD area (OECD 2009).

In the Netherlands, several measures have been introduced in recent years to reduce tax wedges on labour. The effective tax rate on labour has decreased gradually since 1995, with a significant reduction occurring as a result of the reform of the personal income tax in 2001. In the same period, the effective tax rate on capital increased significantly (from 17.2% to 22.3%). Among other things, this was due to taxes levied on dividends. The major tax reform of 2001 was intended to stimulate employment and to improve the country's international competitiveness – which, it was supposed, would also raise employment. Another aim of the reform was to reduce the tax burden on labour, notably on low incomes, in part by the introduction of a work tax credit. High incomes also benefitted considerably, while for average incomes the net increase has been quite moderate (Visser & Yerkes 2008: 222).

Overall, the biggest share of social security contributions has shifted from employees to employers, and in general the contributions have decreased somewhat since 1990. To combat unemployment, tax incentives for people employed in low-paid jobs had already been implemented in the 1990s. And after the 2001 tax reform, a new tax plan was approved for 2002. To tackle labour market problems, the government introduced a number of tax measures to encourage job seekers and promote labour market participation such as tax credits for certain benefit claimants taking a job and for other people re-entering the labour force. Employers employing these people also received tax advantages. Reducing long-term poverty by enhancing employment has been an essential aspect of Dutch social policy in the broad sense (including economic and tax policy) in the 1990s and 2000s (OECD 2004: 95).

In recent years, the idea of a flat tax (i.e. one identical bracket for everyone) has been the subject of serious discussion in Dutch social policy circles. Nonetheless, and despite the general movement in a liberal direction, the social security and tax system is still based on the notion that 'the strongest shoulders carry the heaviest load'.

Schematically presented in Table 5.4, we can identify the overall developments and trends in our two countries.

Table 5.4   Overall trends in welfare state development

	Belgium	*The Netherlands*
Ideological orientation	Increased emphasis on individual responsibility and on activation (from welfare to 'workfare')	Increased emphasis on individual responsibility and on activation (from welfare to 'workfare')
Benefit cuts	Nearly no cuts	Modest cuts
Eligibility criteria for benefits	Tightened	Tightened
Early exit	Phased out	Phased out
Tax incentives	Tax credits for low-wage jobs, after 2005 work bonuses; tax relief for households employing unemployed people for caring tasks	Tax credits for low-wage jobs; also for firms employing unemployed low-skilled workers
Peculiarities		Flexicurity for temporary work

Going liberal along different lines?

Belgium and the Netherlands have similar positions in the global economy, a shared assumption of economic vulnerability among the political-economic elite and a tradition of corporatist industrial relations. The trend of development during the 1990s and 2000s is also similar – and not fundamentally different from that in surrounding countries: both political economies have liberalised but corporatist relations and the redistributive welfare system have shown a notable institutional resilience. However, one has to add that Belgian corporatism has suffered from the tension between the Flemish and Wallonian parts of the country, which has made it more difficult to reach agreement. Where institutional changes took place, it remarkably happened almost irrespective of the political parties in power. This points to the ideological dominance of neo-liberalism. Whether neo-liberalism has been weakened by the global financial crisis and economic downturn after 2008 and whether alternative discourses will gain influence remains to be seen.

In corporate governance one can observe in both countries a trend – influenced by the EU and in particular the European Court of Justice – towards the Anglo-Saxon shareholder formula, although the market for companies is still far from fully liberalised. Sharing in the general trend of emphasising competitiveness and the importance of attracting foreign direct investment, the standard employment relationship has been eroded, the strictness of overall employment protection legislation has been somewhat weakened and the tax regime has been partially adjusted to these goals. In order to raise employment, guarantee the sustainability of the welfare state and cope with the financial effects of demographic ageing, both countries have also embarked on more supply-side activation programmes on the labour market. Regarding employees older than 55 years, developments in both countries have been similar too: early retirement schemes have been curbed.

The overall trend is somewhat ambiguous. On the one hand, there seems to be more path continuity in Belgium: its wage bargaining is still largely centralised, welfare cuts have been limited, and family-controlled holdings are still pivotal financial stakeholders in business. In the Netherlands, by contrast, wage bargaining has the form of guided decentralisation (or indirect centralisation), cuts to welfare have taken place, and shareholder capitalism has grown stronger in this country with many – some large – multinational companies. On the other hand, in relative terms liberalisation in Belgium appears to have been somewhat stronger than in the Netherlands (see Table 1.6 and Figure 1.5 in chapter 1).

Most importantly, in effective terms Belgian corporatism has eroded considerably – to a lower level than Siaroff calculated in 1999 on the basis of data from the 1980s and early 1990s (see Table 1.1 in the introductory chapter) – and statism has increased. Primarily, this change seems not to be the result of global competition, neoliberal dominance and an autonomous radicalisation of the still strong unions, but to the tensions between

Flanders and Wallonia, the federal character of the polity since 1994 and the accompanying fragmentation of corporatist negotiations. Reaching consensus has become very difficult in this context. In the unitary Netherlands, unionisation has declined, neoliberal thinking is relatively strong, and perhaps some acquiescence of the weaker Dutch unions is involved, but reforms took place in a policy environment still largely characterised by high trust, coupled with a discourse on vulnerability to global pressures and the unavoidability of adjusting the Dutch political economy in line with these pressures.

Even though both countries share a tradition of social partnership, Dutch industrial relations have historically evolved towards the 'institutionalisation of cooperation', while Belgian industrial relations took the trajectory of an 'institutionalisation of conflict' (Therborn 1992). Currently, this difference seems to be truer than ever.

Note

1 The *Belfry model* is referring to the characteristic belfries in the Flemish urban landscape (and Brussels), which are added to the UNESCO's list of World Heritage Sites and that represented the power of the merchants in medieval times.

6   Small Countries, Big Countries under Conditions of Europeanisation and Globalisation

Vivien A. Schmidt

Small countries, we know, are small. Big countries are big. The European Union has had a significant impact on both, as has globalisation. The question is: does size make any difference as to how these countries adjusted their political economies and policies in response to European integration as well as globalisation?

In recent years, the smaller countries of Western Europe – consisting of all Nordic EU member states plus non-member Norway, the Continental countries of Austria, the Netherlands, Belgium, Luxemburg, plus non-member Switzerland – appear to have adjusted their political economies more quickly and more effectively to the new globalised and Europeanised environment than the bigger EU member states of Continental Europe like Germany, France and Italy. The smaller countries have higher GDP per capita, similar if not higher rates of productivity and lower rates of unemployment than these bigger states. And they accomplished this with more cooperative and better-coordinated relations between firms, labour and the state through corporatist concertation. Moreover, the small countries' political economic adjustment has not been accompanied by any serious undermining of their welfare states. The Nordic and Continental small states have all largely avoided both the problems of poverty, inequality and lack of job security plaguing Anglophone Europe and, in many cases, also the insider-outsider division of the labour market of the bigger Continental and Mediterranean countries (see Table 7.3 in the concluding chapter). In addition, they have introduced flexibility into labour markets without jeopardising security, increased the sustainability of pension systems without seriously affecting pensioners' income, and reduced the generosity of social assistance programmes without reneging on commitments to equality, universality and/or solidarity. Among

Anglophone countries, however, Ireland as a small state with a more recently open economy has also managed to address problems of poverty and inequality (at least until the current economic crisis) while improving labour relations through a move to a kind of state-led corporatism.

The smaller Nordic and Continental countries of Western Europe also have had a better scorecard with regard to EU-related policies (see the statistical data presented in chapter 7). In the Single Market, they tend to have higher rates of compliance with EU economic policy directives, in particular the Scandinavian member countries. Their performance with regard to the Open Method of Coordination has also been generally better than that of the bigger countries, with their 'best practices' seen as models for the larger member states. Moreover, smaller countries that have participated in the European Monetary Union (EMU), including the Netherlands, Austria, Finland and Belgium, have been quicker and more successful in putting their macroeconomic houses in order and in meeting the Stability and Growth Pact (SGP) criteria than bigger countries like (again) Germany, France and Italy. Equally significantly, however, those smaller member states that have stayed out of EMU – Sweden and Denmark – have nonetheless consistently met the SGP criteria without any warnings from the Commission, in contrast with the other West European non-member, Britain, which has received warnings on its deficit spending. And those smaller countries that have stayed out of Europe – Switzerland and Norway – could have joined EMU without much difficulty.

So what is it about the smaller states that might explain their better performance in Europe? Scholars have suggested any number of possible generalisations, many of which apply to many of the smaller states, but none of which covers all cases. These include small countries' very smallness and economic openness; their better-coordinated political economic institutions; their more generous and supportive socio-economic provisions; their stronger state institutions; their better policy responses; their cultural homogeneity, more innovative ideas and/or more inclusive communicative interactions. We could add that they all share a clear perception of what they are – small states in the open world economy – and therefore what they must do in response to outside pressures: that is, to do all that is necessary to promote economic competitiveness while maintaining public acceptance.

In addition, Europeanisation itself – whether understood as the indirect pressures of increasing competition from market integration, the more direct pressures of macroeconomic adjustment resulting from European monetary integration, the very direct pressures of European directives and European Court of Justice decisions related to the development of the Single Market (see Becker in the introductory chapter to this volume) – has had a differential impact on the small West European countries. In response to such pressures, whether direct or indirect, the small countries – much like the larger ones – have responded differently, with major, minor or no transformation, depending upon a host of factors related to the institutional 'fit' with policies and preferences, and the capacity to respond institutionally and politically, where politics is understood not only in terms of interests and power but also of ideas and discourse.

In what follows, I consider all of the above generalisations, in terms of openness, institutions, culture, discourse and the direct and indirect effects of Europeanisation in order to show that they neither apply to all small West European countries nor do they exclude ex ante the bigger countries. I illustrate throughout with cases of small countries in contrast to big countries. I conclude with some preliminary suggestions about what ideal-typically makes small West European countries not just small but successful, despite the empirical differences.

Small West European countries in a globalising world

Does smallness matter for West European small states' successful adjustment patterns in an increasingly internationalised world, from the postwar period forward? And if it does, what are the characteristics of small states that account for this success? Some scholars emphasise economic openness tied to coordinated action within political economic institutions, others the nature of political institutions, and yet others cultural homogeneity, common ideas or discursive interactions. As we shall see, these all offer clues to the success of small states, but none are entirely satisfactory on their own.

Economic openness and political economic institutions

Economic openness has been one of the longest-standing explanations for small countries' economic success. Peter Katzenstein (1985) was one of the first to show that one of the main characteristics of small West European states was their openness to international markets. Small countries as different in their cultures and political institutions as Sweden, Austria, Switzerland, Belgium, Denmark and the Netherlands all experienced significant growth throughout the postwar period despite – or is it because – they were small countries open to the world economy. One could even argue that Ireland joined this group more recently, having gone from one of the poorest and least developed of West European countries to one of the richest (at least until the financial crisis beginning in 2008) and most developed, with a major factor being its economic openness to global forces plus massive structural funds from the EU that helped promote economic development.

Economic openness alone, however, is no guarantee of performance. If it were, then how would we explain the poor performance of small states at various junctures in time – e.g., the Netherlands in the 1970s, Denmark and Ireland in the 1980s, Sweden and Finland in the early 1990s, and Ireland again today? Moreover, if it is economic openness on its own that counts, what makes small states any different from big ones that are equally if not more open, like the UK beginning with the Thatcher era which, according to Hirst and Thompson (2000), has been the only truly globalised economy among advanced industrialised countries? Equally importantly, European economic integration has increased the openness of all member states to one another as well as to the global economy, thereby diminishing the importance of openness *per se* as a distinguishing characteristic.

For Katzenstein (1985: ch. 1), economic openness was only one of a bundle of factors that together made small states competitive globally. Political economic institutions, in particular those of corporatism, as fostered in small states, was the most important among these factors. Corporatism was characterised by centralised systems of business interests and unions, voluntary coordination of conflicting interests through political bargaining by management, labour and (often) the state, plus an ideology of social partnership. This system enabled the social partners and government of small states with open economies in the post-war years to cooperate and to coordinate their responses to the adjustments required by external economic pressures – in monetary policy, as the social partners responded to the signals of central monetary authorities and moderated their wage rises in response; in industrial relations, wages and work conditions; and in pensions and social policy. The result, as Katzenstein found, was highly generous welfare states, highly stable labour relations and highly competitive economies.

Since the early 1980s when Katzenstein wrote *Small States*, much has changed, as all European countries have opened up their economies to globalisation and some non-corporatist countries have become quasi-corporatist (e.g. Italy, Spain as well as Ireland) while others have altered their form of corporatism (e.g. Sweden). In the mainstream, the theoretical categories for capitalism, moreover, have moved from a tripartite division of capitalism consisting of liberal, corporatist and statist market economies into a binary division, as elaborated by the Varieties of Capitalism school (Hall & Soskice 2001).

The Varieties of Capitalism school identifies a binary division of capitalism split between 'liberal' and 'coordinated' market economies. Whereas in liberal market economies, business and labour relations are competitive, market-based and arbitrated by a liberal state, in coordinated market economies, cooperative management-labour relations appear alongside non-market managed business relations, all of which may be facilitated by an 'enabling' state (Hall & Soskice 2001). In the VoC classification, Ireland along with the US, UK and other Anglophone countries belong to the liberal type, whereas all the smaller West European countries identified by Katzenstein plus Germany are labelled as coordinated market economies.

But at the point at which all European economies are now open to globalisation and many more became more corporatist, we have to reopen our question about the factors that make small states special. Moreover, if we look closely at the small states across time, we can see that in some small states, even corporatism is not what it was, if it ever was what it was ideal-typically supposed to be. This raises a number of questions with regard to our original discussion of small states as successful because they are corporatist open economies.

For example, what do we do with Belgium which, as a result of the weak coordinating capacity of the social partners (Hemerjick et al. 2000), has never been as highly corporatist as the Netherlands or Sweden? Moreover, how do we account for the diverse ways in which coordination has changed even among the traditionally corporatist countries, given the increasing differentiation in wage-bargaining systems, some of which maintained their centralism (e.g. Finland and Norway), some of which have decentralised yet indirectly centralised (e.g. Denmark, the Netherlands and Sweden; see the respective country chapters and Table 1.7 in the introductory chapter to this volume)? The way Becker has dealt with these changes in the introductory chapter is an option, but the discussion of the questions posed here has just started.

A related question is what do we do with the general shift in relative power from labour to business in bargaining relations, or the growing role of the state in influencing the bargains (e.g. Austria, the Netherlands) or even in setting them (i.e. Belgium) (Hemerjick et al. 2000)? And how do we distinguish small states from big ones, given that Germany is also a highly corporatist market economy?

Equally importantly, how do we deal with Ireland, which is more of a liberal market economy with market-driven business relations but which, nonetheless, has since the late 1980s developed cooperative management-labour relations led by the state in something akin to corporatism (Hardiman 2004; Teague & Doneaghy 2004)? And where do we place other countries that have recently managed to institute a form of state-led corporatism, like Italy and Spain (Royo 2002, 2008; Molina & Rhodes 2007)? These bigger Mediterranean countries do not fit the binary division of the Varieties of Capitalism school; nor does France which, unlike its other Mediterranean counterparts, has instead radically decentralised its labour markets. Rather than consigning these countries to a mixed category of uncertain coordination called mixed market economies (MMEs) by the Varieties of Capitalism school, I see them as approximating a third type of capitalism: 'state-influenced market economies' (SMEs). Characterised by hierarchically-based business and labour relations enhanced or hindered by an 'influencing' state (Schmidt 2002a: ch. 3, 2008b), it resembles the statist capitalist variety as presented by Becker in the introduction to this volume. Greece, arguably a small state, along with Portugal as well as most of the small Central and East European countries, could also be categorised as cases approximating the SME type (Pagoulatos 2003). And to what degree the SME type applies to the small West European states considered herein is a task for future research.

Does the configuration of socio-economic institutions also play a role, since all such countries, with the exception of Ireland, have high levels of welfare provision and security? Even here, though, no single generalisation works, since the smaller states are divided between the traditionally social democratic Scandinavian countries, which have maintained similar systems despite cost-cutting and rationalisation, and the traditionally conservative Continental small states, which have changed (or not) in very different ways (e.g. the Netherlands vs. Austria). Notably, the Netherlands is now often categorised with the Scandinavian countries when considered in terms of measures of redistribution and equality (via the Gini coefficient) (see Table 7.3 in the next chapter).

Political institutions

But what can we say of political institutions, and the role of the state more specifically, with regard to the small West European states? One of the problems of the Varieties of Capitalism school is its scant attention to state action, defined as government policies and practices that emerge out of the political interactions among public and private actors in given political institutional contexts (Schmidt 2009). There is in fact a growing literature in political economy that has increasingly paid attention to the role of the state in structuring markets, developing new missions and making critical choices that are the 'product of power and politics, not just path-dependence and employer "coordination"' (Levy 2006). The state is significant, moreover, not only for its political economic institutions and its policies but also its political institutional configuration (polity) as well as politics, understood not only in terms of power and interest but also in terms of the power of ideas and discourse (Schmidt 2009). In this, smaller West European countries are no different.

Significantly, in fact, political economic success is sometimes attributed to the unitary nature of the state. Having a unitary state with autonomous decision-making capacity makes a difference in cases where the social partners are unwilling or unable to play their role in negotiating social policy change, which was true in the 1990s for both the Netherlands and Sweden with regard to reforms of the welfare state (Schmidt 2003). This said, having a weaker unitary state, due to minority-led governments, may also promote reform. In Denmark, for example, beginning in the early 1980s, minority governments were able to reform not despite but rather because of governmental disunity, which enabled reform after reform to be negotiated by *ad hoc* government coalitions that engaged in 'policy and party shopping' (Vad & Benner 2000).

Moreover, centralised corporatism combined with a unitary state, however weak, also seems to be a key to success. Whereas in Sweden, the state had to go it alone with regard to welfare state reform in the 1990s once the social partners had pulled out of centralised national level corporatist mechanisms of negotiation, in Denmark the reform process was facilitated by the continuation of centralised coordination, enabling the state to negotiate far-reaching reforms cooperatively with the social partners (see the respective country chapters in this volume). The Danish state's success in actively promoting policy change through national level coordination mechanisms, using firms in order to achieve its goals of bringing the long-term unemployed into the economy, contrasts markedly with the lack of success in Germany, in which the state was unable to mobilise the social partners for solidaristic purposes, and instead German firms worked through the state to achieve their goals of shedding unproductive labour (Martin & Thelen 2007). This said, if Denmark were compared with the German states of Baden-Württemberg or Bavaria – both with more than twice as many inhabitants as Denmark – the contrasts would not be striking. This helps explain Becker's cautiousness on comparing small and big states (see Becker 2009: 141)

But if it were all about political institutions and the contrast between unitary and federalised states or ongoing centralised and decentralised coordination systems, how do we explain Switzerland and Belgium, both highly federalised systems with weak states and weak corporatist relations in which the state nevertheless managed to achieve significant reform success? In Belgium in the 1990s, for example, the incapacity of the social partners to reach agreement in wage bargaining or of the state to impose a negotiated solution led to the system of wage setting by government decree. Moreover, we still know little about *why* countries reformed in the ways they did, which raises questions regarding culture, ideas and discourse.

Political culture

Political culture has for a long time been out of favour with political scientists as an explanation for why countries or people are what they are or do what they do, mainly because in the past it was used as a heavily value-laden catch-all explanandum, as notably in Banfield's study of Italy, *The Moral Basis of a Backward Society* (1958/1970). For the small countries, it was sometimes used by scholars as a way of pointing to their success while denying the replicability of that success. These explanations were often tautological, such as: Sweden is social democratic because it has an egalitarian culture; Switzerland manages the complexities of a highly federalised society cooperatively because it has long had a consensual culture. These kinds of explanations deny the difficulties involved in creating and maintaining such 'cultures', while culture itself remains unexplained.

More recently, however, culture has been reintroduced to the field of political science. Among the three traditional 'new institutionalisms' in political science (see Hall & Taylor 1996), it serves as an active concept in 'sociological institutionalism'. In rational choice and historical institutionalism, by contrast, culture has remained a residual category, often

used as part of the background characteristics of path-dependent (historical) institutions or 'nested' (rational choice) incentive structures, and
generally serving as unexamined claims about institutions rather than as
something to be studied. In sociological institutionalism, by contrast, culture plays an important role in framing action and (social) institutions.
Barbier (2008) melds this with a more dynamic ideational approach to ex-
plore the political cultures within which normative frameworks based on
common sets of values and norms are institutionalised for given periods
in policies and practices in particular countries, as in the case of notions
of precariousness in Denmark and the Netherlands.

Culture, however, is not always congruent with given countries, since
some countries are culturally homogeneous and some culturally heterogeneous, with small countries more often the former and big countries the
latter. John Campbell and John A. Hall (2006), for example, show quantitatively that small countries that are culturally homogeneous have stronger economic performance than bigger homogeneous countries, and that
even smaller countries that are culturally heterogeneous do at least as well
as the bigger homogenous countries, let alone the bigger heterogenous
ones. In a qualitative case study of Denmark, moreover, they demonstrate
that the cultural origins of homogeneity go a long way back, and that such
homogeneity has contributed to other qualities, such as effective coordination. But if successful adjustment is the result of their cultural homogeneity, what then do we do with culturally heterogeneous countries like
Switzerland or Belgium, which have also been successful?

Moreover, cultural homogeneity has also been linked to outcomes that
are not always positive. These include the rise of anti-immigrant right
wing extremist parties, whether in Denmark, where extremist discourse
has focused on outsiders (read Muslims) exploiting the generosity of the
welfare state, or in the Netherlands, where Pim Fortuyn's discourse (per-
versely) in the 2002 election campaign built on Dutch values of tolerance
to argue that they had to be intolerant of the intolerant (read Muslims) in
order to protect their tolerant society (Schmidt 2006: ch. 4). Intolerance,
however, is not a characteristic linked exclusively to homogeneous cultures – witness the rise of the extreme right in Switzerland and in Belgium
– or of small states, given the Le Pen phenomenon in France. The fact that
the extreme right in France has more recently been losing its appeal in
response to President Sarkozy's construction of a discourse that appealed
to Le Pen voters on security and immigration issues, suggests another differentiating factor related to the politics of ideas and discourse.

Political ideas and discourse

'Discursive institutionalism' – the term I use as an umbrella concept to describe the wide range of approaches that focus on the substantive content of ideas and the interactive processes of discourse – also deals with culture. But culture is not always the main object of study for discursive institutionalists. Although it is primary for those discursive institutionalists who come out of the sociological institutionalist tradition (e.g. Barbier 2008), it is not for discursive institutionalists who engage with rational choice and historical institutionalist traditions and therefore concern themselves with ideas about interests and (historical) institutions instead. This said, culture naturally frames the ideas and discourse studied by all discursive institutionalists, giving the 'ideational structures' of meaning that underpin agents' 'background ideational abilities' to make sense of the world, which are based in language and culture, as well as agents' 'foreground discursive abilities', which enable them to articulate, communicate and criticise those ideas in order to take collective action to change (or maintain) them even while they use them (Schmidt 2008). But most importantly for discursive institutionalists, and not always for sociological institutionalists, what is important is how ideas and discourse serve to (re)frame culture.

Thus, for example, Bo Rothstein, a 'discursive institutionalist' who engages with the rational choice institutionalist tradition, emphasises the importance of collective memories in Sweden to explain the long-term survival of cooperative collective bargaining – as opposed to the neutral incentive structures of rational choice institutionalism. Thus, he explains the history of institutions as the carriers of ideas or 'collective memories' about the trustworthiness of collective-bargaining institutions that were generated at certain critical junctures (Rothstein 2005). In Sweden, the decade of the 1930s was the moment at which Swedish collective bargaining evolved into a trusted 'public institution' based on peaceful and collaborative industrial relations. The defining moments came first in the early 1930s when, in response to a violent strike in which five people were killed, a successful coordinative discourse among policy actors was joined by a persuasive, cooperation-oriented communicative discourse by the prime minister who evenhandedly condemned the violence of the military while also chiding the strikers. This then became the basis for a collective memory that in the late 1930s, at the time of agreements on collective bargaining institutions, served to remind all parties to the discussions that cooperation was both possible and desirable. This collective memory continues to underpin the collective bargaining system today, even though the bargaining system has changed greatly, in particular since the employers pulled out of the national central system, but continue to participate in sectoral bargaining (Rothstein 2005: 168-98).

Discursive institutionalism also lends insight into the dynamics of change in the 1990s in Sweden, which were discussed above primarily in historical institutionalist terms. What is described by historical institutionalists as a shift from social partner coordination to state action as a result of the failure of social concertation in the reform of the welfare state – without any account of why and how the state then acted in the way it did – is explained by discursive institutionalists in terms of ideas and discourse. The generation of the policy ideas can be attributed to the epistemic communities of policy experts and specialised politicians that informed the coordinative discourse of the policy sphere (Marier 2008). The subsequent successful communication and legitimation of those ideas to the general public, by contrast, can be attributed to the social democratic party in power at the time which, in the absence of the social partners, engaged in a communicative discourse with the public in the political sphere by creating public forums through which to inform, discuss and revise the policies before they were implemented (Schmidt 2000).

The Netherlands offers yet another example of the usefulness of turning to the interactive processes of discourse to explain the dynamics of change in welfare states. While our earlier historical institutionalist discussion of the welfare reforms of the 1990s described the significant changes that came about, it did little to explain the dynamics of change endogenously. Discursive institutionalism can help, by pointing to the 'crisis narrative' developed by the government in power and articulated by Prime Minister Ruud Lubbers that the Netherlands was a 'sick country' given that one in seven workers were on disability benefits (Kuiper 2004; Schmidt 2000). But while cognitive arguments about the necessity of reform enabled the government to push through major changes in the disability and pensions systems, the lack of normative legitimisation led to the government's massive defeat in 1994. It was only when a new government was able to argue credibly that it had not only ensured a better economy with 'jobs, jobs and more jobs' but that it safeguarded social equity even as it produced liberalising efficiency, that reform gained public acceptance, as confirmed by the government's landslide electoral victory in 1998 (Levy 1999; Schmidt 2000). As the economy turned around, the 'Dutch miracle' became the talk of the world, and its origins were traced back to the Waasenaar Agreement of the 1980s.

The Dutch miracle, however, may be less about the success of particular policies than it is about the success of a 'miracle' discourse beginning in the mid to late 1990s that led people to believe that success was tied primarily to wage restraint, as Becker (2005) argues. In fact, whatever the contribution of wage restraint to export-led growth, it has also contributed to making the labour market one in which more jobs are divided among more people, with fewer working hours for everyone and lower incomes, in particular for the 'outsiders' with part-time jobs – mainly women, youth and immigrants (Becker 2005; Salverda 2005). This said, however misguided the discourse may have been and however problematic its policy prescriptions turned out for the long term, it involved the creation of a 'collective memory' that contributed to labour peace and the successful negotiation of major reforms of the work and welfare regimes.

Since the mid 1990s, moreover, Dutch governments have continued broad-scale liberalisation programmes, ensuring that the Netherlands, once categorised as a conservative welfare state, is seen as somewhere between the British liberal paradigm – given pension privatisation and high labour-market flexibility – and the Scandinavian social-democratic paradigm – given a high basic pension and labour market 'security' for part-time and temporary jobs (regular social benefits and a top-up in pension if necessary at the end of work life; see the contribution of Houwing and Vandaele in this volume). Moreover, it has managed to liberalise without jeopardising commitments to social equality, as is evident from its low measure of inequality (see Table 7.3 in the next chapter). As a consequence, the public has come to see economic success as linked to neo-liberal reform and, despite economic stagnation in recent years, continues to support it as well as to maintain a positive attitude toward globalisation. Attitudes toward Europeanisation have also been largely positive, at least until the negative vote in the referendum on the Constitutional Treaty which reflected concerns about immigration and the inflationary impact of the euro as well as the desire to punish an unpopular government unable to articulate the case for Europe (WRR 2007b).

Ideas and discourse about economic openness, or globalisation, represent another differentiating factor for small states, accompanying the (historical) institutional facts of economic openness plus corporatism and generous welfare states that served to distinguish small states in the early postwar years until the 1980s. Because globalisation has been a sine qua non of economic life for small West European states throughout the postwar period, it has become such a part of the background assumptions that national leaders have not even felt it necessary to address the issue. By

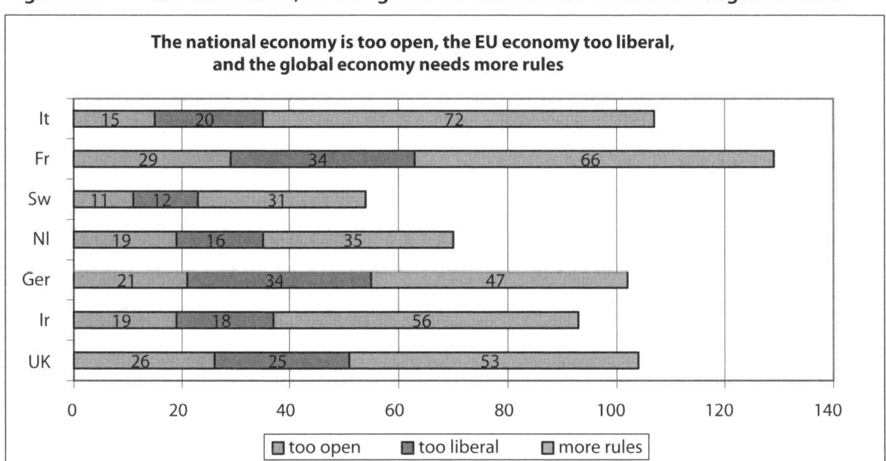

Source: Eurobarometer 2003 (Flash EB no. 151b pp. 9-11, 33)
The questions include:
Q3. Currently, do you consider that our country's economy is too open, too closed or is suited to the development of the worldwide economy?
Q4. And generally speaking, would you say that the European Union is too protectionist or on the contrary too liberal or neither too protectionist nor too liberal?
Q5. Would you say that more regulation or less regulation is needed, or that the current regulation is sufficient in order to monitor the development of globalisation?

contrast, political leaders in Ireland as well as Britain have felt the need to articulate a specifically pro-global discourse, whereas in countries like France, they have been decidedly anti-global in their discourse, and the public has been the most negative (Schmidt 2007). This is illustrated in Figure 6.1, which shows the responses to a range of Eurobarometer questions about attitudes toward globalisation. The smaller states generally have more pro-globlisation views than the bigger countries, and France is off the charts.

For example, in Sweden, even at moments of major economic crisis and reform, in the early 1990s when the country's real estate bubble burst, public attitudes toward globalisation have not been affected. This is because such reforms resulted in some liberalisation but did little to fundamentally jeopardise the basic postwar paradigm of the social-democratic welfare state, with its commitment to equality and universality of access (see the contribution of Lindgren in this volume). The reforms managed to maintain a very high level of benefits and services despite moderate cuts and the introduction of modest user fees (Benner & Vad 2000). Thus, in their communicative discourse, social democratic governments consistently presented themselves as defending basic welfare state values of equality, even as they cut benefits in order to 'save the welfare state' (Schmidt 2000). For the Swedish public, Europeanisation has been much more in question than globalisation, mainly because of fears of the negative impact of the European Monetary Union on the welfare state, as evidenced by the fact that referenda on EMU membership have repeatedly failed. Even the eastward enlargement of the EU related to the insourcing of workers has not been much of an issue (Sweden was only one of three countries, along with the UK and Ireland, to open its doors to the 2004 accession countries; see Schmidt 2007). But immigration more generally, in particular as it relates to third-country nationals, has become an issue, with anti-immigrant feeling growing with regard to immigrants' potential demands on the welfare state if they are jobless and without skills. Sweden, however, has been much less xenophobic in this regard than Denmark (as noted above), which recently instituted the most draconian immigration rules in all of Europe.

The Europeanisation of small West European countries

For further insights, we now turn to how small countries have responded to the pressures of Europeanisation.

In response to the pressures of globalisation, small countries with open economies and corporatist institutions have fared reasonably well from the early postwar years to today, but it is impossible to say why exactly, other than to cite the range of characteristics related to openness, social concertation, political institutions, cultures and ideas and discourse that have played a role in small countries' adjustment. Much the same could be said for the pressures of Europeanisation.

Europeanisation, defined here as the top-down impact of the EU on national policies (following Ladrech 1994; Héritier 2001; Radaelli 2003; Börzel & Risse 2000; Schmidt 2002a), has had a differential impact on the smaller West European countries. Although the process of European integration, defined as the bottom-up influence of the member states on Europe, along with the feedback loop from Europeanisation, is equally important to the smaller European countries' experience in the EU, the formulation I use here is most suited for the study of how the smaller countries have adjusted to Europe. It enables us to consider the different kinds of impact that EU policies and policymaking have on national policy, including the indirect pressures from EU economic integration, the more direct pressures from EU institutional rules and rulings, and the indirect pressures of EU 'new governance' methods of 'policymaking without policies'.

Theorising the impact of Europeanisation on small states

To provide a systematic analysis for why the smaller countries responded in the way they have to EU policies requires a differentiation of the kinds of pressures exerted by the EU rules as well as the identification of the range of national mediating factors affecting countries' responses. First of all, it is important to take note of the kinds of decision rules which frame the EU policy. These include highly specified rules that impose certain policies, as in the Maastricht criteria in the run-up to EMU; less specified rules that allow a certain amount of leeway in the transposition of EU policies, as with the deregulation of the telecommunications or electricity sectors; suggested rules such as in the Open Method of Coordination, in which compliance is voluntary and there are no sanctions other than 'naming and shaming'; or no rules at all, as when the Directorate General for Competition demands only an opening up to competition (Schmidt 2002a: ch. 2).

Secondly, we need to consider the range of nationally specific factors that may affect country responses to European policies. While goodness of fit or misfit of EU policies with national policy legacies may set the stage (see Börzel & Risse 2000; Héritier et al. 1996; Cowles et al. 2001), policy preferences based on national actors' ideas about interests or values dictate whether misfit is seen as a problem or an opportunity, political institutional capacity reflects the institutional arrangements and the political interactions that affect state and societal actors' ability to respond more or less effectively, and the quality of national actors' ideas and the persuasiveness of their discourse enhances the capacity to respond by altering perceptions of legacies and by influencing preferences (Schmidt 2002a: ch. 2). As a result, while in some sectors, the interaction effects of the EU and national policies may be significant, entailing the transformation of national practices, in others the EU may have only a minor impact, with the absorption by national practices of any EU-related changes, and in yet others the EU may have almost no impact at all, as national practices show inertia with regard to the EU (see Héritier et al. 1996; Héritier 2001; Schmidt 2002a: ch. 2).

Market and monetary pressures of Europeanisation

Europeanisation as a driving force for change can be highly varied, in particular where it is understood as the indirect pressures of increasing competition resulting from market integration. These hit early on, beginning with the elimination of European tariff barriers (from 1969), continuing with the Single Market Act, with 1992 as the target date for the elimination of non-tariff barriers, as well as with the increasing harmonisation of those products that could not circulate EU-wide on the basis of mutual recognition alone. All of this was intensified by the first and second oil shocks, which added globalisation alongside Europeanisation as a form of competitive pressure bearing down on all European countries.

For the small West European countries, these pressures were arguably more intense than for the bigger countries, since they have all had very open economies since the early postwar years. But this did not mean that they all responded well or quickly. The Netherlands was a basket case in the 1970s, both in terms of economic performance and corporatist relations, but began its recovery in the 1980s. Denmark had current account difficulties in the 1970s which only worsened in the 1980s. Belgium was in even worse shape than either of these two countries in terms of both performance and corporatism, and did not recover nearly as rapidly (Hemerijck et al. 2000). None, however, were in as parlous a state as the UK, which had to request an IMF loan in 1976.

By contrast, some smaller countries did reasonably well in macroeconomic terms for quite a while, like Sweden and Austria, both of which were outside the EU as well as the European Monetary System (EMS) until 1995. Sweden performed well economically while remaining the last of the neo-Keynesians until the real estate bubble burst in the late 1980s, producing an economic meltdown in the early 1990s that ultimately led to their request for entry into the EU. Sweden's labour relations, however, experienced a major crisis already in the early 1980s when the employers' association withdrew from the centralised bargaining process, although sectoral bargaining continued without difficulty (Vad & Benner 2000). Austria managed the transition from Austro-Keynesian monetary policy reasonably smoothly and with no significant problems in its labour relations, albeit relatively late (mid-1980s) (see Afonso & Mach in this volume as well as Hemerijck et al. 2000).

Europeanisation may secondly be seen to include the more direct pressures of macroeconomic adjustment resulting from European monetary integration through the EMS and the EMU (see the discussion in Becker's introduction, this volume). Here, the small countries that have joined EMU have generally responded well, but not always without difficulty. In the run-up to EMU, although the Netherlands and Austria had little problem meeting the Maastricht criteria for membership, Belgium, like Italy, had a very high public debt. This would have excluded it from membership in the eurozone had the member states in their wisdom not decided to reinterpret the 60% public debt criterion of the Maastricht Treaty to mean moving in the direction of 60% (mainly to ensure Belgium's participation). This said, meeting the deficit criterion was not so easy at the last minute not only for Italy, which was castigated by Germany for fiddling with the figures, but even for France and then Germany, both of which were also caught moving money from one account into another in order to make their books look right.

Moreover, once EMU was established along with the Stability and Growth Pact (SGP), Ireland was in trouble early on because of a rate of inflation (around 4%) higher than the 3% required at the time. The Netherlands struggled with a slow economy in the early to mid-2000s, engaging in significant belt-tightening in order to stay within the SGP criteria. This helps to explain the irascibility of Dutch politicians (along with that of the Dutch president of the European Central Bank) in response to German and French lack of adherence to the SGP criterion on deficit for a number of years running as a result of recessionary pressures in their economies. It also explains Dutch unwillingness to accommodate their demands for a more flexible interpretation of the criteria, although the two bigger countries ultimately won out since punishing France and Germany made no ultimate sense given that these are the two largest economies in the Eurozone and the motors of growth.

Not all smaller European countries, of course, are in EMU. Denmark obtained an opt-out from EMU in its second referendum on the Maastricht Treaty, after the first failed in part as a result of fears of the impact of monetary integration on the welfare state along with concerns about sovereignty and identity. And yet Denmark could easily be part of the euro, given its imported 'hard money' policy, which began in the early 1970s when it stayed in the EMS 'currency snake' (a band within which currencies were permitted to fluctuate) and shadowed the Deutschmark. Sweden, unlike Austria and Finland, did not join EMU when it entered the EU in 1995. But although this de facto opt-out was never specified in writing, as Commission officials sometimes remind its leaders, Sweden continues to resist joining because of public fear of the euro's impact on the welfare state and the economy more generally. Since Norway and

Switzerland are not part of the EU, they have no need to follow the requirements of EMU. And yet both have also largely shadowed the euro in order to protect their currencies from excessive volatility.

In the light of the current financial market crisis, membership in EMU has also represented a kind of insurance policy against excessive currency volatility and speculative pressure. The experience of another very small Nordic state, Iceland, which found its currency near collapse once its major banks had failed, is a case in point. The plans of its newly elected government to join the EU and EMU, although still in their preliminary stages, suggest that at least one very small Nordic 'outsider' has revised its views of the costs and benefits of joining the EU. Norway, by contrast, has not considered revising either its stance on membership in the EU or EMU for the moment; but it does not have the economic problems of Iceland, given its oil revenues.

Institutional pressures of Europeanisation

Europeanisation also encompasses the very direct pressures of European directives and European Court of Justice decisions meant to promote the completion of the Single Market. Here, harmonisation of the rules related to the freedom of movement of goods began in earnest in the mid-1980s with the push to complete the Single Market. At the same time that the principle of 'mutual recognition' ensured that most goods that met the standards of one member state could be sold across the EU, those products that affected health or safety standards would still have to be harmonised. And it is in the industrial standards committees that we find that smaller countries have much less influence than the bigger countries, if judged by their control of the secretariats (see Table 6.1).

The pressures of Europeanisation intensified in the 1990s as the Commission moved from focusing on harmonising the rules of free movement of goods to freedom of movement of services and people, and as it promoted deregulation in public utilities services and the liberalisation of public and private services. This meant that areas such as telecommunications, postal services, electricity and energy were deregulated while public procurement markets and services more generally were to be opened up. Significantly here, smaller states with more liberalising tendencies in recent years, including Denmark, Sweden, and the Netherlands, were less affected by the regulations than countries like Austria and Belgium, which had been slower to deregulate in these industries, as the country chap-

Table 6.1   Small states' control of secretariats of standardisation committees

Countries	CEN (279 secretaries)		CENELEC (108 secretariats)		ETSI (17 chairs)	
	#	(%)	#	(%)	#	(%)
Germany	77	(27.6%)	28	(26%)	3	(18%)
UK	55	(19.8%)	38	(35%)	4	(23.5%)
France	52	(18.6%)	13	(12%)	4	(23.5%)
Italy	30	(10.8%)	13	(12%)	2	(12%)
NL	21	(7.5%)	2	(~2%)	1	(6%)
Belgium	10	(3.6%)	2	(~2%)		
Sweden	10	(3.6%)	1	(~1)		
Spain	7	(2.5%)	7	(6.4%)	1	(6%)
Switzerland	4	(1.4%)	1	(~1)		
Finland	3	(1%)				
Norway	1	(0.4%)	3	(2.7%)		
Greece	1	(0.4%)				
Portugal	1	(0.4%)			1	(6%)
Ireland	1	(0.4%)				
Austria					1	(6%)

1 CEN: European Committee for Standardisation
2 CENELEC: European Committee for Electrotechnical Standardisation
3 ETSI: European Telecommunications Standards Institute
Source: CEN Technical Committee List, 03/03/2005; CENELEC Directory 2005, Issue 1; ETSI website, Organisational Chart

ters in this volume tell us. Importantly, however, the countries with the most significant influence on the content of the reforms were the bigger member states, and in particular Germany and France in all of these areas (Thatcher 2002; Eising & Jabko 2001).

Implementation and compliance patterns also differ with regard to social policy. In gender-related and parent-related social policies, for example, Gerda Falkner and her associates (Falkner et al. 2005: ch. 15) show that across a number of specific policy directives, member states exhibit patterns of reactions that suggest that there are three 'worlds of compliance'. Nordic countries are the only ones that fit the 'world of law' in which whatever the misfit with policy legacies or preferences, the directives are transposed and implemented in a timely fashion. Austria, the Netherlands and Belgium fit the 'world of domestic politics' in which delays are related to partisan politics, much as in the UK, Germany and Spain. The 'world of neglect' is made up of Ireland – which although in the 'world of politics' with regard to transposition, scores poorly in terms of the implementation of directives, much like Italy – and Luxemburg, which although an effective enforcer is a bad transposer, as is France, because of its consistent unwillingness to comply, regardless of the politics. Greece and Portugal, by contrast, are bad at both transposition and enforcement (Falkner et al. 2005: ch. 15).

In addition, we should not forget that Norway and Switzerland, although not part of the EU, have nonetheless had to sign up to the full range of Single Market rules without having a vote on those rules. In the case of Switzerland, for example, whereas its officially stated policy is 'participation without integration,' the reality has been much more one of 'integration without participation' (Kux & Sverdrup 2000: 254). Its laws are largely harmonised with the EU, with 85% of Swiss market legislation EU-compatible. EU directives on competition law, for example, are copied verbatim into Swiss law, while EU technical annexes form an integral part of Swiss laws and decrees. Moreover, in order to gain access to the European clearing system TARGET, Swiss banks have also established a Swiss euro clearing bank in Frankfurt (Kux & Sverdrup 2000: 251-252). In addition, in its bilateral agreements with the EU, access to markets and/or to other policy areas generally come with a quid pro quo. For example, Swiss participation in the Schengen/Dublin system came with concessions on banking secrecy – including imposing a withholding tax on citizens with tax residency in EU member states. The result is that bilateral negotiated agreement takes the place of institutional voice and vote, which would come from sitting around the table in Brussels.

Institutional voice and vote, however, mean little when it comes to action by the Commission or the ECJ that follows from their autonomous treaty-based powers. And for some small states, the impact of EU decisions has been very significant indeed. One such set of decisions involves those that run counter to the country's moral values. For example, the EU's decision that the restrictive alcohol policies of Finland and Sweden violated rules regarding competition policy and the free movement of goods challenged Nordic values that saw such restrictions as necessary 'for the good of society' – to curb the excessive drinking which was stereotypically assumed to be the product of citizens' attempts to overcome 'communication anxiety.' Similarly, the EU's opposition to the tolerant drug policy of the Netherlands – problematic within the context of the Schengen agreement because it clashed with other countries' drug laws

– ran counter to deeply-held Dutch convictions that moral decisions in areas of so-called 'victimless crimes' are a private affair. In these cases, the driver of change was less the EU imposing change from the outside than the opportunities the EU created on the inside, serving more to empower groups from the inside supportive of change (Kurzer 2002).

EU moves to liberalise the provision of social services, moreover, have also had a significant impact on the Scandinavian countries generally, given their tradition of high paid, high quality public services, especially in contrast to, say, Belgium, Austria or Ireland, which have comparatively little in the way of public sector caring services. The recent services directive, that allows for competition between private and public caring services, is a challenge to the Scandinavian countries and has some worried about the development of a two-tiered system in which the rich go private and the public system therefore loses the kind of universal support necessary for its continued existence.

But whereas directives at least give small countries an opportunity to have a say in the decisions, given their seat at the Council table, in the COREPER, and in comitology, ECJ decisions do not. And recent cases have hit the smaller countries very hard, in particular where they jeopardise national industrial relations systems by limiting social rights such as the right to strike or national education and health systems by upholding market-based rights of free movement. The Laval case – which pitted labour's right to strike against businesses that pay and protect posted workers less against businesses' freedom of movement – directly affects Denmark and Sweden. This is because the ruling mainly applies to countries without laws governing all business pay and protection, and thus it hits the long-standing practice of autonomous business-labour negotiations in Denmark and Sweden, but not Finland or Norway (Dolvik 2008). This decision is a problem for Germany as well, however, which also has autonomous wage-bargaining, and no minimum wage in certain sectors, e.g. the construction industry. Other ECJ decisions like the Viking case – which effectively curtailed unions' right to strike in areas where it affects the free movement of business – have also been of greatest concern to Scandinavian countries (Höpner & Schäfer 2007). However, the ECJ's decisions, which uphold market-based rights of free movement, also undermine national education and health systems by imposing undue costs – e.g. Austria's resistance to the voiding of its admission restrictions on German medical students and Luxemburg's concerns about reimbursement for medical products purchased in Belgium in the eyeglasses case – and could threaten the very sustainability of small states' welfare states (Scharpf 2009).

New modes of governance

Finally, Europeanisation consists of 'softer' modes of governance – the so-called 'new governance' – and in particular the Open Method of Coordination (OMC) in social and employment policy based on self-set targets and voluntary compliance (De la Porte & Pochet 2002; Mosher & Trubek 2003). This can be seen as 'policymaking without policies' (Schmidt 2002a: ch. 2) given the vague language in which reform goals are set, such as 'flexibility' and 'employability', which allow for very different interpretations and policy programmes from one country to the next (Barbier 2008). Although the OMC has great potential in areas where national divergence makes EU-level decision-making difficult if not impossible, the very vagueness of the targets and the self-reporting nature of the exercise could mean that much of it may just be smoke and mirrors – as countries set National Action Plans (NAPs) that reflect what they are already doing. This is especially true for those countries such as Sweden or Denmark that are seen as models for the other countries on such things as labour market activation policy, female workforce participation, investment in education and/or in research and development.

Here, too, however, there are big differences among the smaller countries in terms of their scores, with the Scandinavian countries and the Netherlands high up there, even though Sweden has been cited for gender imbalance in certain sectors (mainly women in the public caring services), and the Netherlands for its low number of working hours per year. The problem with the OMC generally, however, is that it is often simply a government exercise, although some countries, like Belgium, have reportedly used it quite effectively to promote reform, in contrast with Germany, for example (De La Porte & Pochet 2005; Zeitlin & Pochet 2005). And yet, the possibility of 'naming and shaming' countries that don't make progress can be very potent, and possibly more in smaller countries where the media is likely to pay more attention to it.

Conclusion

Thus, while generalisations related to institutional, cultural and discursive characteristics are very important in trying to make sense of what makes small states successful, these take us only so far. Small West European countries are indeed smaller than bigger countries, which makes it easier for those that are culturally homogeneous to reach agreements among social partners when they are being cooperative, especially when the state, if unitary, can facilitate such cooperation or take action in its absence, and when ideas and discourse can be more reinforcing of the positive characteristics over time. But the identification of such characteristics is not on its own enough to enable us to explain small states' success. And it is certainly not enough to explain responses to the EU. Europeanisation has led to different responses from small countries, depending upon policy area and decision rules.

But despite the fact that we are left with no easy generalisations, it is clear that there is still something about these small countries in particular that makes their responses worth studying – if only because they are too often neglected in favour of the larger, and dare I say it, more predictable, member states.

7 The Small Corporatist Political Economies as European Socio-Economic Model?*

Uwe Becker and Kees van Kersbergen

The political economies of the small, largely corporatist countries analysed in the contributions to this volume have not been immune to the pressures to liberalise that have sprung up notably since the early 1990s. And indeed, liberalisation has taken place to differing degrees. The contributions also show, however, that this process has remained limited. The countries still reveal a high degree of corporatism, and their welfare systems are still considerably more generous than those in countries such as the US in particular, which approximates the liberal type of capitalism. Their labour markets as well as product and company markets are still far removed from the liberal ideal. The exceptions are Switzerland – which generally combines a strong liberal stance with corporatism – and Denmark due to their relatively flexible labour markets, while in Belgium corporatism has suffered due to Flemish-Wallonian tensions. But these exceptions do not change the overall picture.

The small corporatist countries have performed as well as or even better than the strongly liberal ones. With the exception of Switzerland, they have all had high rates of GDP growth per capita as well as per hour; all of them except Belgium have medium to high employment rates; their inequality and poverty rates are relatively low; their concern for the environment is more serious than average (but still not serious enough); and half of them belong to the most innovative – and in that sense most competitive – countries in the world. Table 7.1 summarises these facts. Moreover, measured in GDP per capita, these countries are richer than all the Anglo-Saxon countries except the US, and some of them roughly equal the US in GDP per hour. When it comes to specific aspects, other countries rank up there with the corporatist 'smalls' – the Anglo-Saxon economies except New Zealand with respect to economic growth; Germany, Japan and the US with respect to innovation and competitiveness;

and with respect to employment, the Anglo-Saxon countries and Japan. Nonetheless, the facts clearly demonstrate that top performances are possible without strong liberalisation. This is particularly true for the Nordic countries (except oil-rich Norway) which belong to the top performers in every respect.

Table 7.1 Economic performances (GDP and productivity growth), 1992-2006; innovative capacity and social indicators (employment, welfare) in the mid-2000s, ordered by most approximated variety of capitalism

Approximately Liberal			*Approximately Corporatist*		
H	M	L	H	M	L
-	CAN, CH, UK, US	AUS, IRL, NZ	DK, FIN, SE	A, GER, NL, N	B

Approximately Statist			*Approximately Meso-communitarian*		
H	M	L	H	M	L
-	-	F, ESP; very low: I	-	J	-

Against this background, we want to ask the question whether the 'smalls' (or at least some of them) qualify as an example of a corporatist European social model (ESM). Since the EU summit in Lisbon in 2000, the ESM has become a hot topic in the ongoing political discussion over the future of work, welfare and competitiveness and whether or not European political economies and welfare systems should move in a liberal direction. The latter has been advised by among others the OECD to meet the challenges of increasing global competition. This has particularly been addressed to European countries that have recently had relatively low employment/high unemployment and low rates of GDP growth, like the bigger countries of France, Germany and Italy. Many European interest organisations and political parties do not want to make the liberal move, however, because of its costs in terms of poverty, material inequality and social insecurity. These groups have therefore launched the European Social Model as an alternative. With the severe financial and economic crisis since 2008, the ESM has gained in importance.

In this concluding chapter, we will briefly clarify the meaning of the concept of a European social model before proposing that it be replaced with the European socio-economic model (ESEM) in the sense of capitalist varieties as described in preceding chapters. Thereafter we will discuss whether and in what respects the small, largely corporatist political economies fulfil the role as example of the ESEM. Finally, we look for the conditions necessary for realising such a model. These are not new questions but we want to bring them together and ask them in the context of the analysis of recent socio-economic performances (most previous studies were published around the turn of the millennium). Moreover, we not only want to stress the importance of the competitiveness of a socio-economic model, we genuinely want to consider it. This aspect, generally the broader varieties of capitalism perspective and the decidedly comparative character of our argument are the *differentia specifica* of this contribution.

The European social model and the European socio-economic model

Very early ideas of a sort of social model for Europe had already been formulated by Guy Mollet back in 1956 (Scharpf 2002: 646) – in a context still considerably determined by the post-Great Depression and post-war ideological climate of that time and before the current national welfare states had taken shape. The theme only returned to the agenda when, in the 1980s and 1990s, the process of European integration had reached the stage where the Single European Market (SEM) was to be realised. Against this background, Jacques Delors, the chairman of the European Commission, launched the idea of a European social model, the main feature of which would have to be its difference with the American model (Jespen & Serrano Pascual 2005: 234) – an aspect that has remained central to the concept ever since. The European Commission's 1994 *White Paper on Social Policy* was also important in this regard, as it defined the ESM as a set of common values including equal opportunities for all, social dialogue, social security and solidarity, in addition to the commitment to democracy and personal freedom.

In the Lisbon Treaty of 2000, then, the scope of the ESM was broadened by stressing research and education and by integrating innovation and competitiveness. European economics would have to be social as well as competitive and provide for sustained economic growth and employment in accordance with environmental objectives. This broader concept – which was, in fact, already a move in the direction of the ESEM – is also reflected in the relevant literature at that time (Esping-Andersen 1999; Ferrera et al. 2001; Black 2002; Scharpf 2002; Whitehead 2003). Also worth mentioning is Anthony Giddens (2006) who, in line with the New Labour philosophy, pleaded for a reformed European social model where individual responsibility and flexibility also have an important place. In sum, what a European socio-economic model achieves, apart from democratic goals, is the combination of:

- high employment;
- generous but conditional benefits for those who have lost their jobs or are unable to work;
- limited material inequality (also between the sexes) and a reasonable equality of condition;
- competitiveness and sustained economic growth;
- protection of the natural environment.

The discussion on the ESM is sometimes somewhat elusive because it is not always clear whether the authors are arguing about empirical reality or a normative model. Empirically, *the* ESM does not exist. Compared with the Anglo-Saxon world, particularly the United States, the common features of continental European political economies might be their higher degree of reliance on the state and less emphasis on individual responsibility. For the rest, however, it is diversity that is colouring the picture.

Geographically, this empirical diversity is somewhat patterned. Roughly, one can distinguish five groups of countries with similar political economies:

- The UK and Ireland, which have already been considerably liberalised, particularly the former (see Tables 1.5a and 1.5b in the introduction to this volume), and approximate the liberal type as defined in the Introduction.
- The Scandinavian countries, with their large public sectors and relatively generous benefits, which approximate the social democratic sub-variety of the corporatist type.
- The 'Rhineland' group (bordering the Rhine including the entire Benelux) plus (also relatively corporatist) Germany and rather statist France. These countries, except Switzerland, combine medium-high employment with relatively generous welfare benefits.
- The Mediterranean countries, which approximate clientelist sub-varieties of statism, with lower but rising welfare benefits and, except in Portugal, a low employment rate.
- The Eastern Europe political economies, which are less consolidated and currently can be sub-divided into two groups: one, including the Czech Republic, Slovakia, Slovenia, Hungary and Poland, that is mov-

ing in the direction of the 'Rhineland' countries and another group (the Baltic states) that is taking the liberal world as their example.

Since the ESEM is not an empirical reality, it must be a normative entity – a model in the proper sense; something we highly value and that *ought to be realised* because it meets our goals. Here, the relevant goals are those formulated in the Lisbon Treaty and similar ones. Such a model might be constructed by mixing elements from several empirical political economies with newly invented ones, but it can also be established by attaching normative status to one of the empirically given political economies/ welfare systems.

In this paper we do not want to go that far. We want to analyse the small countries' political economies and their accomplishments and ask to what extent they can serve as examples of a normative model for Europe. We would hesitate to answer this question positively with respect to all of the small, largely corporatist, political economies. All of them have a good system of social security, and their corporatist arrangements enable them mutually to adjust economic and social goals, but they are too diverse and not all of them perform economically well. Some of them – Austria, Belgium, the Netherlands and particularly oil-producing Norway – are considerably less innovative than others. Belgium is a low-employment country, the Netherlands only has a high employment rate because of its very large number of often tiny part-time jobs (although in principle, part-time work is a viable way of allocating scarce jobs), Austria has an extremely low employment rate of persons older than 55 years, and Switzerland has been a low-growth country during the period since 1990 and is a special case because of its protection of regional Swiss markets (cf. Schulte 2004). Finally, Norway's oil revenues give it special status and render it unsuitable for comparison or discussions of models.

What remains as a potential cohesive case for constructing the ESEM is Scandinavia (largely excluding Norway). Any perfect model case does not exist, but the Scandinavian political economies come closest to the goals mentioned above. Related to their still highly developed corporatism, they feature a form of stakeholder capitalism in which a comparatively remarkable level of co-determination is a sort of natural thing. In Denmark, Norway and Sweden it is most pronounced (as in Austria and Germany), and in Finland (as in the Netherlands) it is somewhat less developed (cf. Jackson 2005: 4). And more than any other region, Scandinavia combines competitiveness and social welfare with high employment for all demographic groups – in spite of the changes described in this volume – and also undertakes more-than-average efforts to protect the environment (which is also true for Austria and Switzerland).

In the past, Scandinavian political economies have more than once been assigned the status of model. In the 1970s and 1980s, Sweden and Denmark enjoyed considerable attention as models of a third way between capitalism and socialism. Because of its 'flexicurity', Denmark has been *the* model country since the mid-1990s, Finland (which together with Sweden experienced a severe economic crisis in the early 1990s) joined the models' club in the late 1990s at the same time that Sweden made a strong comeback. And while other countries fell into a period of stagnation in the years up to 2006, Scandinavia showed robust growth, moved up into the leading group of innovative countries, maintained its welfare state, and found its way back to high employment – although Finland and Sweden never returned to their 1980s levels. In the global financial and economic crisis that started in 2008, the Scandinavian economies have been hit as hard as or even harder than other Western economies (on an annual basis, Swedish GDP declined by 6.5% in the first quarter of 2009 – press release of *Statistics Sweden* on May 29) but these developments were not homemade and at the time of writing (late 2009) it is too early to evaluate them in comparative perspective.

Liberals are right in stressing that welfare benefits or income taxation should neither undermine employment nor competitiveness and that benefits should not be unconditional. They assume a trade-off between generous welfare systems, employment protection and progressive redistributive taxation on the one hand and the employment rate and competitiveness on the other. However, the Scandinavian political economies (and to a lesser degree those of the other countries studied in this book) appear to demonstrate that this assumption is not generally true, and show that economic and social targets are conciliable. We will have to see to what extent this also holds for economic and environment objectives.

Employment and social performance in international comparison

The high employment level is the most remarkable aspect of the Scandinavian political economies. With the exception of Finland, it is running at around 75% (see Table 7.2) of the working-age population (15 to 64 years of age). The only other countries to reach anything like this level are the Netherlands – although this is qualified by the very high number of part-time jobs – Switzerland and the Anglo-Saxon countries (Iceland, which is

Table 7.2   Employment rates (%)

| | Employment rate, 15-64 year | | | | | | FTE | Employment rate | | | SUR | LTU |
| | General | | | Women | | Women, PT | | 15-24 | 55-64 | PS | | |
	1983	1990	2007	1990	2007	2007	1999	2007	2007	2005	2007	2007
Australia	62,5	67,9	72,9	57,0	66,1	38,5	56	64,2	56,7	-	4,4	15,5
Austria	62,9	65,5	71,4	-	66,4	31,5	64	55,5	38,6	12,9	4,4	26,8
Belgium	53,5	54,4	61,6	40,8	54,9	32,9	53	26,8	33,8	18,3	7,5	50,0
Canada	-	70,3	73,6	62,7	70,1	26,1	63	59,5	57,1	-	6,0	7,5
Denmark	71,8	75,4	77,3	70,6	73,3	23,9	70	67,4	58,7	30,4	3,8	18,2
Finland	73,2	74,1	70,5	71,5	68,5	15,5	-	46,4	55,0	25,6	6,9	23,0
France	62,0	59,9	64,4	50,3	59,8	23,1	56	31,2	37,9	23,0	8,3	#42,2
Germany	62,2	64,1	68,9	51,2	62,9	39,2	59	44,9	52,0	11,1	8,4	56,6
Ireland	54,0	52,1	69,0	36,6	60,3	35,6	56	48,8	54,1	12,0	4,6	30,3
Italy	55,0	52,6	58,7	36,2	46,6	29,9	-	24,7	33,8	16,0	6,1	49,9
Japan	-	-	70,7	-	59,9	32,6	61	41,4	66,1	8,7	3,9	32,0
Netherlands	52,0	61,8	74,1	47,5	68,1	60,0	58	65,4	50,1	11,0	3,2	41,7
New Zealand	61,6	67,3	75,4	58,5	69,0	34,7	60	58,7	72,0	-	3,6	5,7
Norway	73,9	73,0	76.9	67,2	74,0	31,6	-	55,1	69,0	-	2,6	8,5
Spain	-	51,1	66,6	31,6	55,5	20,9	-	42,9	44,6	15,0	8,3	27,6
Sweden	80,2	83,1+	75,7	81,0+	73,2	19,7	66	46,3	70,1	31,7	5,1	13,0
Switzerland	-	78,2	78,6	66,4	71,6	45,6	-	62,6	67,2	-	3,6	40,8
UK	67,0	72,5	72,3	62,8	66,3	38,6	61	55,9	57,4	18,8	5,3	24,7
US	68,0	72,2	71,8	64,0	65,9	17,9	67	53,1	61,8	15,7	4,6	10,0

Note: PT = part-time; PS = public sector; FTE = full-time equivalent; SUR = standardised unemployment rate; LTU = long-term unemployment rate (≥ 1 year)

+ = statistical break after 1990

= 2006

Sources: OECD 2003: 175 and Statistical Annex ; OECD 2006a: Statistical Annex; OECD 2008a: Statistical Annex

also Scandinavian but very small, has the highest level). France, Italy and Belgium stand in strong contrast (although the percentage for Flanders is considerably higher than that for Wallonia), while Austria and recently Germany have established themselves in the upper middle band, reaching Finnish levels. The picture is similar with respect to unemployment, and here too Finland performs slightly worse than the other Scandinavian countries. Finland is still dealing with its economic collapse at the beginning of the 1990s when not only house prices and demand collapsed, as in Sweden, but also the immensely important Soviet market was for the most part lost. GDP fell and unemployment rose rapidly to over 20%. Since around 1995, Finland has improved continuously on all fronts (cf. Kiander 2005).

If one goes more into detail, it turns out that Scandinavian long-term unemployment is also much lower than in most European countries. Austria is an exception here, but many potential long-term unemployed are probably hidden due to the very high rates of early retirement there. This suggests that employment rates are more important indicators than unemployment rates, because in cases of high employment hidden unemployment in the form of early retirement and disability is naturally lower, as is the number of those discouraged from seeking employment. Furthermore, it turns out that the employment of women and of persons between 55 and 64 is also very high in Scandinavia – the latter nearly 50% higher than in Belgium, the Netherlands and Germany and about twice as high as in Austria, France and Italy (countries which were called 'pensioners states' by Esping-Andersen [1990] for this reason). As a consequence, problems with pension financing and unemployment among older workers in the Scandinavian countries are less severe than in the rest of Europe. Also, apart from Norway, the female part-time employment rate is relatively low, above all in Finland, thereby qualifying that country's somewhat lower employment rate. Given that the difference between women's and men's wages is smaller than the European average (cf. European Commission 2003), one may conclude that women have attained economic independence at least to some extent.

With respect to part-time work, the Netherlands and Switzerland are contrasting cases. Part-time jobs are often related to a lack of child care, and perhaps they might be part of an employer's strategy to create flexibility without changing the law. In a less work-centred society – a classification particularly true for the Netherlands; in Switzerland the working week is considerably longer – it could also be the basis for a focus on other objectives, provided that this society is able to stay productive and competitive. Perhaps less emphasis on work and GDP growth could be another feature of a future ESEM.

Alongside and in connection with high rates of female employment, the employment of almost one third of all working people in the public sector (in Finland one quarter) is the most characteristic feature of the Scandinavian political economies. Most women are employed in this sector, particularly in labour-intensive health care, social services and education (one occasionally hears the expression 'state feminism' in this connection). While in the US low-paid service jobs are at the basis of the high employment rate and while in the Netherlands it is part-time work, high employment rates in Scandinavia stem from the large number of public jobs.

The data in Table 7.3 show that the percentage of limited employment contracts (temporary work) in Scandinavia is not lower than the continental European average (leaving apart the extremely high Spanish percentage). One could however add that this has, together with the percentage of part-time work, gone down during the past decade in Denmark, Finland and Norway. This is also true for Switzerland. In most other West European countries, the percentage has risen – this was also the case in Sweden – while it has remained low in the Anglo-Saxon world (Canada is the exception). It seems that employers regard flexwork as less necessary when dismissal rules are flexible. By contrast, the low-wage sector is big in the Anglo-Saxon countries and small, even if it has slightly increased, in Scandinavia. One could add that a small low-wage sector is of course part of the 'Nordic model'.

The employment-centred welfare state is supported by social benefits and a tax policy based on the principle of equality of condition. For 'social citizenship', this equality of condition is more important than the equality of opportunity as stressed by liberalism. The Scandinavian political economy and welfare philosophy imply the approval of the market – with the exception of Norway in the 1920s, revolutionary socialism has always been weak – but it is also critical of it. Corrections in accordance with the equality principle are considered essential (Esping-Andersen 1985). Social benefits are therefore high, income taxes progressive, and both together have a greater redistributive effect than the social systems of almost all other countries (cf. the first two columns in Table 7.3).

Denmark is the most egalitarian country in social terms, followed by Sweden and, trailing at some distance, Finland and Norway. Outside the

Table 7.3   Basic social data

	Temporary work (%)		Low-wage sector (%)		Gini coefficient		Decile ratio 9/5	Poverty rates# (%)	Replace- ment rates* 2004 Start 60 months		Employment protection** (index)
	1994	2004	1994	2004	mid-90s	mid-00s	2006	mid-2000s			2003
Australia	-	-	13,5	13,6	0,309	0,301	1,90	12,4 / 1,0	45/ n	46	1,2
Austria	6,0	8,9	-	-	0,251	0,265	-	6,6 / 1,9	63/ 9	57	2,2
Belgium	5,1	8,7	13,3	12,5	0,268	0,271	-	8,8 / -0,3	61/ u	61	2,5
Canada	11,3	12,8	22,3	22,3	0,283	0,317	1,87	12,0 / 2,5	63/ n	48	0,8
Denmark	12,0	9,8	7,3	9,3	0,221	0,232	1,73	5,3 / 0,6	70/48	70	1,8
Finland	18,3	16,2	-	-	0,228	0,269	1,75	7,3 / 2,4	70/23	65	2,1
France	11,0	12,3	13,9	14,0	0,281	0,281	1,98	7,1 / -0,4	75/23	57	2,9
Germany	10,3	12,2	11,6	15,8	0,278	0,298	1,73	11,0 / 2,5	69/12	66	2,5
Ireland	9,5	3,5	23,5	13,7	0,349	0,328	2,05	14,8 / 4,4	49/15	64	1,3
Italy	7,3	11,9	8,1	7,5	0,348	0,352	-	11,4 / -2,8	54/ 6	22	2,4
Netherlands	10,9	14,6	11,0	16,6	0,282	0,271	1,76	7,7 / 0,6	74/24	66	2,3
New Zealand	-	-	14,5	14,7	0,335	0,335	1,79	10,8/ 2,4	56/ n	54	1,5
Norway	12,9	9,9	-	-	0,256	0,276	1,47	6,8 / - 0,3	68/36	56	2,6
Spain	33,7	30,4	17,7	15,2	0,319	0,319	2,14	14,1 / 1,9	67/21	49	3,1
Sweden	14,6	15,1	5,7	6,4	0,211	0,234	1,67	5,3 / 1,7	75/28	63	2,6
Switzerland	12,9	12,3	-	-	-	0,276	1,81	8,7 / 1,2	77/24	69	1,6
UK	6,5	5,7	19,5	23,4	0,354	0,335	1,98	8,3 / -1,5	54/ 6	53	1,1
US	-	4,0	25,1	23,3	0,361	0,381	2,30	17,1 / 0,4	54/ 6	36	0,7

= 60% of median income. The figure after the dash gives the change in percentage points since the mid-1990s.

* Average of different household types/income groups. The first column gives the replacement rate at the start of unemployment, and the duration of the payment of benefits (n = no specific rules; u = unlimited); the second column gives the percentage of last-earned income to be received as unemployment/social benefits after 60 months of unemployment.

** The higher the value (maximum 6), the stricter the protection.

Sources: Förster & Mira d'Ercole 2005; OECD 2006a (wage replacement); OECD 2004b (level of employment protection); Begg et al. 2007: 100 (deciles); OECD 2008c: 53 (Gini), 127 (poverty)

Nordic region, Austria and the Netherlands are at a level comparable to that of the latter two Nordic countries. The situation concerning poverty is similar, although in the Netherlands as well as in Belgium and Switzerland the rates are higher. Poverty in Denmark, Finland and Sweden has, however, followed the international trend and, accompanied by modest cuts in social benefits (Korpi & Palme 2003), has increased since the mid-1990s. Importantly, however, child poverty has constantly remained low, a feature that according to Esping-Andersen (2007: 643f) is causally related to female employment.

Table 7.3 lists the wage replacement rates of social benefits. These are no longer significantly higher than in some other countries in Europe, although the Danish top rate of 90% for lower incomes is achieved nowhere else. However, it is the whole package of social benefits and services that is important. This includes the extensive public childcare facilities such as day-care centres, after-school day-care and other possibilities to remain in school after hours, available to almost half of all children. In a broader sense, the school and training system also belongs to social services. The international PISA studies, comparatively testing intellectual capacities of fifteen year old pupils, regularly report on the high quality of these systems. Finally, employment protection belongs to social services, since it indicates the extent to which labour has become a commodity. With the exception of Denmark and, with qualifications, Finland, the figures for Nordic countries (the data in the table are compiled from several components) are not much different from the continental European average, which is described by liberal critics as both rigid and an obstacle to growth and employment.

Danish 'flexicurity', more extensively described in Mailand's contribution to this volume, deserves special attention again. It is a system that combines relaxed employment protection, high wage replacement rates in the case of unemployment, and the obligation of the unemployed to participate in retraining. In 2004 the Danish prime minister proudly announced that 'by international standards, we have a very flexible labour market. It is actually highly praised abroad and the envy of many other countries (...). It is, however, only possible because we have a high level of social security' (Bredgaard et al. 2005: 21). Indeed, in a broad international comparison of the connection between labour market structure, social security and employment, Denmark came out as the 'best case' (Bradley & Stephens 2007: 1505).

The basic form of this system has existed since 1994 and has been modified several times. A further element of this system comprises special leave of up to one year for educational or parental purposes (up to 1999 there was also a sabbatical year in the strict sense of the term), with job retention and payment of (currently no more than) 60% of the wage replacement given in the case of unemployment. Eligibility requirements are a minimum age of 25 years and several years of employment experience. In the international discussion on flexicurity, leave schemes are barely mentioned – perhaps because in contrast to the looser employment protection it is costly and does not fit in the dominant paradigm. However, it is a central element because many unemployed take up jobs left temporarily vacant by those on special leave (on this set of issues as a whole, see Compston & Madsen 2001; Abrahamson 2006).

The last relatively positive performance – with the emphasis on relative – of the Nordic countries to be mentioned regards the environment. Possible indicators we can use are the 'ecological footprint' (GFN 2006), which is a measure of human demand on the Earth's ecosystems (expressed in hectares per capita), and the Environmental Performance Index (EPI 2008) which includes indicators such as biodiversity and the use of forests. The EPI favours countries with a low population density. Thus the densely populated, geographically monotonous Netherlands, while boasting a small ecological footprint, is a laggard in terms of its EPI score (ranked number 55 with a score of 78.4, while much bigger polluters such as the US and Australia are ranked 39 and 41 respectively with scores of 81.0 and 79.8; Switzerland, ahead of Norway, Sweden, Finland and Austria, is ranked #1 with a score of 95.5). Alternative indicators are data on emissions of pollutants such as CO_2, sulphur and nitrogen oxides (cf. Becker 2009: 165). They do not take into account, however, what a country is specialised in in the international division of labour. Because of its specialisation in minerals, sparsely populated Australia is polluter number one, but its ecological footprint and its value in the EPI makes it comparable to the Nordic countries. Table 7.4 (ibid: 131) which summarises pollution data therefore has to be taken with a grain of salt. Nonetheless, it is not

Table 7.4   Summarised ranking of polluters

Very High	AUS, CAN, US
High	NZ, ESP
Medium	B, FIN, GER, IRE, I, NL
Relatively Low	A, DK, F, J, N, SE, UK
Lowest	CH

far-fetched to say that Switzerland and the Nordic countries (with Finland as slight exception) are environmentally speaking the cleanest in the economically developed world. Britain, France and Japan also belong to the group of relatively low polluters (leaving aside nuclear energy). The biggest polluters are the strongly liberal countries (except Britain).

Criticisms

One of the most criticised aspects of the Nordic political economies is their high public sector employment and the costs related to this. High public spending and taxes are generally a thorn in the side of liberals, but high public sector employment in Scandinavia is perceived as a particularly egregious example of inefficiency. According to recent ECB data, the Swedish public sector was half as efficient as that of the US, and the Danish public sector is not much better (*The Economist*, 9 September 2006: 27). Even if this is the case, one might ask whether public sector employment could be justified for the sake of employment – at least as long as the market sector remains in a position to pay for it. After all, unemployment is not cost-free, and public employment of the Scandinavian sort also guarantees poorly qualified workers an honest income. Efficiency is a necessary economic criterion, but not the only one. And the ideological dominance of social democracy – even if social democrats currently are not in power – means that considerable weight is given to social criteria.

A further point of criticism is the high level of sick leave in Scandinavia, particularly in Sweden, which is also said to illustrate inefficiency and to distort employment levels. In fact, Sweden loses 26 days due to sick leave per year and employee, Norway 21, and Finland 15. Not far behind these frontrunners are Belgium and France with 16 days, the Netherlands with 14 and the UK with 13 days, while Denmark, with an average of 'only' 10 days, is at the same level as Austria. Sick leave is even lower in the US (9 days), Germany (8), Switzerland (7), Italy (7) and Ireland (6) (Rae 2005a: 5). Looking for reasons for the high sick leave in notably Sweden, the cause must probably be sought in lax regulation. 'Getting sickness benefit appears to be much easier in Sweden than in other countries', writes Rae (2005a: 13). And perhaps a culture has grown in which sick leave is considered 'normal'. It does not appear to have much connection with the health of the Swedish people because, with an average of only three visits to the doctor a year (Rae 2005b: 13), they are among the most healthy in the world.

Above-average sick leave points to hidden unemployment and an inflated employment rate. For example, the Swedish total of registered unemployment and sick leave of a week or more is as high as the corresponding total in Germany, a much larger country in terms of population (Hesselius 2006: 28). Some form of hidden unemployment exists in virtually all countries, however. Often, early retirement takes large segments of people out of unemployment. Sometimes (as in the Netherlands and Italy) a disability scheme is doing this job, while in Sweden (where the number of persons unable to work due to disability has recently even been growing; cf. Hesselius 2006: 10f) and in Norway it is the high level of sick leave (and to a somewhat lesser degree also in Belgium, France, the Netherlands and the UK). Regarding Denmark, one might point to the above-mentioned special leaves of up to one year as a kind of hidden unemployment (purely in quantitative relation to employment and unemployment; apart from the fact that these leaves can be classified as socially desirable), while in the US it is the high number of persons incarcerated – 762 persons per 100,000 inhabitants, which is 1.4% of the labour force (Schmitt 2007: 3) and eight to twelve times higher than in Japan and the continental European countries (ICPS 2008). So, alongside the special case of Switzerland, only Finland remains as a country with a relatively high employment rate in which there is no category of hidden unemployment worth mentioning. Finnish employment, however, is somewhat lower than in the other Nordic countries, and overt unemployment is higher.

A final criticism concerns Sweden's overall economic performance. Thanks to its oil reserves, Norway is very rich, while Denmark belongs to the countries with the highest per capita income in the world. In the meantime, the former model country Sweden has been overtaken not only by some German *Länder* but also, if only slightly, by the UK, Ireland, Belgium, Austria and the Netherlands (*The Economist,* 9 September 2006: 26). And Finland, which never belonged to the richest countries, has almost caught up with Sweden. The criticism is justified, but the long process of Sweden's alignment to the average up to the beginning of the 1990s is less a sign of that country's decline and more a sign of the other countries catching up. The following years indeed illustrate a period of crisis – in 1992 alone, 600,000 jobs were lost (Plougmann & Madsen 2002: 6). Since about 1995, Sweden has, however, like Denmark and Finland, experienced an upswing that was only broken when a global crisis emerged in 2008. And in terms of competitiveness, it became stronger.

Competitive – even if with a little luck!

The Nordics are doing almost everything that, according to neo-classical textbooks, will lead inevitably to poor growth and reduced competitiveness: taxes are high, social services generous, the public sector is large and to some extent inefficient, wage dispersion is relatively flat, and employment protection is – apart from the special case of Danish flexicurity – by no means weak. Moreover, wage development is almost classically Keynesian, running parallel with that of productivity (on this point the situation in liberal countries such as the UK and the US is similar). The sole exception was Finland in the second half of the 1990s. Growth, competitiveness and employment have not suffered due to these 'sins'. All four countries are of course competitive in their own ways, although Norway, which is largely excluded here from our comparative analysis, is not competitive at all, apart from its oil and some other, smaller branches. This holds at least when competitiveness in technologically advanced markets – where the developed economies of the West and East Asia largely have to operate in – is understood as a country's capacity to: a) host and facilitate a relatively large number of innovative companies and primarily to export goods and services because of their quality and productivity in the sense of the product/price relation,[2] and b) acquire comparative advantages by specialising in the international division of labour.

Obviously, a country can maintain its competitiveness without excessive wage restraint of the Austrian or German (and, in earlier years, Dutch) variety. Decisive for competitiveness, alongside the very important factors of quality and specialisation, are unit wage costs as well as productivity development based on innovation. Disadvantages on the part of Denmark, Finland and Sweden are not apparent here – the two latter countries have even achieved particularly strong productivity gains. In addition, demand – both foreign and domestic – is important for economic growth and, as a consequence, for employment.

If one looks closely at Table 7.5, it turns out that there appear to be several ways to competitiveness and growth: via increased productivity per hour (UK, Sweden and the US 1995-2006), via wage restraint (Belgium and the Netherlands 1995-2000; Spain 1997-2006; Austria 2002-2006), and a combination of the two factors (Finland and Austria 1995-2001; Ireland 1995-2006; Japan 2002-2006). There are, of course, cases in which neither wage restraint (Germany and Italy 2002-2006), nor a combination of wage restraint and a strong increase in productivity (Japan 1995-2000) meet with success. The simple cause of this phenomenon could be that

Table 7.5 Basic economic data (percentages of average annual changes)

	GDP (per capita)			Productivity (GDP per hour)			Real wages		Unit labour costs		Private consumption	
	92-96	97-01	02-06	90-95	95-00	00-06	97-01	02-06	97-01	02-06	97-01	02-06
Australia	-	-	1,8*	2,0	2,5	1,5	1,9[#]	1,7[#]	-	-	-	-
Austria	1,4	2,4	1,3	-	2,1	1,0	0,5	0,5	-0,7	-0,9	1,7	1,4
Belgium	1,2	2,4	1,5	2,4	1,9	0,9	1,0	0,3	0,0	-0,9	2,3	1,3
Canada	-	-	1,7*	1,4	2,3	1,0	2,0[#]	2,5[#]	-	-	-	-
Denmark	2,2	2,1	1,6	2,7	1,1	1,0	1,7	1,9	0,3	-0,4	1,0	3,2
Finland	0,8	4,3	2,7	2,9	2,7	2,2	0,8	2,0	-1,3	0,3	3,2	3,5
France	0,8	2,4	1,0	1,9	2,1	1,4	1,2	1,4	-0,3	-0,1	2,8	2,2
Germany	0,9	1,9	0,9	2,9	2,0	1,4	1,3	0,2	-0,1	-1,0	1,9	0,1
Ireland	5,6	7,7	3,4	3,7	5,4	2,8	0,9	2,7	-2,7	-0,3	6,3	4,8
Italy	1,1	2,1	0,2	2,1	0,9	0,2	-0,3	0,6	-2,5	0,5	2,4	0,8
Japan	1,1	0,2	1,7	2,3	2,1	2,1	0,3	0,0	-0,4	-1,5	0,6	1,3
Netherlands	1,9	3,1	1,1	2,5	1,7	0,7	1,2	1,2	-0,4	-0,4	3,9	0,3
New Zealand	-	-	1,8*	0,9	1,4	0,9	-	-	-	-	-	-
Norway	-	-	1,8*	3,3	2,3	2,2	1,9[#]	3,3[#]	-	-	-	-
Spain	1,3	3,7	1,7	1,9	0,2	0,9	-0,3	-0,1	-0,7	-1,5	4,3	3,6
Sweden	0,7	3,1	2,7	2,0	2,4	2,9	2,6	1,8	0,7	-1,2	3,0	2,5
Switzerland	-	-	0,9*	-	1,6	1,1	1,0[#]	1,2[#]	-	-	-	-
UK	2,2	2,8	2,1	2,8	2,3	2,0	3,0	2,3	0,9	-0,1	3,9	2,7
US	2,0	2,4	1,8	1,1	2,2	2,1	2,4	1,6	0,6	-0,8	4,2	3,1

* 2001-2006

1995-2000 and 2000-2006

Sources: European Commission 2008: 139ff; OECD 2007a, 2008a: 359, 2008b: 14

additional factors, e.g. the costs of German reunification, have played a role and that in relation to growth, all ways have advantages and disadvantages which balance out in the final analysis.

The sole unambiguous (though by economic theory underrated) factor has been private consumption. When it is high, growth is also high. Some qualifications in relation to Denmark in the 1997-2001 period are needed, but French, Dutch, Austrian, Swedish, US, UK, Finnish, Irish and Spanish data verify this causal nexus. In all these cases – except for the UK, the US and Sweden – the increase in consumption is clearly higher than wage growth. Conversely, where private consumption increases only modestly, as in Germany and the Netherlands, economic growth is very low. Since wages and consumption are often disconnected, in the light of the above-mentioned thesis that several ways lead to economic growth, this is not necessarily a call for a Keynesian wage policy, but rather for paying attention to demand as an independent factor in macroeconomic processes.

The decoupling of wages and consumption since the mid-1990s means that consumers have been breaking into their savings or have increasingly been getting into debt. The latter has happened above all in those countries in which house prices have risen strongly since the mid-1990s – in the Anglo-Saxon countries, Scandinavia, and the Netherlands; at the end of the decade also in France, Italy and above all Spain (see OECD 2006c: 18) – and that offer the opportunity of tax relief on mortgage interest payments. This is the case in the US, the Netherlands (up to 100% tax relief) and to a lesser extent in the other Anglo-Saxon countries, Spain and Scandinavia. In this group, the sharp rises in house prices have not only resulted in a so-called wealth effect but also in the option of engaging in consumption with mortgage loans subject to tax benefits. This was taken up particularly in the Netherlands (see Becker 2005: 1092ff) as well as in the UK, Spain and the US, but also Denmark and Sweden.

House price trends and related demand bubbles have of course not been the result of wise policies. They have simply been favourable circumstances in which the Scandinavian countries shared – at least until 2008 when the bubble started to burst. It was also fortunate that Denmark found North Sea oil in the early 1990s, which accounted for a full percentage point added to GDP growth (Andersen 1997: 46). The image of quality attached to Scandinavian, particularly Danish products ('Danish design'), is a further element of fortune, even if it was hard work in the past that achieved it. As in the case of Swiss products, this reputation makes high premium prices possible (one might mention such products as Carlsberg beer, Bang & Olufsen or Lego) and positions the producers to some extent outside international competition. Finally, one can ask whether the rise of Nokia from an unknown TV and tire producer to global number one in mobile telephony is the product of the coincidence of a number of lucky circumstances.

This does not mean that politics has not been uninfluential. We have already mentioned the Danish reform programme of 1994, which introduced flexicurity with its three elements. Whether this promoted economic dynamism or not remains an open question, but it cannot be denied that it had some effect on employment (cf. Green-Pedersen & Lindbom 2005). And the fact that wages in the Scandinavian economies (apart from Finland 1996-2000) have risen more strongly than in the rest of the European continent is due not only to the higher level of unionisation but also to lessons learned in the crisis at the beginning of the 1990s, above all in Sweden and Denmark.

In these countries, too, particularly under pressure from the Maastricht criteria, most economists made the turn to neo-liberalism and monetarism, but Keynesian approaches receded later than in other countries, and never to the same extent (for Sweden, see Blyth 2002: ch. 7). Therefore, this had some influence on the analysis of this crisis, which was interpreted not only as a financial and debt crisis but also as a crisis based on inadequate private demand (Lindvall 2004: 118ff). The 1990 bursting of the house-price bubble and mortgage-induced demand in Sweden (and Finland and, to some extent, Denmark) had in any case demonstrated that demand should not be neglected. In Denmark, this led to an easing of interest rates in 1993, and in Sweden to debates on how demand could be stimulated and indirectly to the legitimation of union demands for considerably higher wage increases – though employers opposed this.

The latter was one of the reasons for continuing the break in the Swedish social partnership at the central level that had been triggered in 1988 by the trade union/social democratic plan to establish workers' funds. This break led to a form of social partnership fraught with strike action. In this respect, Scandinavian corporatism is far less friendly than that of the German-speaking countries or the Benelux states (cf. Aarvaag Stokke & Thörnqvist 2001: 249). It represents an interplay between open conflict and talking to one another, a constellation that could be called the consensualism of two strong partners.

Where the social partners do talk to one another, the topic of competitiveness is at the top of the agenda, above all in Finland (see Kettunen 2004) and Sweden (see Elvander 2002). The times in which competitiveness could be restored by means of devaluations of the national currency are over, due to the opening up of markets and accession to the EU. It is also clear that the expensive welfare state can be borne only by a highly productive private sector. These insights were translated into action and, as a consequence, the two countries find themselves highly ranked in the innovation league. R&D expenditure – at more than 4% in Sweden and 3.5% in Finland – is about double that of the EU average and considerably higher than that of the US (see Table 7.6). Denmark, which is rather reliant on small businesses, has less specifically designated R&D expenditures and has to rely more on informal innovation in the course of the work process. An important aspect of this is the importance attached to regular re-schooling/training on the basis of a high general level of education. In comparative perspective, Denmark – and to a lesser degree also Finland and Sweden – has a considerable edge in this respect (Gallie 2007: 92).

Denmark, not ranking at the top of the Innovation Index in the narrow sense, has recently been in the top five (third in 2007) of the World Economic Forum's Global Competitiveness Index, together with the US, Switzerland, Finland and Sweden. In the Innovation Index and in terms of patents – more specifically, Triadic Patent Families (TPFs), i.e. patents registered at all of the three main patent offices: those of the EU, Japan and the US – it does not belong to the top, but Finland and Sweden do, although Finland performs less in the patent field. In what is arguably the most comprehensive index – the European Innovation Scoreboard (EIS) – Denmark, Sweden and Finland belong once again among the top, together with Germany, Japan, South Korea (not mentioned in Table 7.6), Switzerland, the UK and the US – with Sweden ranking number one. In the EIS, five dimensions are used to determine innovative capacity: 1) the structural conditions for innovation, 2) R&D investment, 3) efforts towards innovation at the firm level, 4) value added in innovative sectors, and 5) results in terms of successful know-how.

One ought not to exaggerate the importance of these indices. Sometimes, as in the case of the World Economic Forum rankings, they are partially based on interviews and have a subjective dimension with often neo-liberal undertones. For another part they consist of input data such as the expenditures for education and R&D. Input does not necessarily say much about output, however. Nonetheless, the high rankings do demonstrate the attempts above all by Finland and Sweden to attain productivity growth by means of innovation. Real development in terms of productivity and unit wage costs (relevant data were presented in Table 7.5) attests to these efforts.

Table 7.6 Indicators of innovative capacity and competitiveness

	Spending on educational institutions as % of GDP, 2005	R&D spending as % of GDP, 2005	Employment in M&HT (%), 2003	Summary Innovation Index of the EIS, 2004, 2005 or 2006 (score and rank)	TPF per 1 mn in-habitants in 2005	GCI 2007 (score and rank)	BCI 2007 (rank)	Innovation Index 2007 (score and rank)
Australia	5,77	1,76*	-	0,36 (20)	20,2	5,17 (19)	18	4,41 (22)
Austria	5,49	2,42	5,2	0,48 (14)	36,5	5,23 (15)	8	4,76 (15)
Belgium	6,13	1,82	5,2	0,47 (16)	31,8	5,10 (20)	15	4,74 (16)
Canada	5,93	1,98	3,9	0,44 (18)	25,4	5,34 (13)	14	5,08 (12)
Denmark	7,01	2,45	5,6	0,61 (5)	40,5	5,55 (3)	5	5,11 (11)
Finland	6,13	3,48	7,0	0,64 (3)	50,3	5,49 (6)	3	5,67 (3)
France	6,31	2,13	5,4*	0,47 (16)	39,3	5,18 (18)	17	4,69 (17)
Germany	5,28	2,46	9,8*	0,59 (7)	76,0	5,51 (5)	2	5,46 (7)
Ireland	4,44	1,26	7,0*	0,49 (13)	14,2	5,03 (22)	24	4,54 (19)
Italy	5,05	1,10	6,5	0,33 (24)	12,2	4,36 (46)	42	3,45 (47)
Japan	4,77	3,33	7,3	0,60 (6)	119,3	5,43 (8)	10	5,64 (4)
Netherlands	4,99	1,78	4,0	0,48 (14)	72,6	5,40 (10)	7	4,88 (13)
New Zealand	6,84	1,15	-	-	15,7	4,98 (24)	22	4,09 (25)
Norway	6,56	1,52	-	0,36 (20)	24,1	5,20 (16)	13	4,60 (18)
Spain	4,71	1,12	5,0*	0,31 (26)	4,6	4.66 (29)	27	3,58 (39)
Sweden	6,74	3,89	7,2	0,73 (1)	72,3	5,54 (4)	4	5,53 (6)
Switzerland	6,54	2,93*	-	0,67 (2)	106,7	5,62 (2)	6	5,74 (2)
UK	6,09	1,78	4,8	0,57 (8)	26,4	5,41 (9)	11	4,79 (14)
US	7,46	2,62	3,8	0,55 (9)	55,2	5,67 (1)	1	5,77 (1)

* One year earlier

Sources: OECD 2007b: 50f and 38f for columns 1 and 2; Begg, Draxler and Mortensen 2007: 111 for column 3, *Employment in Medium and High Tech Manufacturing* (% of total employment); Pro Inno Europe 2007, Figure 1 for column 4 (*Summary Innovation Index* – scale 0-1 – of the European Innovation Scoreboard): OECD Science, Technology and Industry Scoreboard 2007/OECD database for column 5, *TPF (Triadic Patent Families)*; WEF 2007/2008 for columns 6-8: BCI (*Business Competitiveness Index*) 2007, GCI (*Global Competitiveness Index*) 2007 and *Innovation Index* 2007; all scaled 1-7.

Nokia's spectacular rise is an example of this and can be understood as something for which the way was paved both politically and by corporatism. Traditionally, Finland's economy has been highly dependent on the timber industry, and while this sector is still the strongest ICT is closing in on it. The ICT sector largely consists of Nokia, which only employs 1% of Finnish workers but accounted for 3% of Finnish GDP, contributed 20% to exports and carried out 35% of the country's R&D in 2002. These percentages do not include the performance of domestic suppliers (Moen & Lilja 2005: 359f; Etla 2003) and illustrate how much Finland depends on one company. In Sweden, the diffusion of economic strengths is much greater.

Nokia benefited from the European Commission's choice of GSM as the standard for mobile telephones. Even more importantly, according to Moen and Lilja (2005), the state as well as capital and labour in the 1990s have pointedly banked on innovation. The establishment of the corporatist Science & Technology Policy Council (STPC) in 1987 is a crucial date in this context, even if the concerted move towards high tech and innovation only took place under the pressure of the economic crisis in the early 1990s. Important activities started by the STPC have been the creation of an IT infrastructure, changes made to the education system, and the opening up of possibilities for international venture capital to invest in Finland. In the context of the general stock market euphoria in the second half of the 1990s, particularly regarding high-tech shares, the country became very attractive for foreign capital.

Conclusion and prospects for a European socio-economic model

With regard to competitiveness and employment, the West is currently confronting major challenges in the form of the rise of new economic powers such as China, India and Brazil, productivity increases exceeding GDP growth, and the relocation of simple work to low-wage countries. The neoliberal solution is to solve these problems by Americanisation – i.e. labour market flexibilisation, the extension of the low-wage sector, and related cuts in the social safety net. Alternatives include the Dutch part-time model and above all the Scandinavian or Nordic formula of high public employment. An important lesson from the Danish, Finnish and Swedish experiences is that the combination of extensive public sector employment, a generous welfare state, workers' rights, high employment protection, and wage increases tied to productivity is affordable when it is tied to a highly competitive market sector. With qualifications, one can say that, to a greater or lesser degree, Denmark, Finland and Sweden have managed to combine high employment, generous but conditional welfare benefits, limited material class and gender inequality, a reasonable equality of conditions, competitiveness, sustained economic growth, and the protection of the natural environment. In other words, if there is such a thing as an empirical basis for a normative European Social Model meeting the Lisbon criteria, for example, then its main characteristics can be observed in the Nordic countries.

Institutionally, Scandinavian capitalism is embedded in a social-democratic variety of corporatism – but this should not be misunderstood as an arrangement of milk and honey. The Swedish tension between labour and capital and the high level of Danish strike activity illustrate this. Nonetheless, society is involved at the macro-level of corporatism by the organisations representing capital and labour, and at the micro-level, employees are, with national variations, involved via co-determination, which provides this corporatism with a democratic flavour. This democratic component and its conditional character for the Nordic socio-economic performances make modern, pragmatic corporatism a good choice for a European socio-economic model, and its social democratic variety stressing equality of condition an even better choice.

Is there, however, any chance to bring strongly liberal or statist political economies onto the path towards corporatism, let alone social democratic corporatism? The installation of a formal-institutional framework would not be sufficient. In rudimentary form, France has such institutions (notably the *conseil du travail*), and Britain has tried them under Labour in the 1970s, but this did not make them countries approximating the corporatist type. Effective, as opposed to only formal-institutional, corporatism requires a high level of social trust, a discursive pattern of conflict resolution, the *norm* of finding compromises and a commitment to the common interest on the part of its players.

In countries such as Denmark and Sweden (Norway, the Netherlands and Switzerland could also be mentioned) – with the absence of deep, long-lasting cleavages in their history and with their evolutionary processes of democratisation – effective corporatism could develop over centuries. However, Finland as well as Austria, with their repressive and revolutionary past, show that, under certain conditions, effective corporatism can develop within a few decades (cf. Smallcons 2003: ch. 6 and 7). To some degree, its emergence in these countries was also the result of institutional learning – learning from relevant neighbours by the political administration that subsequently pushed the country in a corporatist direction, with capital and labour accepting and then embracing this turn. The Finnish and Austrian cases could be important examples for political economies where a majority of the population and a large part of the relevant political players feel unsatisfied with the current situation and would like to change the institutional structure. With a slight affinity with consensualism as a starting point, such change is perhaps possible – even if at this moment it is difficult to imagine that countries with a rather confrontationalist political culture, such as that of France, or with a culture of individual competition tending towards anti-statism, like that of the UK, would move this way.

Another condition of effective corporatism is a certain balance of power between capital and labour. When one part is structurally weaker than the other, the existence of corporatism is in danger. This balance is difficult to accomplish, but with strong unions critically accepting capitalism, the Nordic countries have demonstrated its feasibility. In recent decades, this balance has been under pressure. The abolition of international trade barriers, the creation of the Single European Market and Europeanisation (see chapters 1 and 6), the emergence of the internet and the hardening of global competition have forced capital to become more mobile and at the same time rendered mobility possible (though it is far from unlimited). Capital mobility and perhaps even more the bare threat of investing abroad has recently tended to be a stronger power resource than the organisational strength of trade unions in many countries. To this redistribution of power resources one has to add that, because of social-structural individualisation and the attractiveness of neo-liberalism for some strata of wage-earners, unions have also weakened from within. A partial remedy against this changing power relations could perhaps be the enhancement of the 'fitness' of the labour force in terms of general and specific qualification. Capital depends on this 'fitness'.

The current global economic crisis, the consequences of which will probably last for some years, might be a moment of change, however. For the time being, capital has become more dependent on the state than vice versa, the failure of exaggerated liberalisation might trigger some ideological change, and unions outside the Nordic region (where they have barely declined in numbers) might regain some of the strength of earlier years. Long-term processes such as social-structural individualisation will not stop, however, and the same is true for capital mobility (unless countries become more protectionist). Factors favourable for neo-liberalism will therefore remain effective. So it is difficult to render the institutional mix of European capitalism *more* corporatist, but for a number of political economies (think of Germany, Ireland, perhaps Italy) it does not seem impossible in the years to come. Some authors (e.g. Zeitlin 2005) think that the European Union can play an important role in this respect, notably via the Open Method of Coordination (OMC) where possible options for socio-economic improvement are discussed at the central level and sent for consideration to the member states. Sovereignty in socio-economic affairs rests, however, at the national level and the soft decision-making process of the OMC has, as has been pointed out by other authors (e.g. Scharpf 2002; Schäfer 2004), only limited effectiveness. So, in the end, as Vivien Schmidt has indicated in the previous chapter, it is up to the member states whether or not to implement the recommendations of the European Commission.

What about the chances of realising the decidedly social democratic sub-variety of corporatism? Will populations outside Scandinavia pay the bill not only for social security but also for a high degree of material equality as well as extensive public employment? In recent years, in Denmark, Finland, Sweden and Norway these features have largely become decoupled from social democratic dominance in parliament, implying that maintaining 'social democratic corporatism' does not require a social democratic government. Independent from party-political commitments, it requires people who are willing to pay for this way, a stance one could call social individualism. Social individualism means that people are aware that they are social beings on the basis of which they would not only support the principles of individual responsibility and meritocracy, but also those of solidarity and collective responsibility for work and welfare. Is this feasible? Survey data (see the introduction to this volume) are mixed and do not allow us to offer a clear conclusion, but this might change if the overall ideological climate changes.

Whether this is going to happen is another question. In the first year of the Obama administration, there were indications of some movement away from strong neo-liberal individualism even in the US, but the distance in empirical terms between the US and social Northwest Europe is still enormous. In his second year Obama adapted to stronger conservative forces, however. And Europeans have recently given their vote to liberal and conservative (and even outspoken rightwing) parties – for example in the 2009 elections for the European Parliament. This can hardly be interpreted as support for social democratic ideas to restructure political economies. For its supporters, changing the ideological climate and the normative reference frame of macroeconomic action must be an important task in itself. In a context where (further) 'corporatisation' and 'social democratisation' are no real options, the discussion on the European socio-economic model Nordic style should perhaps first of all be seen as a contribution to this endeavour.

Notes

*   For critical suggestions we would like to thank Brian Burgoon and Barbara Vis.

1   This table is taken from Becker 2009: 130 and based on chapter 6 of that book.

2   Regularly, productivity is simply measured as pecuniary output per hour and does not necessarily reflect efficiency. When the oil price increases, but the number of hours Norwegians work and the quantity of exported oil remain constant, then Norwegian productivity rises. As a rule, however, western countries will have to increase their productivity by improving efficiency. A remedy against this could perhaps be the enhancement of the 'fitness' of the labour force in terms of the general and specific qualifications capital depends on.

About the Authors

Alexandre Afonso is a Max Weber Postdoctoral Fellow at the European University Institute in Florence, Italy. He received his PhD in political science from the University of Lausanne in June 2010, and has been a visiting researcher at AIAS, University of Amsterdam, between 2008 and 2010. His fields of research include comparative political economy, industrial relations, European integration, welfare state reform, labour market policies, interest groups and labour migration policy. His work has been published in the *European Journal of Industrial Relations, Social Policy and Administration, Policy and Politics* and the *Swiss Political Science Review*. Besides working on the publication of a revised version of his dissertation, he is developing a new research project entitled "The Polanyian politics of European integration", which investigates national policy responses to the integration of labour markets in the European Union.

Uwe Becker is associate professor in Political Science at the University of Amsterdam. He has been a visiting scholar at i.a. the European University Institute, the Wissenschaftszentrum Berlin and the Center for European Studies at Harvard University as well as coordinator of an EU-financed research project on *The Consensual Political Cultures of the Small West European Countries in Comparative and Historical Perspective*. His main fields of work are Comparative Politics and Comparative Political Economy, recently also including the so-called BRIC countries. He has published in journals such as *Politics & Society, Journal of European Social Policy, Journal of European Public Policy, New Political Economy, Socio-Economic Review* and *Review of International Political Economy*. Recent books include *Employment 'Miracles': A Critical Comparison of the Dutch, Scandinavian, Swiss, Australian and Irish Cases versus Germany and the US* (Amsterdam University Press 2005; ed. with Herman Schwartz), *Open Varieties of Capitalism: Continuity, Change and Performances* (Palgrave 2009) and *Het Obama experiment: Hoop in tegenslag* (Het Spinhuis 2010).

Hester Houwing is a scientific advisor at the Administrative Authority for Employee Insurances (UWV) in the Netherlands. Her fields of specialisation are 'flexicurity', flexible employment relations and social security. She studied sociology of labour markets and organisations at the University of Amsterdam, where she also defended her PhD thesis on *Flexibility and Security in the Dutch Labour Market* on 26 February 2010. After obtaining her PhD, Hester worked on a project for the European Commission on flexicurity and social partners at the *ReflecT Institute* of Tilburg University and at the Dutch Social and Economic Council, directorate of social affairs.

Kees van Kersbergen studied political science at the University of Amsterdam (the Netherlands) and Social and Political Sciences at the European University Institute in Florence (Italy), where he obtained his PhD in 1991. He has held positions as full professor at VU University Amsterdam and the University of Nijmegen. Currently he is professor of Comparative Politics at the Department of Political Science of Aarhus University in Århus (Denmark). His main research interests lie in comparative politics, comparative political economy and comparative political sociology. He is the author of *Social Capitalism* (1995) and winner of the Stein Rokkan Prize in Comparative Social Science. He has published in the *European Journal of Political Research*, the *European Journal of International Relations*, *Party Politics*, *Acta Politica*, the *Journal of European Public Policy*, the *Journal of Common Market Studies* and the *Journal of Theoretical Politics*, among others.

Karl-Oskar Lindgren is Assistant Professor of Political Science at Uppsala University. He is also affiliated as a research fellow at the Uppsala Center for Labor Studies (UCLS). His main research interests are in political economy, political representation and EU politics. He is the co-author of *Participatory Governance in the EU: Enhancing or Endangering Democracy and Efficiency* (forthcoming Palgrave MacMillan), and articles appearing in journals such as *Comparative Political Studies*, *European Union Politics*, *Journal of European Public Policy* and *Social Networks*. Currently, he runs a research project studying the political and economic consequences of the design of the unemployment insurance system.

André Mach is senior lecturer in comparative political economy and Swiss politics at the Institute of Political and International Studies (University of Lausanne). His areas of specialisation include comparative political economy, economic sociology, elites sociology, industrial relations, corporate governance, competition policy, interest groups, Swiss politics and the impact of globalisation on national politics and policies. He has recently published in *Business and Politics*, *World Political Science Review*, *Swiss Political Science Review* and *Journal of European Public Policy*. He is currently directing a three-year research project on Swiss elites called *Les élites suisses au 20e siècle: un processus de différenciation inachevé?* [Swiss Elites during the 20th Century: An Incomplete Process of Differentiation?], funded by the Swiss National Science Foundation (SNF).

Mikkel Mailand is head of research and associate professor at the Employment Relations Research Center (FAOS), Department of Sociology, University of Copenhagen. His present research interests cover employment policy, neo-corporatism, flexicurity, EU-level labour market regulation and public sector industrial relations. Among his publications are the book *Coalitions and Policy Coordination – Revision and Impact of the European Employment Strategy* (DJØF Publishing, 2006) and the journal articles "Different Routes, Common Directions? Activation Policies for Young People in Denmark and the UK" (*International Journal of Social Welfare*, 2004); "Social Dialogue in Central and Eastern Europe – Present State and Future Development" (*European Journal of Industrial Relations*, 2004); "The Uneven Impact of the European Employment Strategy on Member States' Employment Policies – A Comparative Analysis" (*Journal of European Social Policy*, 2008); and "The Common European Flexicurity Principles: How a Fragile Consensus was Reached" (*European Journal of Industrial Relations*, 2010).

Vivien Schmidt is Jean Monnet Chair of European Integration, professor of International Relations and Political Science, and chair of the Center for International Relations at Boston University. She has published extensively in the fields of European political economy, institutions and democracy as well as on institutional theory. Recent publications include *Debating Political Identity and Legitimacy in the European Union* (co-edited with S. Lucarelli and F. Cerutti; Routledge 2011), *Democracy in Europe* (OUP 2006), *The Futures of European Capitalism* (OUP 2002), *Welfare and Work in the Open Economy* (with F.W. Scharpf; OUP 2000), "Discursive Institutionalism", *Annual Review of Political Science* (2008), "Putting the Political Back into Political Economy by Bringing the State Back in Yet Again", *World Politics* (2009) and "Re-Envisioning the European Union", *Journal of Common Market Studies* (2009). Recent distinctions include an honorary doctorate from the Free University of Brussels, the Franqui Interuniversity Chair of Belgium, and Senior Visiting Scholar at the Free University of Berlin.

Kurt Vandaele is a political scientist and senior researcher at the European Trade Union Institute (ETUI) in Brussels, Belgium. The thesis for his PhD, obtained from Ghent University in 2004, examined the reasons for the relatively high union density found in Belgium. He has written a number of articles and book chapters on Belgium's trade unionism, industrial relations and social security system, in addition to which he co-edited the volume *Strikes Around the World, 1968-2005* (Amsterdam: Aksant, 2007). His current research is focused on industrial action in Europe, the 'organising model' and its rising influence in continental Europe, and the morphology of the trade unions in the new member states of the European Union.

Bibliography

Aanstad, S. and P. Koch (2005) *Foreign Takeovers in the Nordic Countries. Summary Report and Policy Recommendations.* FOTON

Aarbu, K.O. and T.O. Thoresen (1997) "The Norwegian Tax Reforms: Distributional Effects and the High-income Response". In: *Discussion Papers No. 207*, December 1997. Statistics Norway, Research Department. Oslo: Statistics Norway

Aarvaag Stokke, T. and C. Thörnqvist (2001) "Strikes and Collective Bargaining in the Nordic Countries". In: *European Journal of Industrial Relations* (vol. 7) (no. 3), pp. 245-267

Abrahamsen, P. (2006) "Welfare Reform. Renewal or Deviation?" In: J.L. Campbell, J.A. Hall and O.K. Pedersen (eds.) *National Identity and a Variety of Capitalism: The Case of Denmark.* Montreal: McGill University Press, pp. 356-374

Afonso, A. (2005) "When the Export of Social Problems is No Longer Possible: Immigration Policies and Unemployment in Switzerland". In: *Social Policy & Administration* (vol. 39) (no. 6), pp. 653-668

Afonso, A. (2007) "Policy Change and the Politics of Expertise. Economic Ideas and Immigration Control Reforms in Switzerland". In: *Swiss Political Science Review* (vol. 13) (no. 1), pp. 1-38

Afonso, A. (2010a) "Europeanisation, Policy Concertation and New Political Cleavages: The Case of Switzerland". In: *European Journal of Industrial Relations* (vol. 16) (no. 1), pp. 57-72

Afonso, A. (2010b) *European Integration, Corporatist Concertation and Labour Market Policymaking in Austria, Switzerland and Ireland.* PhD Dissertation, University of Lausanne

Aiginger, K. (1999) "The Privatisation Experiment in Austria". In: *Austrian Economic Quarterly* (vol. 4) (no. 1), pp. 261-70

Allard, G. (2005) "Measuring Job Security Over Time: In Search of a Historical Indicator for EPL (Employment Protection Legislation)". In: *IE Working Paper* nr. 17

Amable, B. (2003) *The Diversity of Modern Capitalis.* Oxford: Oxford

University Press

Anchordoguy, M. (2005) *Reprogramming Japan: The High Tech Crisis under Communitarian Capitalism*, Ithaca, NY: Cornell University Press.

Andersen, P. (1997) "Wonderful Denmark?" In: *CPB Report* 97/2, S. 46-47

Anderson, K.M. (2001) "The Politics of Retrenchement in a Social Democratic Welfare State". In: *Comparative Political Studies* (vol. 34) (no. 9), pp. 1063-1091

Andersen, T.M. and M. Svarer (2008) "Flexicurity – Labour Market Performance in Denmark". In: *CESifo Economic Studies*, doi:101093/cesifo/ifm015

Anxo, D. and H. Niklasson (2002) *The Swedish Model in Turbulent Times: Decline or Renaissance?* Labour and Employment Relations Association Series. Proceedings of the 59th Annual Meeting

Arbeids- og Sosialdepartementet (2005) *Country note* – Norway. Oslo: Arbeids- og Socialdepartementet.

Arcq, E. and P. Blaise (2007) *Les organisations syndicales et patronales.* Bruxelles: Centre de recherche et d'information socio-politiques

Armingeon, K., M. Gerber, P. Leimgruber and M. Beyeler (2007) *Comparative Political Data Set 1960-2006.* Bern: Institute of Political Science, University of Berne

Arnoldus, D., K. Davids, G. Vercauteren and I. Wijnens (2004) "De groei van de overlegeconomie in Nederland en België. Een overzicht van ontwikkelingen in het onderzoek". In: *Tijdschrift voor Sociale en Economische Geschiedenis* (vol. 1) (no. 1), pp. 76-109

Arnoldus, D. (2007) *In goed overleg? Het overleg over de sociale zekerheid in Nederland vergeleken met België, 1967-1984.* Amsterdam: Aksant

Asplund, R. (2007) "Finland: Decentralisation Tendencies within a Collective Wage Bargaining System". In: *ETLA Discussion Paper* No. 1077

Bacarro, L. (2003) "What is Dead and what is Alive in the Theory of Corporatism?" In: *British Journal of Industrial Relations* (vol. 41) (no. 4), pp. 683-706

Banfield, E. ([1958] 1970) *The Moral Basis of a Backward Society.* New York: Free Press

Barbier, J.C. (2008) *La longue marche de l'Europe sociale.* Paris: PUF

Becker, U. (2005) "An Example of Competitive Corporatism? The Dutch Political Economy 1983-2003 in Critical Examination". In: *Journal of European Public Policy* (vol. 12) (no. 6), pp. 1078-1102

Becker, U. (2007) "Open Systemness, Contested Reference Frames and Change. A Reformulation of the Varieties of Capitalism Theory". In: *Socio-Economic Review* (vol. 5) (no. 2), pp. 261-286

Becker, U. (2009) *Open Varieties of Capitalism. Continuity, Change and Performance*. Basingstoke: Palgrave Macmillan

Becker, U. and C. Hendriks (2008) "'As the Central Planning Bureau Says'. The Dutch wage restraint paradigm, its sustaining epistemic community and its relevance for comparative research". In: *Review of International Political Economy* (vol. 15) (no. 5), pp. 826-850

Beer, P. de and T. Schils (2009) "Introduction: achieving an optimal social policy mix". In P. de Beer and T. Schils (eds.) *The labour market triangle. Employment protection, unemployment compensation and activation in Europe*. Cheltenham: Edward Elgar

Begg, I., J. Draxler and J. Mortensen (2007) *Is Social Europe Fit for Globalisation? A Study on the Social Impact of Globalisation in the European Union*. Centre for European Policy Studies (CEPS). Brussels: European Commission

Benner, M. (2003) "The Scandinavian Challenge: The Future of Advanced Welfare States in the Knowledge Economy". In: *Acta Sociologica* (vol. 46) (no. 2), pp. 132-149

Berger, S. (2005) *How We Compete. What Companies Around the World are Doing to Make it in Today's Global Economy*. New York: Currency/Doubleday

Bergholm, T. (2007) *From Hesitation to Promotion – European Integration and the SAK*. Unpublished manuscript, University of Helsinki

Bertozzi, F., G. Bonoli, and B. Gay-des-Combes (2005) *La Réforme de L'état Social en Suisse. Vieillissement, Emploi, Conflit Travail-Famille*. Lausanne: PPUR

Blanchflower, D.G. (2007) "International Patterns of Union Membership". In: *British Journal of Industrial Relations* (vol. 45) (no. 1), pp. 1-28

Blom-Hansen, J. and C. Daugbjerg (1999)(eds.) *Magtens Organisering – Stat og interesseorganisationer i Danmark*. Århus: Systime

Blyth, M. (2002) *Great Transformations: Economic Ideas and Institutional Change in the Twentieth Century*. Cambridge: Cambridge University Press

Bocksteins, H. (2006). "Het collectief onderhandelen in cijfers". In: Cox G., M. Rigaux and J. Rombouts (eds.) *Collectief onderhandelen*. Mechelen: Kluwer

Bonoli, G. (1999) "La Réforme de L'etat Social Suisse: Contraintes Institutionnelles et Opportunités de Changement". In: *Revue Suisse de Science Politique* (vol. 5) (no. 3), pp. 57-77

Bonoli, G., and A. Mach (2000) "Switzerland: Adjustment Politics Within Institutional Constraints." In: *Welfare and Work in the Open Economy* (ed.) F.W. Scharpf and V. Schmidt. Oxford: Oxford University Press, pp. 131-173

Boréus, K. (1994) *Högervåg: nyliberalismen och kampen om språket i svensk debatt 1960-1989*. Stockholm: Rabén & Sjögren

Börzel, T. and T. Risse (2000) "When Europe Hits Home: Europeanisation and Domestic Change". In: *European Integration Online Papers* (EIOP) (vol. 4) (no. 15), http://eiop.or.at/eiop/texte/2001-006a.htm

Boyer, R. (2004) *Why and how capitalisms differ*. Working Paper. CEPRE-MAP, Paris

Boyer, R. (2005) "Coherence, Diversity, and the Evolution of Capitalisms – The Institutional Complementarity Hypothesis". In: Evolutionary and Institutional Economics Review (vol. 2) (no. 1), pp. 43-80

Bradley, D.H. and J.D. Stephens (2007) "Employment Performance in OECD Countries. A Test of Neoliberal and Institutional Hypotheses". In: *Comparative Political Studies* (vol. 40) (no. 12), pp. 1486-1510

Bredgaard, T., F. Larsen and P.K. Madsen (2005) "The Flexible Danish Labour Market". In: *Carma Research Papers* 2005:01. Alborg University

Bredgaard, T., F. Larsen and P.K. Madsen (2006) "Opportunities and challenges for flexicurity – Danish examples". In: *Transfer* (vol. 12) (no. 1), pp. 61-82

Bruff, I. (2008), *Culture and Consensus in the European Varieties of Capitalism*, Houndmills: Palgrave.

Bruno, M. and J. Sachs (1985) *The Economics of Worldwide Stagflation*. Cambridge: Harvard University Press

Campbell, J.L. (2004) *Institutional Change and Globalisation*. Princeton: Princeton University Press

Campbell, J.L. and J. Hall (2006) *The Political Economy of Scale and Nation, with Special Reference to Denmark*. Paper presented at the annual meeting of the American Sociological Association, TBA, New York, New York City Online. 2010-10-24 from http://www.allacademic.com/meta/p175811_index.html

Campbell, J., J. Hall and O.K. Pedersen (2006) (eds.) *National Identity and the Varieties of Capitalism. The Danish Experience*. Montreal: McGill University Press

Campbell, J. and O.K. Pedersen (2007) "The Varieties of Capitalism and Hybrid Success: Denmark in the Global Economy". In: *Comparative Political Studies* (vol. 40), pp. 307-333

Carlsson, R.H. (2007) "Swedish Corporate Governance and Value Creation: Owners Still in the Driver's Seat". In: *Corporate Governance: An International Review* (vol. 15) (no. 6), pp. 1038-1055

Cawson, A. (1986) (ed.) *Organised Interests and the State. Studies in Meso-corporatism*. London: Sage

Cerny, P. (2000) "Globalisation and the Restructuring of the Political Arena: Paradoxes of the Competition State. In: R. Germain (ed.) *Globalisation and Its Critics*. Houndsmill: Palgrave Macmillan, pp. 117-138

Christensen, P.M., A.S. Nørgaard, II. Rommertvedt, T. Svensson, G. Thesen and P.O. Øberg (2008) *What is Corporatism, and Why Should We Care? With Examples from Scandinavia*. Unpublished paper

Christensen, P.M., A.S. Nørgaard and N.C. Sidenius (2004) "Hvem Skriver Lovene?" In: *Interesseorganisationer og politiske beslutningsprocesser*. Magtudredningen. Aarhus: Aarhus Universitetsforlag

CoE (2003) *Recent demographic developments in Europe*. Council of Europe Publishing: Strasbourg

Compston, H. and P.K. Madsen (2001) "Conceptual Innovation and Public Policy: Unemployment and Paid Leave Schemes in Denmark". In: *Journal of European Social Policy* (vol. 11) (no. 2), pp. 117-132

Conway, P., V. Janod and G. Nicoletti (2005) "Product Market Regulation in OECD Countries: 1998 to 2003". In: *OECD Economics Department Working Papers* (no. 419). Paris: Organisation for Economic Cooperation and Development

Corporate Governance Committee (2003) *The Dutch corporate governance code. Principles of good corporate governance and best practice provisions*. Available at http://www.corpgov.nl

Corporate Governance Committee (2009) *The 2009 Belgian code on corporate governance*. Brussels: Corporate Governance Committee

Cowles, M.G., J. Caporaso and T. Risse (2001) *Transforming Europe: Europeanisation and Domestic Change*. Ithaca, NY: Cornell University Press

CRB (2008) *Technisch verslag van het secretariaat over de maximale beschikbare marges voor de loonkostontwikkeling. Volledig verslag*. 4 november 2008. Brussel: Centrale Raad voor het Bedrijfsleven

CRB (2009) *Analyse van de loonvormingsmechanismen in België. Resultaten van de enquête*. Brussel: Centrale Raad voor het Bedrijfsleven

Crepaz, M. (1994) "From Semi-sovereignty to Sovereignty. The Decline of Corporatism and Rise of Parliament in Austria". In: *Comparative Politics* (vol. 27) (no. 1), pp. 45-65

Crouch, C. (2005) *Capitalist Diversity and Change. Recombinant Governance and Institutional Entrepreneurs*. Oxford: Oxford University Press

Crouch, C. and W. Streeck (1997) "Introduction: The Future of Capitalist Diversity". In: C. Crouch and W. Streeck (eds.) *Political Economy of Modern Capitalism*. London: Sage, pp. 1-18

Csonka, A. (1992) *Når virksomheder rekrutterer*. København: Socialforskningsinstituttet

Culpepper, P. (2007) "Small States and Skill Specificity: Austria, Switzerland, and Interemployer Cleavages in Coordinated Capitalism". In: *Comparative Political Studies* (vol. 40) (no. 6), pp. 611

Daems, H. (1998) *De paradox van het Belgische kapitalisme. Waarom bedrijven financieel goed scoren en toch strategisch slecht spelen*. Tielt: Lannoo

Dagens Nyheter (1992) "Facken enade i massiv protest", 7 October

David, T., and A. Mach (2004) "The Specificity of Corporate Governance in Small States: Institutionalisation and Questioning of Ownership Restrictions in Switzerland and Sweden." In: Aguilera R., and M. Federowicz (eds.), *Corporate Governance in a Changing Economic and Political Environment. Trajectories of Institutional Change on the European Continent* . London: Palgrave, pp. 220-246

Debacker M., L. De Lathouwer and K. Bogaerts (2004) *Time credit and leave schemes in the Belgian welfare state*. Paper presented at the TLM.net conference. Antwerpen: Centrum voor Sociaal Beleid

Deeg, R. (2007) "Complementarity and Institutional Change in Capitalist Systems". In: *European Journal of Public Policy* (vol. 14) (no. 4), pp. 611-630

Deeg, R. and G. Jackson (2007) "Towards a More Dynamic Theory of Capitalist Variety". In: *Socio-Economic Review* (vol. 5) (no. 1), pp. 149-179

Delsen, L. (2002) *Exit polder model? Socioeconomic changes in the Netherlands*. Westport: Praeger Publishers

Deschouwer, K. (2002). "The color purple. The end of predictable politics in the Low Countries". In: P. Webb, I. Holliday and D. Farrell (eds.) *Political parties in democratic societies*. Oxford: Oxford University Press

Dice Report (2001) "Collective Bargaining Coverage in the OECD from the 1960s to the 1990s". In: *CESIFO Forum*. IFO Institute, pp. 2

DI & CO-industri (2007) Organisationsaftale om industriens kompetenceudviklingsfond. København: DI & CO-industri.

Dølvik, J.E. (2007) "The Nordic regimes of labour market governance: From crises to success story". In: *FAOS rådsprogram* 2006-08. Oslo: FAFO

Dolvik, J.E. (2008) "The Negotiated Nordic Labour Markets: From Bust to Boom." Paper presented for the Conference: "The Nordic Models: Solutions to Continental Europe's Problems?" Center for European Studies, Harvard University (Cambridge, MA, 9-10 May)

Dølvik, J.E. and F. Martin (2000) "A Spanner in the Works and Oil of Troubled Waters: The divergent Fates of Social Pacts in Sweden and Norway". In: G. Fajertag and P. Pochet (eds.) *Social Pacts in Europe – New Dynamics*. Brussels: ETUI

Dore, R. (2006/2007) "Japan's Shareholder Revolution". In: *CentrePiece* (vol. winter 2006/2007), pp. 22-24

Due, J., J.S. Madsen, C. Strøby Jensen and L.K. Petersen (1993) *Den danske model. En historisk sociologisk analyse af det kollektive aftale system.* København: DJØF

Due, J. and J.S. Madsen (2003) *Fra magtkamp til konsensus – arbejdsmarkeds pensionerne og den danske model.* København: Jurist- og Økonomforbundets Forlag

Due, J. and J.S. Madsen (2006) *Fra storkonflikt til barselsfond – Overenskomstfor-handlingerne 1998, 2000, 2004.* København: Jurist- og Økonomforbundets Forlag

Due, J., J.S. Madsen and A. Kolstrup (2005) *Overenskomsternes bestemmelser om efteruddannelse mv.* FAOS, Sociologisk Institut, Københavns Universitet

Dutch Ministry of Finance (2005) *De lessen uit de Nordics.* GT/BFB/0505

Ebbinghaus, B. (2002) *Varieties of Social Governance: comparing the social Partners' Involvement in Pension and Employment Policies.* Cologne: Max Planck Institute for the Study of Societies

EC (2007) *Towards Common Principles of Flexicurity. More and better jobs through flexibility and security.* Brussels: European Commision, DG Employment, Social Affairs and Equal Opportunities

Edbalk, Per Gunnar (2007) *Staten, arbetsmarknadens parter och sjukersättningen 1992-2005.* Working paper 2007: 2, Socialhögskolan, Lunds universitet

EIRO (2001) "Social Partners Agree Pension and Unemployment Insurance Reforms", December 5, http://www.eurofound.europa.eu/eiro/2001/12/inbrief/fio112120n.htm

EIRO (2005) "Austria: Industrial Relations Profile". *European Industrial relations observatory online*

EIRO (2006) "Union Crisis Puts Social Partnership At Risk". *European industrial relations observatory online* 2006 (5)

EIRO (2007) "Austria: Social Partners Agree to Minimum Wage Increase". *European industrial relations observatory online* 2007 (7)

EIRO (2008a) "High Pay Increases agreed in 2007 Sectoral Bargaining Round", January 14, http://www.eurofound.europa.eu/eiro/2007/12/articles/fio712049i.htm

EIRO (2008b) "European Court Ruling on the Laval Case Will Restrict Right to Industrial Action", March 10, http://www.eurofound.europa.eu/eiro/2008/01/articles/seo801019i.htm

EIRO (2008c) "Austria: Wage Flexibility and Collective Bargaining". *European Industrial relations observatory online* 2008 (3)

Eising, R. and N. Jabko (2001) "Moving Targets: Institutional Embeddedness and Domestic Politics in the Liberalisation of EU Electricity Markets". In: *Comparative Political Studies* (vol. 34) (no. 7), pp. 742-767

Elvander, N. (1988) *Den svenska modellen: Löneförhandlingar och inkomstpolitik 1982-1986*. Stockholm: Allmänna förlaget

Elvander, N. (2002a) "The Labour Market Regimes in the Nordic Countries: A Comparative Analysis". In: *Scandinavian Political Studies* (vol. 25) (no. 2), pp. 117-37

Elvander, N. (2002b) "The New Swedish Regime for Collective Bargaining and Conflict Resolution: A Comparative Perspective". In: *European Journal of Industrial Relations* (vol. 8) (no. 2), pp. 197-216

Encyclopedia Britannica Online, o.J., Chicago: Encyclopedia Britannica

Engelen E., M. Konings and R. Fernandez (2008) "The rise of activist investors and patterns of political responses: lessons on agency". In: *Socio-Economic Review* (vol. 6) (no. 4), pp. 611-636

EPI (2008) *Environmental Performance Index*. New Haven and New York: Yale and Columbia Universities. http://epi.yale.edu/Home

Esping-Anderson, G. (1985) *Politics Against Markets: The Social Democratic Road to Power*. Princeton, N.J.: Princeton University Press

Esping-Andersen, G. (1990) *The Three Worlds of Welfare Capitalism*. Cambridge: Polity Press

Esping-Andersen, G. (1999) *Social Foundations of Post-industrial Economies*. Oxford: Oxford University Press

Esping-Andersen, G. (2007) "Sociological Explanations of Changing Income Distribution". In: *American Behavioral Scientist* (vol. 50) (no. 5), pp. 639-658

Etla (2003) *Nokia in the Finnish Economy*. http://brieetla.org/_pdf/wef_rouvinen_yla-anttila_wireless_finland.pdf

Eurobarometer (2002) *Eurobarometer 56.1: Social Precarity and Social Integration*. Brussels: European Commission

European Commission (1994) *White Paper – European Social Policy: a Way Forward for the Union*. Luxembourg: Office for Official Publications of the EC

European Commission (2003) *The Social Situation in the European Union*. Brüssel: Europäische Kommission

European Commission (2003) *Implementing lifelong learning strategies in Europe: Progress report on the follow-up to the 2002 council resolution (Norway)*. Bruxelles: European Commission

European Commission (2008) *Spring Economic Forecasts 2008*. Brusssel, Directorate-General for Economic and Financial Affairs

Eurostat (2004) *Living conditions in Europe. Statistical Pocketbook, Edition 2003*. Brussels: European Commission http://epp.eurostat.cec.eu.int/cache/ITY_OFFPUB/KS-53-03-831/EN/KS-53-03-831-EN.PDF

EVS (1990) *European Values Studies, second wave 1990*. www.europeanvalues.nl

EVS (2000) *European Values Studies, third wave 1999-2000*. www.europeanvalues.nl

Faccio, M. and L.H.P. Lang (2002) "The Ultimate Ownership of Western European Corporations". In: *Journal of Financial Economics* (vol. 65) (no. 3), pp. 365-395

Falkner, G. and S. Leiber (2004) Europeanization of Social Partnership in Smaller European Democracies? *European Journal of Industrial Relations*, 10, (no. 3), pp. 245-266.

Falkner, G., O. Treib, M. Harlapp and S. Leiber (2005) *Complying with Europe: EU Harmonisation and Soft Law in the Member-States*. Cambridge: Cambridge University Press

Ferrera, M., A. Hemerijck and M. Rhodes (2001) "The Future of the European "Social Model" in the Global Economy". In: *Journal of Comparative Analysis: Research and Practice* (vol. 3) (no. 2), pp. 163-190

Fischer, A., S. Nicolet, and P. Sciarini (2002) "Europeanisation of Non-EU Countries: The Case of Swiss Immigration Policy Towards the EU" In: *West European Politics* (vol. 25) (no. 4), pp. 143-170

Fluckiger, Y. (1998) "The Labour Market in Switzerland: The End of a Special Case?" In: *International Journal of Manpower* (vol. 19) (no. 6), pp. 369-395

Fluder, R. and B. Hotz-Hart (1998) "Switzerland: Still as Smooth as Clockwork?" In: Ferner, A. and R. Hyman (eds.), *Changing Industrial Relations in Europe*. Oxford: Blackwell, pp. 262-281

Förster, M. and M. Mira d'Ercole (2005) "Income Distribution and Poverty in OECD Countries in the Second Half of the 1990s". In: *OECD Social Employment and Migration Working Papers* (no. 22) OECD.

Gallie, D. (2007) "Production Regimes and the Quality of Employment in Europe". In: *Annual Review of Sociology* (vol. 33), pp. 85-104

Genschel, P. (2002) "Globalisation, Tax Competition, and the Welfare State". In: *Politics & Society* (vol. 30) (no. 2), pp. 245-275

GFN (2006) *Ecological Footprint*. Oakland/Brussels/Zürich: Global Footprint Network, http://www.footprintnetwork.org/

Giddens, A. (2006) "A Social Model for Europe?" In: A. Giddens, P. Diamond and R. Liddle (eds.) *Global Europe Social Europe*. Cambridge: Polity Press, pp. 14-36

Goyer, M. (2006) "Varieties of Institutional Investors and National Models of Capitalism: The Transformation of Corporate Governance in France and Germany". In: *Politics and Society* (vol. 34) (no. 4), pp. 399-430

Green-Pedersen, C. and A. Lindbom (2005) "Employment and Unemployment in Denmark and Sweden: Success or Failure for the Universal Welfare Model?" In: U. Becker and H. Schwartz (eds.) *Employment Miracles. A Critical Comparison of the Dutch, Scandinavian, Swiss, Australian and Irish Cases versus Germany and the US*. Amsterdam: Amsterdam University Press, pp. 65-85

Gugler, K., S. Kalss, A. Stomper and J. Zechner (2001) "The Separation of Ownership and Control in Austria". In: F. Barca and M. Becht (eds.), *The Control of Corporate Europe*. Oxford: Oxford University Press, pp. 46-70

Hagberg, T., L. Jonung, J. Kiander and P. Vartia (2006) "Den ekonomiska krisen i Finland och Sverige". In: Aunesluoma, J. and S. Fellman (ed.) *Från olika till jämlika*. Stockholm: Atlantis förlag

Hall, P.A. (2007) "The Evolution of Varieties of Capitalism in Europe". In: B. Hancké., M. Rhodes and M. Thatcher (eds.) *Beyond Varieties of Capitalism: Contradictions, Complementarities & Change*. Oxford: Oxford University Press, pp. 39-88

Hall, P.A. and D.W. Gingerich (2004) "Varieties of Capitalism and Institutional Complementarities in the Macroeconomy. An Empirical Analysis". In: *MPIfG Discussion Paper* 04/5. Cologne: Max-Planck-Institut für Gesellschaftsforschung

Hall, P.A. and D. Soskice (2001) "An Introduction to Varieties of Capitalism". In: P.A. Hall and D. Soskice (eds.) *Varieties of Capitalism: Institu-*

tional Foundations of Comparative Advantage. Cambridge: Cambridge University Press, pp. 1-78

Hall, P. and R.Taylor (1996) "Political Science and the Three New Institutionalisms". In: *Political Studies* (XLIV), pp. 952-973

Hall, P.A. and K. Thelen (2009) "Institutional Change in Varieties of Capitalism". In: *Socio-Economic Review* (vol. 7) (no. 1), pp. 7-34

Halvorsen, R. and P. H. Jensen (2004) "Activation in Scandinavian Welfare Policy. Denmark and Norway in a comparative perspective". In: *European Societies* (vol. 6) (no. 4), pp. 461-483

Hancké, B., M. Rhodes and M. Thatcher (2008) (eds.) *Beyond Varieties of Capitalism: Conflict, Contradictions, and Complementarities in the European Economy*. Oxford: Oxford University Press

Hardiman, N. (2004) "Which Path? Domestic Adaptation to Economic Internationalisation in Ireland". Paper prepared for delivery to the National Meetings of the American Political Science Association (Chicago, Ill, Sept. 2-5)

Hauser, H. and S. Bradke (1992) *EWR-Vertrag, EG-Beitritt, Alleingang: Wirtschaftliche Konsequenzen für die Schweiz. Gutachten zu Handen des Bundesrates*. Chur Zürich: Rüegger

Häusermann, S. (2009) "Reform Opportunities in a Bismarckian Latecomer: Restructuring the Swiss Welfare State". In: Palier, B. (ed.) *A Long Good-bye to Bismarck? The Politics of Welfare Reform in Continental Europe*. Amsterdam: Amsterdam University Press

Häusermann, S., A. Mach, and Y. Papadopoulos (2004) "Social Policy Making under Strain in Switzerland". In: *Swiss Political Science Review* (vol. 10) (no. 2), pp. 33-59

Havik, K. and K. McMorrow (2006) "Global Trade Integration and Outsourcing: How Well is the EU Coping with the New Challenges?" In: *Directorate-General for Economic and Financial Affairs, Economic Papers*. Brussels: European Commission

Heemskerk, E.M. (2007) *Decline of the corporate community. Network dynamics of the business elite*. Amsterdam: Amsterdam University Press

Heidrick and Struggels (2009) *Boards in turbulent times. Corporate governance report 2009* http://www.heidrick.com/PublicationsRports/PublicationsReports/CorpGovEurope2009.pdf

Hemerijck, A. and I. Marx (2010) "Continental welfare at a crossroads. The choice between activation and minimum income protection in Belgium and the Netherlands". In: Palier, B. (ed.) *A long goodbye to Bismarck? The politics of welfare reform in continental Europe*. Amsterdam: Amsterdam University Press, pp. 129-155

Hemerijck, A., B. Unger, and J. Visser (2000) "How Small Countries Negotiate Change: Twenty-Five Years of Policy Adjustment in Austria, the
Netherlands, and Belgium". In: F.W. Scharpf and V.A. Schmidt (eds.)
*Welfare and Work in the Open Economy. Volume II: Diverse Responses
to Common Challenges.* Oxford: Oxford University Press

Hemerijck, A. and J. Visser (2000) "Change and immobility. Three decades of policy adjustment in the Netherlands and Belgium". In: *West
European Politics* (vol. 23) (no. 2), pp. 229-256

Hendriks, C. (2005) *Stability through change: towards indirect centralisation and coordination. Explaining the "relative stability" of Dutch
consensual corporatism.* Amsterdam: University of Amsterdam

Henrekson, M. (1996) "Sweden's Relative Economic Performance: Staying
on Top or Lagging Behind?" In: *Economic Journal* (vol. 106) (no. 439),
pp. 1747-1759

Héritier, A. (2001) "Differential Europe: New Opportunities and Restrictions for Policy-Making in Member-States". In: Héritier, A. et al. (eds.),
*Differential Europe: European Union Impact on National Policy-Mak-
ing* (eds.) Boulder, CO: Rowman & Littlefield.

Héritier, A., C. Knill and S. Mingers (1996) *Ringing the Changes: Regulatory
Competition and the Transformation of the State.* Berlin: De Gruyter

Hesselius, P. (2006) *Work Absence and Social Security in Sweden.* Department of Economics. Uppsala University, www.sns.se/document/
nber2_ph.pdf

Hirst, P. and G. Thompson (2000) "Globalisation in One Country? The
Peculiarities of the British". In: *Economy and Society* (vol. 29) (no.3),
pp. 335-356

Hohnen, P. (2002) *Aftale baserede skånejob – en kvantitativ analyse.*
København: Socialforskningsinstituttet

Hollingsworth, R. and R. Boyer (1997) "Coordination of economic actors
and social systems of production". In: J.R. Hollingsworth and R. Boyer,
Contemporary Capitalism. The Embeddedness of Institutions. Cambridge: Cambridge University Press 1997, pp. 1-47

Honkapohja, S. and E. Koskela (1999) "The Economic Crisis of the 1990s
in Finland". In: *Economic Policy* (vol. 14) (no. 29), pp. 401-436

Höpner, M. (2005a) "What connects industrial relations and corporate
governance? Explaining institutional complementarity". In: *Socio-
Economic Review* (vol. 3) (no. 2), pp. 331-358

Höpner, M. (2005b) "Politisch-institutionelle Determinanten aktionärs-
orientierter Reformen". In: *MPIfG Working Paper* 05/10. Cologne:
MPIfG

Höpner, M. and A. Schäfer (2007) "A new Phase of European Integration. Organised Capitalisms in Post-Ricardian Europe". In: *MPIfG Discussion Paper* 2007/4. Köln: Max-Planck-Institut für Gesellschaftsforschung

Houwing, H., E. Verhulp and J. Visser (2007) "Chapter 4: The Netherlands". In: *Flexibility and Security in Temporary Work: A Comparative and European Debate*. B.C.a.S. Sciarra. Catania. WP C.S.D.L.E. "Massimo D'Antona". INT-56/2007, pp. 59-78

Houwing, H. (2010) *A Dutch approach to Flexicurity? Negotiated change in the organisation of temporary work*. PhD Thesis, University of Amsterdam

Howell, C. (2003) "Varieties of Capitalism: and Then There was One?" In: *Comparative Politics* (vol. 36) (no. 1), pp. 102-124

Huber, E. and J.D. Stephens (2001) *Development and Crisis of the Welfare State*. Chicago: University of Chicago Press

ICPS – *International Center for Prison Studies 2008, World Prison Brief*. London: Kings College. http://www.kcl.ac.uk/depsta/law/research/ icps/worldbrief/wpb_stats.php

IMF (2007) *World Economic Outlook 2007. Spillovers and Cycles in the Global Economy*. Washington: International Monetary Fund

Immergut, E.M. (1992) *Health Politics: Interests and Institutions in Western Europe*. Cambridge: Cambridge University Press

ITUC (2007) *Where the House Always Wins. Private Equity, Hedge Funds and the New Casino Capitalism*. Brussels: International Trade Union Federation (www.ituc-csi.org)

Iversen, T. and J.D. Stephens (2008) "Partisan Politics, the Welfare State, and Three Worlds of Human Capital Formation". In: *Comparative Political Studies* (vol. 41) (no. 4/5), pp. 600-637

Jackson, G. (2005) "Employee Representation in the Board Compared: A Fuzzy Sets Analysis of Corporate Governance, Unionism and Political Institutions". In: *Industrielle Beziehungen* (vol. 12) (no. 3), pp. 1-28

Jensen, A.H. (2001) "Summary of Danish tax policy 1986-2002". In: *Working paper no. 2/2001*. Copenhagen: Finansministeriet

Jepsen, M. and A. Serrano Pascual (2005) "The European Social Model: An Exercise in Deconstruction". In: *Journal of European Social Policy* (vol. 15) (no. 3), pp. 231-245

Jones, E. (2008) *Economic adjustment and political transformation in small states*. Oxford: Oxford University Press

Jud, W. (1994) "Institutional Investors and Corporate Governance: The Austrian View". In: T. Baums (ed.) *Institutional Investors and Corporate Governance*. Berlin: De Gruyter, pp. 465-488

Kaahr, R. van het and M. Grünell (2004) *Occupational pensions and industrial relations*. www.eiro.eurofound.eu.int

Katzenstein, P.J. (1984) *Corporatism and Change: Austria, Switzerland, and the Politics of Industry*. Ithaca, London: Cornell University Press

Katzenstein, P.J. (1985) *Small States in World Markets: Industrial Policy in Europe*. Ithaca, New York: Cornell University Press

Kauppinen, T. (1994) *The Transformation of Labour Relations in Finland*. Helsinki: Ministry of Labour

Kenworthy, L. (2001) "Wage-Setting Measures: A Survey and Assessment". In: *World Politics* (vol. 54) (no. 1), pp. 57-98

Kenworthy, L. (2006) "Institutional Coherence and Macroeconomic Performance". In: *Socio-Economic Review* (vol. 4), pp. 69-91

Kettunen, P. (2004) "The Nordic Model and Consensual Competitiveness in Finland". In: Anders Castén et al. *Between Sociology and History. Essays on Micro-History, Collective Action, and Nation-Building*. Helsinki. SKS

Kiander, J. (2005) "The Evolution of the Finnish Model in the 1990s: From Depression to High-Tech Boom". In: U. Becker and H. Schwartz (eds.) *Employment Miracles. A Critical Comparison of the Dutch, Scandinavian, Swiss, Australian and Irish Cases versus Germany and the US*. Amsterdam, Amsterdam University Press, pp. 87-106

Korpi, W. (1983) *The Democratic Class Struggle*. London: Routledge

Korpi, W. and J. Palme (2003) "New Politics and Class Politics in the Context of Austerity and Globalisation: Welfare State Regress in 18 Countries, 1975-95". In: *American Political Science Review* (vol. 97), pp. 425-446

Kuipers, S. (2006) *The crisis imperative. Crisis rhetoric and welfare state reform in Belgium and the Netherlands in the early 1990s*. Amsterdam: Amsterdam University Press

Kurzer, P. (1993) *Business and Banking: Political Change and Economic Integration in Western Europe*. Ithaca: Cornell University Press

Kurzer, P. (2002) *Markets and Moral Regulation: Cultural Change in the European Union*. Cambridge: Cambridge University Press

Kux, S. and U. Sverdrup (2000) "Fuzzy Borders and Adaptive Outsiders: Norway, Switzerland and the EU". In: *Journal of European Integration* (vol. 33) (no. 3), pp. 237-270

Kvam, B. (2001) "Council of Nordic Trade Unions: Full Steam Ahead?" In: *Nordic Labour Journal* (vol. 6). Oslo: The Work Research Institute

Ladrech, R. (1994) "Europeanisation of Domestic Politics and Institutions: The Case of France". In: *Journal of Common Market Studies* (vol. 32) (no. 1), pp. 69-88

Larsen, K.A. (2006) Contribution to the EEO Autumn Review 2006 'Flexicurity'. http://www.eu-employment-observatory.net/

Larsen, F. and M. Mailand (2007) "Danish activation policy – the role of the normative foundation, the institutional set-up and other drivers". In: A.P. Serrano and L. Magnusson (eds.) *Reshaping Welfare States and Activation Regimes in Europe*. Brussels: P.I.E. Peter Lang

Lash, S. and J. Urry (1987) *The End of Organised Capitalism*. Madison: University of Wisconsin Press

Leboutte, R., J. Puissant and D. Scuto (1998) *Un siècle d'histoire industrielle (1873-1973). Belgique, Luxembourg, Pays-Bas: industrialisation et sociétés*. Paris: SEDES

Leimgruber, M. (2008) *Solidarity Without the State? Business and the Shaping of the Swiss Welfare State, 1890-2000*. Cambridge: Cambridge University Press

Levy, J.D. (2005) "Redeploying the State: Liberalisation and Social Policy in France". In: W. Streeck and K. Thelen (eds.) *Beyond Continuities. Institutional Change in Advanced Political Economies*. Oxford: Oxford University Press, pp. 103-126

Lijphart, A. (1999) *Patterns of Democracy: Government Forms and Performance in Thirty-Six Countries*. New Haven: Yale University Press

Lilja, K. (1998) "Finland: Continuity and Modest Moves Towards Companay-level Corporatism". In: A. Ferner and R. Hyman (eds.) *Changing Industrial Relations in Europe*. Oxford: Blackwell Publishers

Liljeblom, E. and A. Löflund (2006) "Developments in Corporate Governance in Finland". In: *International Journal of Disclosure and Governance* (vol. 3) (no. 4), pp. 277-287

Lindbeck, A. (1997) "The Swedish Experiment". In: *Journal of Economic Literature* (vol. 35) (no. 3), pp. 1273-1319

Lindbom, A. (2001) "Dismantling the Social Democratic Welfare Model? Has the Swedish Welfare State Lost Its Defining Characteristics?" In: *Scandinavian Political Studies* (vol. 24) (no. 3), pp. 171-193

Lindgren, K.O. (2006) *Roads from Unemployment: Institutional Comple-*

mentarities in Product and Labour Markets. Doctoral Thesis, Department of Government, Uppsala University

Lindvall, J. (2004) *The Politics of Purpose: Swedish Macroeconomic Policy After the Golden Age.* Göteborg: Göteborg Studies in Politics 84

Lismoen, H. (2002) 2001 *Annual Review from Norway. European Industrial Relations Online.* www.eurofound.eu.int

Lismoen, H. (2007) 2006 *Annual Review from Norway. European Industrial Relations.* www.eurofound.eu.int

Lismoen, H. (2008) 2007 *Annual Review from Norway. European Industrial Relations.* www.eurofound.eu.int

LO-Tidningen (2007) "LO-förbunden som trotsar industrin", 16 November

Luyten, D. (2006) "Corporatisme, neocorporatisme, competitief corporatisme: sociale regulering sinds 1945". In: E. Witte and A. Meynen (eds.) *De geschiedenis van België na 1945.* Brussel: Vubpress

Mach, A. (2006) *La Suisse Entre Internationalisation et Changements Politiques Internes. Les Relations Industrielles et la Législation Sur Els Cartels Dans Les Années 1990.* Chur: Ruegger

Mach, A. and D. Oesch (2003) "Collective Bargaining Between Decentralization and Stability: A Sectoral Model Explaining the Swiss Experience During the 1990s". In: *Industrielle Beziehungen* (vol. 10) (no. 1), pp. 160-182

Mach, A., S. Häusermann and Y. Papadopoulos (2003) "Economic Regulatory Reforms in Switzerland: Adjustment Without European Integration, Or How Rigidities Become Flexible". In: *Journal of European Public Policy* (vol. 10) (no. 2), pp. 301-318

Mach, A., G. Schnyder, T. David, and M. Lüpold (2007) "Transformations of Self-Regulation and New Public Regulations in the Field of Swiss Corporate Governance (1985-2002)". In: *World Political Science Review* (vol. 3) (no. 2), pp. 1-30

Maggetti, M., A. Afonso, and M.C. Fontana (2010) "The More it Changes, the More it Stays the Same? Liberalisation and Re-Regulation in Switzerland in Comparative Perspective". In: C. Trampusch and A. Mach (eds.) *Switzerland in Europe: Continuity and Change in the Swiss Political Economy.* London: Routledge

Mailand, M. (2005) "The involvement of Social Partners in Active Labour Market Policy – do the Patterns fit Expectations from Regime Theories?" In: T. Bredgaard and F. Larsen (eds.) *Employment Policy from Different Angels.* Copenhagen: DJØF Publishing

Mailand, M. and J. Due (2003) "Partsstyring i arbejdsmarkedspolitikken

– perspektiver og alternativer". In: L. Petersen and P. K. Madsen (eds.) *Drivkræfter bag arbejdsmarkedspolitikken*. København: SFI

Mailand, M. (2008) *Regulering af arbejde og velfærd – mod nye arbejdsdelinger mellem staten og arbejdsmarkedets parter*. København: Jurist- og Økonomforbundets Forlag

Marier, P. (2008) "Empowering Epistemic Communities: Specialized Politicians, Policy Experts and Policy Reform". In: *West European Politics* (vol. 321) (no. 3), pp. 513-533

Mcrrien, F.X. and U. Becker (2005) "The Swiss Miracle: Low Growth and High Employment." In: U. Becker and H. Schwartz (eds.) *Employment Miracles*. Amsterdam: Amsterdam University Press

Merton, R.K. (1957) *Social Theory and Social Structure*, 2nd eds. Glencoe IL: Free Press

Ministry of Finance (2007) The Norweigian Tax Reforms 2004-2006. www.regeringen.no

Moen, E. and K. Lilja (2005) "Change in Coordinated market Economies: The Case of Nokia and Finland". In: G. Morgan et al., *Changing Capitalism*. Oxford: Oxford University Press, pp. 352-379

Molina, O. and M. Rhodes (2007) "Conflict, Complementarities and Institutional Change in Mixed Market Economies". In: B. Hancké, M. Rhodes and M. Thatcher (eds.) *Beyond Varieties of Capitalism*. Oxford: Oxford University Press

Mujagic, E. and A. Zweers (2004) "Sociale economie: polderakkoord mist essentie". In: *FEM Business* (vol. 7) (no. 46)

Navrbjerg, S.E. (2006) *Ledelse på tværs af grænser – konsekvenser af virksomhedsovertagelser i Danmark*. FAOS forskningsnotat nr. 67. FAOS, Sociologisk Institut, Københavns Universitet

Neergaard, K. (2004) *Controversial pension reform proposed*. European Industrial Relations Online. www.eirofound.eu.int

Nickell, W. (2006) "The CEP-OECD Institutions Data Set (1960-2004)." In: *CEP Discussion Paper* No. 759

Niemelä, J. (1999) "Organised Decentralisation of Finnish Industrial Relations". Paper presented at the 21st Conference of the International Working Party on Labour Market Segmentation, Bremen, September 9th to 11th 1999

Niemelä, H. and K. Salminen (2006) *Social Security in Finland*. Helsinki: The Social Insurance Institution (Kela), The Finnish Centre for Pensions (ETK), The Finnish Pension Alliance (TELA) and The Finnish Ministry of Social Affairs and Health

Nowotny, E. (1998) "Privatisation, Deregulation, Reregulation – Experiences and Policy Issues in Austria". In: *Journal for Institutional Innovation, Development, and Transition* (vol. 2), pp. 235-248

Obinger, H. (1998) "Federalism, Direct Democracy, and Welfare State Development in Switzerland". In: *Journal of Public Policy* (vol. 18) (no. 3), pp. 241-263

Obinger, H. and E. Talos (2006) *Sozialstaat Österreich Zwischen Kontinuität Und Umbau. Eine Bilanz der ÖVP/FPÖ/BZÖ Koalition.* Wiesbaden: VS Verlag für Sozialwissenschaften

Obinger, H. and E. Talos (2009) "Janus-Faced Developments in a Prototypical Bismarckian Welfare State. Welfare Reforms in Austria Since the 1970s". In: B. Palier (ed.) *A Long Good-bye to Bismarck? The Politics of Welfare Reform in Continental Europe.* Amsterdam: Amsterdam University Press

Obstfeld, M. and A.M. Taylor (2004) *Global Capital Markets, Integration, Crisis, and Growth.* Cambridge: Cambridge University Press

OECD (1994) *The OECD Jobs Study: Facts, Analysis, Strategies*, Paris, Organisation for Economic Coordination and Development.

OECD (2003) *Employment Outlook 2003.* Paris: Organisation for Economic Cooperation and Development

OECD (2004a) *Education at a Glance.* Paris: Organisation for Economic Cooperation and Development

OECD (2004b) *Employment Outlook 2004.* Paris: Organisation for Economic Cooperation and Development

OECD (2004c) *Figure 1. Tax Revenue of main headings as percentage of total tax revenue.* http://www.oecd.org/dataoecd/18/23/35471773.pdf

OECD (2004d) *Recent tax policies trends and reforms in OECD countries.* Paris: Organisation for Economic Coordination and Development

OECD (2005) *Employment Outlook 2005.* Paris: OECD

OECD (2006a) *Employment Outlook 2006.* Paris: Organisation for Economic Cooperation and Development

OECD (2006b) *Economic Outlook 79.* Paris: Organisation for Economic Cooperation and Development

OECD (2006c) *Economic Outlook 80.* Paris: Organisation for Economic Cooperation and Development

OECD (2006d) *OECD Database.* Paris: Organisation for Economic Cooperation and Development. http://dx.doi.org/10.1787/184587347336

OECD (2007a) *Statistics Portal. Productivity Database*, April 2007. Paris: Organisation for Economic Cooperation and Development. http://stats.oecd.org/WBOS/Index.aspx?DatasetCode=PDYGTH

OECD (2007b) *OECD in Figures 2007*. Paris: Organisation for Economic Cooperation and Development

OECD (2007c) *Employment Outlook 2007*. Paris: Organisation for Economic Cooperation and Development

OECD (2007d) *Lack of Proportionality Between Ownership and Control: Overview and Issues for Discussion*. Report from the OECD Corporate Affairs Division

OECD (2007e): Revenue Statistics. Paris: Organisation of Economic Cooperation and Development. http://stats.oecd.org/Index.aspx?DataSetCode=REV

OECD (2008a) *Economic Outlook 83*. Paris: Organisation for Economic Cooperation and Development

OECD (2008b) *Growing Unequal? Income Distribution and Poverty in OECD Countries*. Paris: Organisation of Economic Cooperation and Development

OECD (2008c) *Employment Outlook 2008*. Paris: Organisation for Economic Cooperation and Development

OECD (2009) *Taxing wages 2008*. Paris: Organisation for Economic Coordination and Development

OECD (n.a.) *Science, Technology and Industry Scoreboard 2007*. OECD Database. Paris: Organisation for Economic Cooperation and Development, www.oecd.org/sti/ipr-statistics

OECD (n.a.) *Benefits and Wage Database*. Paris: Organisation for Economic Cooperation and Development

OECD (n.a.) *Database on the Incidence of Temporary Employment*. Paris: Organisation for Economic Cooperation and Development

OECD (n.a.) *Financial Market Trends* (various issues), Paris, Organisation for Economic Coordination and Development.

Oesch, D. (2007) "Weniger Koordination, Mehr Markt? Kollektive Arbeitsbeziehungen Und Neokorporatismus in der Schweiz seit 1990". In: *Swiss Political Science Review* (vol. 13) (no. 3), pp. 337-368

Oosterlynck, S. (2006) *The political economy of new regionalism in Belgium. Imagining and institutionalising the Flemish regional economy*. Doctoral Thesis. Lancaster: Lancaster University

Pagoulatos, G. (2003) *Greece's New Political Economy: State Finance and Growth from Postwar to EMU*. Basingstoke: Palgrave Macmillan

Palme, J., A. Bergmark, O. Bäckman, F. Estrada, J. Fritzell, O. Lundberg, O. Sjöberg, and M. Szebehely (2002) "Welfare Trends in Sweden: Balancing the Books for the 1990s". In: *Journal of European Social Policy* (vol. 12) (no. 4), pp. 329-346

Pedersen, O.K. (2006) "Corporatism and Beyond: The Negotiated Economy". In: J. Campbell, J. Hall and O.K. Pedersen (eds.) *National Identity and the Varieties of Capitalism. The Danish Experience.* Montreal: McGill University Press

Pedersen, T. and S. Thomsen (1999) "Economic and Systemic Explanations of Ownership Concentration among Europe's Largest Companies". In: *International Journal of Business* (vol. 6) (no. 3), pp. 367-381

Pekkarinen, J. and K. Alho (2005) "The Finnish Bargaining System: Actors' Perceptions". In: Pekkola, Hannu and Kenneth Snellman (ed.) *Collective Bargaining and Wage Formation.* Hamburg: Springer Verlag

Pelinka, A. (2008) "Gesetzgebung im Politischen System Österreichs". In: W. Ismayr (ed.) *Gesetzgebung in den Staaten der Europäischen Union.* Wiesbaden: VS Verlag für Sozialwissenschaften, pp. 431-462

PEW (2007) *Trends in Political Values and Core Attitudes: 1987-2007. Political Landscape More Favorable To Democrats.* Washington: The Pew Research Center for the People & the Press. http://people-press.org/report/312/trends-in-political-values-and-core-attitudes-1987-2007

Piotet, G. (1987) *Restructuration et Corporatisme. Le Cas de L'horlogerie En Suisse, 1974-1987.* Lausanne: Imprivite SA

Plougmann, P. and P.K. Madsen (2002) "Flexibility, Employment development and Active Labour Market Policy in Denmark and Sweden in the 1990s". In: *CEPA Working Paper* 2002-04. New York: New School University, Center for Economic Policy Analysis

Pochet, P. (2004) "Belgium: monetary integration and precarious federalism." In: Martin, A. and G. Ross (eds.) *Euros and Europeans. Monetary integration and the European model of society.* Cambridge: Cambridge University Press

Pochet, P. and G. Fajertag (2000) "A New Area For Social Pacts in Europe". In: G. Fajertag and P. Pochet (eds.) Social Pacts in Europe – New Dynamics. Brussels: ETUI

Polanyi, K. (1957 [1944]) *The Great Transformation. The Political and Economic Origins of Our Time.* Boston: Rinehart

Pontusson, J. (1997) "Between neo-liberalism and the German model: Swedish capitalism in transition". In: C. Crouch and W. Streeck (eds.) *Political Economy of Modern Capitalism. Mapping Convergence & Diversity.* London: Sage

Pontusson, J. and P. Swenson (1996) "Labour Markets, Production Strategies, and Wage Bargaining Institutions." In: *Comparative Political Studies* (vol. 29) (no. 2), pp. 223-250

Poutsma, E. and G. Braam (2005) "Corporate governance and labour management in the Netherlands: Getting the best of both worlds?" In: H. Gospel and A. Pendleton (eds.) *Corporate Governance and Labour Management. An international comparison.* Oxford: Oxford University Press, pp. 148-172

Pro Inno Europe (2007) *European Innovation Scoreboard 2007.* Brussels: European Commission

Puype, J. (2005) *De elite van België. Welkom in de club.* Leuven: Van Halewyck

Radaelli, C.M. (2003) "The Europeanisation of public policy". In: K. Featherstone and C.M. Radaelli (eds.) *The Politics of Europeanisation.* Oxford: Oxford University Press, pp. 27-56

Rae, D. (2005a) *How to Reduce Sickness Absences in Sweden: Lessons from International Experience.* OECD, Economics Department, Working Paper 442. Paris: Organisation for Economic Cooperation and Development

Rae, D. (2005b) *Getting Better Value for Money From Sweden's Health Care System.* OECD, Economics Department, Working Paper 443. Paris: Organisation for Economic Cooperation and Development

Regeringen (2007) *Danmarks Nationale Reform Program – An den Fremskridtsrapport.* København: Regeringen.

Rehn, O. (1996) *Corporatism and Industrial Competitiveness in Small Europeand States: Austria, Finland and Sweden 1945-95.* Thesis, Oxford University

Reman, P. and P. Pochet (2005) "Transformations du système belge de sécurité sociale". In: P. Vielle, P. Pochet and I. Cassiers (eds.) *L'état social actif. Vers un changement de paradigme?* Bruxelles: Peter Lang

Rothstein, B. (1992) *Den Korporativa Staten: Interesseorganisationer och Statsforvaltning i Svensk Politik.* Stockholm

Rothstein, B. (2005) *Social Traps and the Problem of Trust.* Cambridge: Cambridge University Press

Royo, S. (2002) *A New Century of Corporatism?* London: Praeger

Royo, S. (2008) *Varieties of Capitalism in Spain.* Basingstoke: Palgrave Macmillan

Rueda, D. and J. Pontusson (2000) "Wage Inequality and Varieties of Capitalism". In: *World Politics* (vol. 52) (no. 3), pp. 350-383

Salverda, W. (2005) "The Dutch Model: Magic in a Flat Landscape", in: U. Becker and H. Schwartz (eds.) *Employment Miracles. A Critical Comparison of the Dutch, Scandinavian, Swiss, Australian and Irish Cases versus Germany and the US*. Amsterdam: Amsterdam University Press, pp. 39-64.

Sandgren, A. (2002) *Verkstadsindustrin och Industriavtalet*. Stockholm: Sveriges Verkstadsindustrier

Sapir, A. (2006) "Globalisation and the Reform of European Social Models". In: *Journal of Common Market Studies* (vol. 44) (no. 2), pp. 369-390

Scarbrough, E. (2000) "West European Welfare States: The Old Politics of Retrenchement". In: *European Journal of Political Research* (vol. 38), pp. 225-259

Schäfer, A. (2004) "Beyond the Community Method. Why the Open Method of Coordination was Introduced to EU Policy-Making". In: *European Integration Online Papers* (vol. 8) (no. 13)

Scharpf, F.W. (1991) *Crisis and Choice in European Social Democracy*. Ithaca: Cornell University Press

Scharpf, F.W. (1993) *Games in Hierarchies and Networks Analytical and Empirical Approaches to the Study of Governance Institutions*. Frankfurt am Main: Campus Verlag

Scharpf, F.W. (2002) "The European Social Model: Coping with the Challenges of diversity". In: *Journal of Common Market Studies* (vol. 40) (no. 4), pp. 645-70

Scharpf, F.W. (2009) "Legitimacy in the Multilevel European Polity". In: *MPIfG Working Paper* 09/1. www.mpifg.de

Schmidt, V.A. (2000) "Values and Discourse in the Politics of Adjustment." In: F.W. Scharpf and V.A. Schmidt (eds.) *Welfare and Work in the Open Economy Vol I: From Vulnerability to Competitiveness*. Oxford: Oxford University Press

Schmidt, V.A. (2002a) *The Futures of European Capitalism*. Oxford: Oxford University Press

Schmidt, V.A. (2002b) "Does Discourse Matter in the Politics of Welfare State Adjustment?" In: *Comparative Political Studies* (vol. 35) (no. 2), pp. 168-193

Schmidt, V.A. (2003) "How, Where, and When does Discourse Matter in Small States' Welfare State Adjustment?" In: *New Political Economy* (vol. 8) (no. 1), pp. 127-146

Schmidt, V.A. (2006) *Democracy in Europe: The EU and National Polities*. Oxford: Oxford University Press

Schmidt, V.A. (2007) "Social Contracts under Siege: National Responses to Globalized and Europeanized Production in Europe". In: E. Paus (ed.) *Global Capitalism Unbound: Winners and Losers of Offshore Outsourcing*, Basingstoke: Palgrave Macmillan, pp. 113-129

Schmidt, V.A. (2008) "Discursive Institutionalism: The Explanatory Power of Ideas and Discourse." In: *Annual Review of Political Science* (vol. 11), pp. 303-26

Schmidt, V.A. (2009) "Putting the Political back into Political Economy by bringing the State back in yet Again." In: *World Politics* (vol. 61) (no. 3), pp. 516-46

Schmitt, J. (2007) "Is the Unemployment Rate in Sweden Really 17 Percent?" In: *CEPR Issue Brief* (June). London: Centre for Economic Policy Research

Schmitter, P.C. (1979) "Still the century of Corporatism". In: I.P.C. Schmitter and G. Lembruch (eds.) *Trends towards Corporatist Intermediation*. London: Sage

Schnyder, G., M. Lüpold, A. Mach, and T. David (2005) *The Rise and Decline of the Swiss Company Network During the 20th Century*. Lausanne: Travaux de Science Politique 22

Schröter, H.G. (1999) "Small European Nations: Cooperative Capitalism in the Twentieth Century". In: A.D. Chandler, F. Amatori, and T. Hikino (eds.) *Big Business and the Wealth of Nations*. Cambridge: Cambridge University Press

Schulte, M. (2004) "Musterland mit Schwächen. Wirtschafts- und Arbeitsmarktentwicklung in der Schweiz". In: *IWG Impulse*. Bonn: Institut für Wirtschaft und Gesellschaft

Scruggs, L. (2005) *Welfare State Entitlements Data Set: A Comparative Institutional Analysis of Eighteen Countries*, Version 1.1

Scruggs, L. and J.P. Allan (2006) "The Material Consequences of Welfare States: Benefit Generosity and Absolute Poverty in 16 OECD Countries". In: *Comparative Political Studies* (vol. 39) (no. 7), pp. 880-904

Sels, L. and G. Van Hootegem (2001) "Seeking the balance between flexibility and security. A rising issue in the Low Countries". In: *Work, Employment and Society* (vol. 15) (no. 2), pp. 327-352

Sennett, R. (2007) *The Culture of the New Capitalism*. New Heaven: Yale University Press

Siaroff, A. (1999) "Corporatism in 24 Industrial Democracies: Meaning and Measurement". In: *European Journal of Political Research* (vol. 36) (no. 6), pp. 175-20.

Siegel, N.A. (2007) "Moving Beyond Expenditure Accounts: The Changing Contours of the Regulatory State, 1980-2003". In: F.G. Castles (ed.) *The Disappearing State. Retrenchment Realities in an Age of Globalisation*. Cheltenham: Edward Elgar, pp. 245-272

Sihvo, T. and H. Uusital (1995) "Economic Crises and Support for the Welfare State in Finland 1975-1993". In: *Acta Sociologica* (vol. 38) (no. 3), pp. 251-262

Simmons, B.A., F. Dobbin, and G. Garrett (2006) "Introduction: The International Diffusion of Liberalism". In: *International Organisation* (vol. 60), pp. 781-810

Skule, S., M. Stuart and T. Nyen (2002) "International briefing 12: Training and development in Norway". In: *International journal of Training and Development* (vol. 6) (no. 4), pp. 263-276

Smallcons (2003) *A Framework for Socio-Economic Development in Europe? The Consensual Political Cultures of the Small West European States in Comparative and Historical Perspective*. State-Of-The-Art Report (FP5 project; ed. U. Becker), University of Amsterdam, http://home.medewerker.uva.nl/k.u.becker/

Smits, H. (2008) "Stroperig poldermodel is dringend aan hervorming toe". In: *CDV* (wintereditie), pp. 64-70

Soskice, D. (1990) "Wage Determination: The Changing Role of Institutions in Advanced Industrialized Countries". In: *Oxford Review of Economic Policy* (vol. 6) (no. 4), pp. 36-61

STAR (2004) *De CAO: Wat en Hoe?* Den Haag: Stichting van de Arbeid

Stokman, F., R. Ziegler, and J. Scott (1985) *Networks of Corporate Power. A Comparative Analysis of Ten Countries*. Oxford: Polity Press

Streeck, W. and K. Thelen (2005) (eds.) "Introduction: Institutional Change in Advanced Political Economies." In: *Beyond Continuity: Institutional Change in Advanced Political Economies*. Oxford: Oxford University Press

Studiecommissie voor de Vergrijzing (2010) *Jaarlijks verslag*. Brussel: Hoge Raad voor Financiën

Sundberg, J. (1993) "Finland". In: *European Journal of Political Research* (vol. 24), pp. 419-423

Svallfors, S. (1995) "The End of Class Politics? Structural Cleavages and Attitudes to Swedish Welfare Policies". In: *Acta Sociologica* (vol. 38) (no. 1), pp. 53-74

Svallfors, S. (1997) "Worlds of Welfare and Attitudes to Redistribution: A Comparison of Eight Western Nations". In: *European Sociological Review* (vol. 13) (no. 3), pp. 283-304

Svallfors, S. (2007) "Convergence in Welfare State Support? A Comparison of Sweden, Germany and the US 1990-2006". Paper prepared for delivery at the 2007 Annual Meeting of the American Political Science Association, Chicago, August 30th-September 2nd, 2007, www.allacademic.com//meta/p_mla_apa_research_citation/2/1/0/2/1/pages210213/p210213-22.php

Swank, D. (2006) "Tax Policy in an Era of Internationalisation: Explaining the Spread of Neoliberalism". In: *International Organisation* (vol. 60), pp. 847-882

Swenden, W. and M. Theo Jans (2006) "'Will it stay or will it go?' Federalism and the sustainability of Belgium." In: *West European Politics* (vol. 29) (no. 5), pp. 877-894

Teague, P. and Donaghey, J. (2004). "The Irish experiment in social partnership". In: H. Katz, W. Lee and J. Lee (eds.) *The New Structure of Labour Relations: Tripartism and Decentralization*. Ithaca: Cornell University Press, pp. 10-36

Thatcher, M. (2002) "Analyzing Regulatory Reform in Europe". In: *Journal of European Public Policy* (vol. 9) (no. 6), pp. 859-872

Thelen, K. (2001) "Varieties of Labour Politics in the Developed Democracies". In: P.A. Hall and D. Soskice (eds.), *Varieties of Capitalism*. Oxford: Oxford University Press

Therborn, G. (1992) "Lessons from 'corporatism' theorizations". In: J. Pekkarinen, M. Pohjola and B. Rowthorn (eds.) *Social corporatism. A superior economic system?* Oxford: Clarendon Press, pp. 24-43

Thompson, M., R. Ellis and A. Wildavsky (1990) *Cultural Theory*. Boulder, Col.: Westview Press

Tijdens, K. and M. van Klaveren (eds.) (2008) *Bargaining issues in Europe: comparing countries and industries*. Brussels: European Trade Union Institute

Trampusch, C. (2007) "Industrial Relations as a Source of Solidarity in Times of Welfare State Retrenchment". In: *Journal of Social Policy* (vol. 36) (no. 2), pp. 197-215

Trampusch, C. (2008a) "Employers, the State, Trade Unions and the Politics of Institutional Change. Varieties of Institutional Change in the Vocational Education and Training Regimes in Austria, Germany and Switzerland". In: *Gemeinsame Tagung von DVPW, ÖGPW und SVPW "Die Verfassung von Demokratien"* (vol. 21) (23.11.2008)

Trampusch, C. (2008b) "Von einem liberalen zu einem post liberalen Wohlfahrtsstaat. Der Wandel der gewerkschaftlichen Sozialpolitik in der Schweiz". In: *Swiss Political Science Review* (vol. 14) (no. 1), pp. 49-84

Traxler, F. (1995) "From Demand-Side to Supply-Side Corporatism? Austria's Labour Relations and Public Policy." In: C. Crouch and F. Traxler (eds.) *Organised Industrial Relations in Europe: What Future?* Aldershot: Ashgate, pp. 271-286

Traxler, F. (1998) "Austria: Still the Country of Corporatism." In: A. Ferner and R. Hyman (ed.) *Changing Industrial Relations in Europe.* Oxford: Blackwell

Traxler, F. (2001) "Die Metamorphosen des Korporatismus: Vom klassischen zum schlanken Muster". In: *Politische Vierteljahresschrift* (vol. 42) (no. 4), pp. 590-623

Trogen, G. (1995) "Avtalsparterna bör avsluta sitt skyttegravskrig". In: Svenska Dagbladet, 28 October

UNCTAD (2008) 2008 World Investment Report, New York, UNCTAD.

Url, T. (2003) "Occupational Pension Schemes in Austria". In: *Austrian Economic Quarterly* (no. 2003/2), pp. 64-70

Uusitalo, H. (1996) "Economic Crisis and Social Policy in Finland in the 1990s". In: *SPRC Discussion Paper* (no. 70)

Vad, T., and M. Benner (2000) "Sweden and Denmark". In: F.W. Scharpf and V.A. Schmidt (eds.) *Welfare and Work in the Open Economy, Volume II: Diverse Responses to Common Challenges.* Oxford: Oxford University Press

Vandaele, K. (2007) "From the 70s strike wave to the first cyber-strike in the 21st century: strike activity and labour unrest in Belgium". In: S. van der Velden, H. Dribbusch, D. Lyddon and K. Vandaele (eds.) *Strikes around the world, 1968-2005. Case-studies of 15 countries.* Amsterdam: Aksant

Vandaele, K. (2009) "The Ghent system, temporary unemployment and the Belgian trade unions since the economic downturn". In: *Transfer* (vol. 16) (no. 3-4), pp. 589-596

Van der Meer, M., R. De Boer, H. Houwing, M. Kahankova, and D. Raess (2004) *The impact of globalisation on industrial relations in multinationals in the Netherlands.* Amsterdam: Federatie Nederlandse Vakverenigingen

Vander Steene, T., L. Sels, G. Van Hootegem, A. Forrier and H. De Witte (2002a) *Cahier 1: Feiten en cijfers van flexibiliteit. Definities van flexibiliteit en een caleidoscopisch flexibiliteitsoverzicht.* Leuven: Katholieke Universiteit Leuven – Steunpunt Werkgelegenheid, Arbeid en Vorming

Vander Steene, T., L. Sels, G. Van Hootegem, A. Forrier and H. De Witte (2002b) *De impact van het institutionele kader op de politiek van flexibiliteit. Een vergelijking België-Nederland.* Leuven: Katholieke Universiteit Leuven – Steunpunt Werkgelegenheid, Arbeid en Vorming

Vanderweyden, K. (2002) *Van loopbaanonderbreking naar tijdskrediet. Een verhaal van een wijzigend maatschappelijk discours.* PSW-paper 2002/6. Antwerpen: Universiteit Antwerpen

Van Gerven, M. (2008) *The broad tracks of path dependent benefit reforms. A longitudinal study of social benefit reforms in three European countries.* Tilburg: University of Tilburg

Van Gestel, N.M., P.T. de Beer and M. van der Meer (2009) *Het hervormingsmoeras van de verzorgingsstaat: Veranderingen in de organisatie van de sociale zekerheid, 1980-2008.* Amsterdam: Amsterdam University Press

Van Gyes, G., J. Segers and E. Hendrickx (2009) "In het gelijke, onze verschillen... Het Belgische collectieve systeem van arbeidsverhoudingen gespiegeld aan Nederland". In: *Tijdschrift voor IIRM* (vol. 12) (no. 1), pp. 67-96

Van het Kaar, R. (1999) *Social partners react critically to cabinet's tax proposals,* European Industrial Relations Observatory; https://eurofound.europa.eu

Van Der Elst, C. (2008) *The Belgian struggle for corporate governance improvements.* Law working paper N°. 114/2008. Brussels: European Corporate Governance Institute

Van Rie, T. (2008) *Sociaal-economische uitkomsten in Nederland, België en zijn gewesten.* Antwerpen: Centrale Raad voor het Bedrijfsleven

Van Ruysseveldt, J. and J. Visser (1996) "Weak corporatism going different ways? Industrial relations in the Netherlands and Belgium". In: J. Van Ruysseveldt and J. Visser (eds.) *Industrial Relations in Europe. Traditions and Transitions.* London: Sage

Van Ruysseveldt, J. (2000) *Het belang van overleg. Voorwaarden voor macroresponsieve CAO-onderhandelingen in de marktsector.* Leuven: Acco

Vaughan-Whitehead, D. (2003) *EU Enlargement versus Social Europe? The Uncertain Future of the European Social Model.* Cheltenham: Edward Elgar

Verbist, G., L. De Lathouwer and A. Roggeman (2007) "Labour market activation policies: a comparison of the use of tax credits in Belgium, the UK and the US". In: J. de Koning (ed.) *The evaluation of active labour market policies. Measures, public private partnerships and benchmarking.* Cheltenham: Edward Elgar

Vercauteren, G. (2007) *In naam van de sociale vooruitgang. De rol van de overheid in het sociaal overleg in België (1944-1981).* Leuven: Acco

Visser, J. (2002) "The first part-time economy in the world: a model to be followed?" In: *Journal of European Social Policy* (vol. 12) (no. 1), pp. 23-42

Visser, J. (2009) *ICTWSS: Database on Institutional Characteristics of Trade Unions, Wage Setting, State Intervention and Social Pacts in 34 Countries between 1960 and 2007.* Amsterdam: Institute for Advanced Labour Studies

Visser, J. and A. Hemerijck (1997) *A Dutch miracle. Job growth, welfare reform and corporatism in the Netherlands.* Amsterdam: Amsterdam University Press

Visser, J. and M. van der Meer (1998) *The structural framework of the Netherlands, National report – part 1.* Amsterdam: University of Amsterdam, Centre for Research for European Societies and Industrial Relations / Institute for Advanced Labour Studies

Visser, J. and M. Yerkes (2008) "Part-Time work and the Legacy of Breadwinner Welfare States: a Panel Study of Women's Employment Patterns in Germany, the United Kingdom, and the Netherlands 1992-2002". In: L. Kenworthy and A. Hicks (eds.) *Method and Substance in Macrocomparative Analysis.* New York, Palgrave Macmillan

Vitols, S. (2008) "Private equity: Financial engineering or solution to market failure?" Forthcoming in: E. Hein, T. Niechoj, P. Spahn and A. Truger (eds.) *Finance-Led Capitalism? Macroeconomic Effects of Changes in the Financial Sector.* Marburg: Metropolis-Verlag

Vogel, S.K. (2005) "Routine Adjustment and Bounded Innovation: The Changing Political Economy of Japan". In: W. Streeck and K. Thelen (eds.) *Beyond Continuities. Institutional Change in Advanced Political Economies.* Oxford: Oxford University Press, pp. 145-168

WEF (2007) *World Competitiveness Report 2007-2008.* Basel: World Economic Forum, www.weforum.org

Widmer, F. (2007) "Stratégies syndicales et renouvellement des élites: Le syndicat FTMH face à la crise des années 1990". In: *Swiss Political Science Review* (vol. 13) (no. 3), pp. 395-431

Wilthagen, T. (1998) *Flexicurity: A new paradigm for labour market policy reform?* Berlin: Wissenschaftszentrum Berlin

Windolf, P. and M. Nollert (2001) "Institutionen, Interessen, Netzwerke: Unternehmensverflechtung im internationalen Vergleich". In: *Politische Vierteljahresschrift* (vol. 42) (no. 1), pp. 51-78

WKO (2003) *Statistisches Jahrbuch 2003*. Wien: Wirtschaftskammern Österreichs

WRR (Wetenschappelijke Raad voor het Regeringsbeleid) (2007a) *Investeren in werkzekerheid*. Amsterdam: Amsterdam University Press

WRR (Scientific Council for Government Policy) (2007b) *Rediscovering Europe in the Netherlands*. Amsterdam: Amsterdam University Press

Zeitlin, J. (2005) "Introduction: The Open Method of Coordination in Question". In: J. Zeitlin and P. Pochet (eds.) *The Open Method of Coordination in Action. The European Employment and Social Inclusion Strategies*. Brussels: Peter Lang, pp. 11-25

Zumbansen, P. and D. Saam (2007) "Volkswagen and European Corporate Law: Reshaping the European Varieties of Capitalism". In: *Comparative Research in Law & Political Economy* (vol. 3) (no. 6), Research Paper 30

Index

CHANGING WELFARE STATES

PREVIOUSLY PUBLISHED

Jelle Visser and Anton Hemerijck, *A Dutch Miracle. Job Growth, Welfare Reform and Corporatism in the Netherlands*, 1997
ISBN 978 90 5356 271 0

Christoffer Green-Pedersen, *The Politics of Justification. Party Competition and Welfare-State Retrenchment in Denmark and the Netherlands from 1982 to 1998*, 2002
ISBN 978 90 5356 590 2

Jan Høgelund, *In Search of Effective Disability Policy. Comparing the Developments and Outcomes of the Dutch and Danish Disability Policies*, 2003
ISBN 978 90 5356 644 2

Maurizio Ferrera and Elisabetta Gualmini, *Rescued by Europe? Social and Labour Market Reforms from Maastricht to Berlusconi*, 2004
ISBN 978 90 5356 651 0

Martin Schludi, *The Reform of Bismarckian Pension Systems. A Comparison of Pension Politics in Austria, France, Germany, Italy and Sweden*, 2005
ISBN 978 90 5356 740 1

Uwe Becker and Herman Schwartz (eds.), *Employment 'Miracles'. A Critical Comparison of the Dutch, Scandinavian, Swiss, Australian and Irish Cases Versus Germany and the US*, 2005
ISBN 978 90 5356 755 5

Sanneke Kuipers, *The Crisis Imperative. Crisis Rhetoric and Welfare State Reform in Belgium and the Netherlands in the Early 1990s*, 2006
ISBN 978 90 5356 808 8

Anke Hassel, *Wage Setting, Social Pacts and the Euro. A New Role for the State*, 2006
ISBN 978 90 5356 919 1

Ive Marx, *A New Social Question? On Minimum Income Protection in the Postindustrial Era*, 2007
ISBN 978 90 5356 925 2

Monique Kremer, *How Welfare States Care. Culture, Gender and Parenting in Europe*, 2007
ISBN 978 90 5356 975 7

Sabina Stiller, *Ideational Leadership in German Welfare State Reform. How Politicians and Policy Ideas Transform Resilient Institutions*, 2010
ISBN 978 90 8964 186 1

Barbara Vis, *Politics of Risk-taking. Welfare State Reform in Advanced Democracies*, 2010
ISBN 978 90 8964 227 1

Bruno Palier (ed.), *A Long Goodbye to Bismarck? The Politics of Welfare Reform in Continental Europe*, 2010
ISBN 978 90 8964 234 9

J. Timo Weishaupt, *From the Manpower Revolution to the Activation Paradigm. Explaining Institutional Continuity and Change in an Integrating Europe*, 2011
ISBN 978 90 8964 252 3